Love Yourself and Be Healed

Awakening

Dr. Jane E. Rackley

www.drJaneRackley.com

Copyright © 2014 by Jane E. Rackley, D.C.

Published by:
Doc of Light Publishing
Newburgh, IN. 47630
www.DrJaneRackley.com

Cover photo: Imagedepotpro   Back cover photo: Tschitscherin

All rights reserved. No part of this book may be reproduced by any mechanical, photographic, or electronic process, or in the form of a phonographic recording; nor may it be stored in a retrieval system, transmitted, or otherwise be copied for public or private use-other than for "fair use" as brief quotations embodied in articles and reviews-without prior written permission of the publisher.

The author of this book does not dispense medical advice, or prescribe the use of any technique as a form of treatment for any physical, emotional, or medical problems without the advice of a physician, either directly or indirectly. The intent of the author is only to offer information of a general nature to help you in your quest for emotional and spiritual well-being. In the event that you use any of the information in this book for yourself, which is your constitutional right, the author and the publisher assume no responsibility for your actions.

Printed in the United States of America

20 19 18 17 16 15 14   1 2 3 4 5

1st printing, October 2014

ISBN: 978-0692312810

Because of the dynamic nature of the internet, any web addresses or links contained in this book may have changed since publication and may no longer be valid.

Dedication

I dedicate my *first* book to my parents, Helen and Neil. You are my constant guides and support throughout my life for all of my *first times* that I did everything. You taught me, and were with me the first time I rode my bicycle. After I crashed into that big tree, you helped me get back up, brush off, and to ride again. Both of you were there for me the first time that I graduated, the first time I left home, the first time I accomplished a dream, and the first time that I failed a dream. Also, you have always been there for me for the second times, third, fourth, and all of the rest of the times of my life. For this and so much more, I am ever so grateful.

Your love and support throughout my life is always steadfast and unconditional. I thank-you for simply allowing me the freedom to make all of my own choices, whether they made any sense to you at the time. Permitting me to journey down my own unique direction, and you both embracing every aspect of who I have become during the years has been such of a blessing to me.

You both have always inspired me in so many different ways; it has always made me strive to become a better person. Every day I see the life-example you always display, and hope that I too, may develop greater unconditional love, compassion, integrity, generosity, and discipline in my life.

I am eternally grateful that you both said yes, and chose to become my parents, my teachers, my way-showers. I love you.

Acknowledgements

I have been very blessed throughout my life to have had so many different teachers. My first, and most important teachers are my parents, Helen and Neil. Without all of your love, teaching me directly and indirectly, I might never have discovered the most important things in life. Your love has always kept me moving, and *your lives* have always inspired me to know I can become more.

I am grateful for all of my formal teachers throughout my grade school, high school, undergraduate college, and graduate school. I am so blessed that I received such an excellent education, which has provided the foundation for so much more to come into my life.

I am thankful for Tony Strawn, my Communications Professor during undergraduate school. During a time when I was lost, and ready to quit college, you were responsible for a major turning point in my life. You pushed me just enough to help me move forward and grow. You gave me assignments on the college newspaper that I had no idea I could do. Your constant guidance and encouragement spurred me on to have greater confidence in my abilities throughout my life.

I am grateful for all of my Professors and education at Logan College of Chiropractic. This experience stretched me beyond everything I had previously imagined. Earning my Doctorate was one of the greatest academic challenges thus far in my life, and I am so thankful for the experience. It is here that I learned another meaning of perseverance and discipline. I am so blessed to have received such a great foundation in the highest understanding of *real* health as possible. I am so thankful that you taught me that the word *Doctor* really means *Teacher*. It is here that I received an even greater understanding of the true meaning of serving others.

I am so thankful that I met Genevive Woingust at the perfect moment in my life when I was stationed in the Army at Heidelberg, Germany in 1984. You were my first Spiritual Teacher. I had given up on the traditional Western religious teachings, and had been stagnant in searching for any answers for at least three years. You were the first to introduce me to the concepts of *karma* and *reincarnation.* At 20 years my senior, you were patient and took the time to sit and explain these over and over to me until I finally got it. You suggested an Edgar Cayce book, which fueled the fire for me to learn more and read nearly all of his books. These books directed me to countless more. You took me under your wing, as an wonderful mentor for over two years. As you were studying *A Course in Miracles,* I recall racing out to buy it right away to read. It remained on my bookshelf unread for nearly 20 years, until I was finally ready for it. Thank-you for being the first to open me up to the vast ocean of spiritual understanding, and directing me back onto my spiritual journey.

During early 2001, I am so grateful for meeting H.H. Sai Maa Lakshmi Devi. You stirred within me an instant recognition of everything that was missing in my life. My heart has a resonance with your heart every time you walk into the room, and I am aroused awake to understand divine love even more than ever before. I am so honored to have you in my life, and all of your love and guidance. My life has continuously transformed in every area through the years because of you. The first time I met you, you removed all of my doubt I apparently had been carrying for a long time. Because of this, the following week I was leading my first spiritual bookstudy group on *A Course in Miracles.* Now I have had the confidence to lead classes and study groups every year since. Throughout the years you have always pushed me- sometimes a little, and other times a lot. Thank-you for always pushing, and helping me to recognize that the only way to *really* obtain all of my possible spiritual growth, is to perform *every* task, and use every spiritual tool *fully*. I am eternally indebted and grateful for all of your love, grace, and wisdom you have shared with me throughout these years.

As the veil becomes thinner between us and all of the beings of light just on the other side, I am grateful for all of the assistance that is being poured over to us every day. Every day I feel your gentle direction and love. The ideas that simply come as a whisper from nowhere; the abundance of light and love that I feel during meditations, and am so honored to receive this divine support.

I am able to recognize the divine purpose behind every event, every career choice, every person, and every experience throughout my life. I know that *everything* is always occurring in my life just like a well-played symphony. Each and every note supports the one next to it, and once several are in the right combination, with perfect spacing it becomes music. I am grateful for *all* of the music in my life.

I am so thankful for all of my grandparents. Each of you through your strength, wisdom, and guidance created the ripples on the water, which greatly influenced me and shall be felt throughout the generations to come.

I am grateful for my oldest brother, Neil Jr. Although you left this planet much sooner than many of us, all of us who were with you were so greatly blessed by your presence. Thank-you for being a complete embodiment of divine, unconditional love. You radiated your love to us all, and in your life of silence you taught me so much.

I am grateful for my older brother, Charles. You always believe in me, and support my decisions. Every time I choose the less beaten path, you always cheer me on, becoming one of my best fans.

I am thankful for all of my family who each weave a unique strand into the tapestry of my life. You each add your own color to the fabric, and we are all strengthened as we all continue to work, and grow together.

Lastly, and certainly not the least, I am grateful for my life partner. The universal dance first brought us together in the cornfields of Kentucky detasseling corn at age 13. I am so glad you became my fast friend through the rest of school and some of college. As we drifted seemingly to different corners of the world to start our lives, the universal dance would bring us together again, and again. The first time I "ran into you," literally, in Germany at the library, the next time was St. Louis, then Kentucky, and finally in Indiana. I am so grateful that over seven years ago, we both for the first time were fully out of our respective marriages or relationships. I am so happy you said yes, that you wanted to move into a relationship with me, and that you would move with me to Colorado to live near my Spiritual Teacher. I am delighted that all of the years we were apart on our own spiritual journeys, our individual paths were not too far away. Now that we are teamed up together, we both have experienced much growth together that I am sure could never have happened apart. I appreciate your willingness to move with me to three different states within seven years. Thank-you for all of your love, patience, and support as you have watched me struggle during these years. You have witnessed me countless times start and stop various writing projects, each ending in frustration. You are always loving and comforting no matter how many times you have seen this happen. Now that the words are flowing, I now appreciate your tolerance with living with me. Thanks for putting up with my "being on a roll" until 2:00 in the morning, or turning down going on a family outing to write. I appreciate your willingness to pretend you might be interested, as I explain such exciting things as ISBN's, the difference between a *foreword* and a *preface*, or my latest studies on *verb* usage from my old college English book. I am so blessed by your presence in my life, my partner, my best friend, and my eternal love. I am so grateful that you choose to continue to dance this dance with me, sharing our lives, and spiritual journey together.

CONTENTS

Dedication……………………………….....................iii
Acknowledgements………………………………...iv
Preface……………………………………………….xi
Chapter 1: It's Time to Wake Up!...................................1
    What is That *Something* Which is Missing?
    Truth vs. Be*lie*f
Chapter 2: What is Awakening?....................17
Chapter 3: Establishing The Framework……………24
    The East Teaches the West
    And Justice for Us All
    Let's Play It Again
    Where's The Proof?
Chapter 4: The Glue That Unites us………………..41
    Are We Harmonizing?
    The Miracle on 34th Street
    Our New Paradigm
    Analysis Of The Invisible
    Simplifying The Science
Chapter 5: Elevating The Love Experience…………..57
    Feeding The Tree Of Love
    Just A Heartbeat Away
    Taming The Beast Within
    Practicing In The Trenches
    Is Love In The Air?
    Interlocking Components of Divine Love
    Living Without Conditions
    Our Furry Friends Are The Way-showers
Chapter 6: Regain Compassion and Giving…..……..93
    "We Can Do Small Things With Great Love"
    First Day on the Street
    Heart-Centered Giving
    Having The Time Of Your Life
    Our Gifts To The World
    The Parable Of The Talents
    The Bulb is Still Burning
    If You Get Into A Ditch, Don't Keep Digging

    Turning Points Are Always Pivotal
Chapter 7: To Thine Own Self-Love.......................140
    What Goes Around
    The Greatest Secret Revealed
    Do You Go To The Bathroom?
    Use Your Imagination
    Remembering Ourself and Others
    What Is So Great?
    Stop Focusing On The Ditch
    Green Eggs and Ham
Chapter 8: Wind Beneath My Wings......................175
    Living On The Edge
    Passion Meets The Pavement
    The 20 Percent Principle
Chapter 9: Wisdom of The Ages..........................190
    Learning To Swim With The River
    Learning To Avoid Distraction
    The Art of *Being* Wisdom
Chapter 10: Master's Of Discipline......................204
    You Are Your Possibilities
Chapter 11: Powertools For The Path....................216
    The Seven Sacred Flames
    The Violet Transmuting Flame
    Benefits and Actions of the Flame
    Clouds and Angels
    Making the Call
Chapter 12: The Spiral Ladder We Climb...............234
    The Perfect Spiral
    The Relationship Diagram
    Analyzing Our Spirals
Afterword: 250
References...255
Suggested Reading 259
About The Author..260

Preface

There are those who stay in the distance, keeping every foreign idea, concept, or aspiration at bay. These are the less adventurous ones who habitually settle on all that is familiar, and that which is in alignment with most of the teachings which were learned growing up.

Then there are those who are adventurous by nature. These are the ones who when they were four, got in trouble because they didn't want to stay by their Mother next to the grocery cart in the grocery store. These are the ones who felt the pull of an insatiable curiosity to wander down each different aisle to investigate what was in every lane. These are the same ones who later in life have the need to fully immerse themselves into an idea, concept, or aspiration to really get the full feel of it, and *then* make the decision whether to embrace it, live it, or not.

I am the latter of these two. This book is for the adventurous types who enjoy exploring, uncovering, and understanding what we *really* are here to accomplish. It is for anyone who has ever asked, *and* tried to find the answer to, *why am I here?* Or, *what is the purpose of my life?*

Once we have chased the dream of obtaining a well-paying career, good marriage, nice house, children, and eventually grandchildren, some finally come to a place of the feeling that there is *something else.* We sooner or later get to the spot where we ask ourselves, *what is missing?*

These are some of the questions that I asked myself early on. I quickly learned that as soon as we ask- the doors become flung open wide, and if we choose, we begin a wonderful journey.

One of the key things I have learned, is what lies on the other side of that door is simply the greatest playing field one can imagine, and even more limitless than that. Once the questions are asked, the right and perfect person shows up and teaches you one concept or idea. Then a situation comes into your life which perfectly illustrates it to you. Next, a friend recommends a particular book for you to read. Then *more* circumstances move into your life to help you experience even greater opportunities for growth. The concepts are often very simple, but are not always easy. There are many times that we may have to have a similar situation repeated for us, perhaps over and over, until we finally master it and are able to move on to the next.

Earlier in my life, I first learned that the only thing that was ever constant in life my was change. I recall working so hard to control everything in my life, and wanting so much for everything to stay the same, for at least a little while. Yet every few months there was some new challenge that rocked my world, and then everything was different. After a couple of years of struggling with this, I finally surrendered to the reality that *life is change.* What I didn't realize was that each and every challenge that I simply dismissed as *another change,* was really giving me a new opportunity to grow. It is easy to see now looking back. But this is one of the *sure* signs when we are truly on that *spiritual journey.*

What I have also come to know is that there isn't *any* end point of the journey. This is such of a huge key concept. No matter how much we grow, there is always room for more. This applies to *everyone* who is here. It is the same whether it is a person who is completely clueless that there is a reason or purpose for life here, or if it is one who is the greatest enlightened master to ever walk on planet earth. Everyone of us are immersed in the vast ocean of prospective growth. It is up to us. Are we fully engaged in living our life, open to discovering everything? Or are we playing it safe, limiting ourselves, and possibly avoiding all that we truly came here to be?

The backstory is that I never expected I would write my first book about spiritual teachings. During the last sixteen years I have actively practiced as a Chiropractic Physician. I am completely immersed in the practice and use of all types of holistic healing treatments. My degrees, certifications, and experience includes Chiropractic, nutrition, genetic testing and dietary therapies, enzyme therapy, frequency specific microcurrent therapy, energetic healing, reconnective healing, and I even recently developed a line of quantum energized specialty waters. Whew! I really expected that my first book most likely would highlight some of my experience regarding holistic health, or possibly a new slant on quantum energetic healing. However, this was simply not the case.

At the age of seven, I first realized that I loved to write. I recall getting in trouble staying up past my bedtime because I wanted to sit at my desk in my room and write. I wrote all kinds of stories for fun. A couple of years later, I learned to take my pad and pencil under the covers with a flashlight.

Finally, once I went off to college I spent the first couple of years there mostly confused, and eventually found my way to obtain my undergraduate degree in Communications. I rediscovered my love for writing, and was one of the feature writers and photo editor for the college newspaper. One time for fun, I wrote a feature article for my local newspaper, and I was delighted when it was published.

After graduation, I searched for employment in the journalism field. I excitedly interviewed with the editor of that same newspaper. It was a smaller, family-run paper, and I had great expectations that I might potentially be hired. I hadn't thought about the fact, that certain key positions in the newspaper were already filled with other members within the same family. My meeting didn't go well at all. This editor told me that I really didn't have any talent as a writer, and I needed to go take more writing classes if I ever wished to work in this field. Also, I was told that the article I had written was published only as a favor to my college instructor, who had worked at this newspaper years earlier. The evidence actually pointed at least somewhat in a different direction, as I had been awarded several *Kentucky Inter-Collegiate Press Association* awards for both my photography and feature articles. This incident happened to me about 30 years ago, and apparently would have a greater impact on me than I ever imagined.

I did go on into the Army after this and became a successful photographer. However, what I didn't realize for the next nearly 30 years, that this would become the cause of a near permanent kind of writer's block for me. I started throughout the years a countless number of writing projects, only to barely get started and quit. I did this over and over again. During the last 15 years, I finally moved slightly forward and found myself writing, and finishing short health articles and newsletters for my patients in my practice. But anytime I had a great idea for a larger project, I always stopped within the first two or three pages.

I first met my most recent Spiritual Teacher, H.H. Sai Maa Lakshmi Devi, in early 2001. Throughout the years, I have attended numerous spiritual retreats with her. It was during one of the more recent programs I attended, that she taught us a very specific method to clear away old, unresolved issues which may still affect us today. These issues may result from various family relationships, other encounters, or events involving other people. She helped us to understand how we tend to take on, and carry much unwanted baggage from these old relationships and events. During the retreat she assists, and teaches us how to clear these away so we no longer are *carrying* these from the past. After attending this retreat, I experienced quite a few major transformations in my life, as I had worked on all of the various people I *realized* that I needed clearing of any previous concerns.

About a year ago, I outlined a new writing project. This time I was determined as ever. I managed to write nearly 20 pages, and once again, became sidetracked and stopped. I was frustrated, and decided I wanted to get to the bottom of *why* I simply couldn't finish writing something, *yet again*.

I finally sat and searched back throughout my past, and I recalled this encounter I had with this editor nearly 30 years ago. I thought, *surely not*? Certainly I didn't give *this* much power of my life over to one single person so long ago? Yet I managed to trace back through my life, and realized that I *never* completed *any* other significant writing task after this encounter. I spent about two or three days doing the work. I did all which Sai Maa taught me, to clear all that occurred between myself and that editor on that day so long ago. Afterwards, I simply went into the silence of meditation, and just surrendered myself. I turned everything over to my higher self, and asked for divine guidance. I decided that if writing was really mine to do, I would know.

Almost immediately, within the next couple of days, during the mornings I started being given ideas, and direction for topics to write. I pulled out my 20 page manuscript written several months earlier, and started. This time, I finished the first chapter, then the second, and when I finished chapter three I knew I had made a breakthrough. I knew that I had really managed to remove a block from 30 years ago, that I didn't previously know had existed.

I decided to take the similar approach I had been taught as a healer to simply keep myself open like a flute, and just allow the energies to flow through to assist others. As I did this, I found that I might wake up in the middle of the night with ideas given to me. The other common time is either immediately after I awaken in the morning, or just after my morning meditation. At first, I was surprised that the topics which were flowing through were all spiritual in nature. But I just kept writing whatever I was guided.

Throughout this book, I did absolutely no pre-planning or outlining ahead of time. Each next portion came to me, just as I finished the previous topic. During this process, I rediscovered my original joy of writing. I found that I still love writing and telling stories.

The format of this book is written in a way which is informative, containing the needed concepts, along with illustrations to help support further understanding. I know that I always learn the best when there is a story that helps to demonstrate the idea. There are many stories woven throughout, some are of the experiences of other famous people, and others are personal events from my life. There are many experiences and teachings I learned directly from Sai Maa. This book would never have been written if it weren't for her being my Spiritual Teacher all of these years. I am so deeply grateful for all that I have learned, and continue learning from her teachings.

There are also several questions throughout the book designed to create further thought, and explorative action within oneself. After the first month of writing, it was revealed that I would also write a companion workbook to accompany this book. I expect to finish and release this within a couple of months, after first publishing this book. I know that I will receive similar guidance with each portion of it until it is finished.

I have met some people who read and study many spiritual books, yet do not actively work to apply the new principles into their life. I strongly recommend for those who really choose to apply these concepts, to obtain the workbook as well. It will help to guide you through specific exercises to facilitate greater growth into your life.

This book may move some out of their comfort zone, and others into saying, "Wow, that really makes sense to me." My intent is to reach as many people who are ready to take the next steps on their path. It is apparent to me that not only are the teachings appropriate for ones who are just beginning to pursue their spiritual journey, but for those who have been on the path for awhile.

As I was writing, I found that there were at least a few things which came through that really surprised me. I had either never quite thought of them in that way, or they were new concepts to me. So I feel that most people will find something new, or at least somewhat different than they have studied previously.

There is one section in the book written about the specific role of our pets in our lives. This information came suddenly out of right field to me, and seemed really different. I had written this section at least a few months previously, when one day a patient came into my office. Out of nowhere, she told me about something she had heard on the radio earlier that day. It was about a new scientific study which had just been released on dogs, and it happened to confirm exactly what I had written a few months earlier. I had no idea until that moment of such research. Fortunately, I hadn't published just yet, so went back and included the new study at the end of that section. This really helped to boost my confidence in the accuracy of some of the seeming tangents which came through, and have been sprinkled here and there.

There was only one modification I intellectually needed to correct in the book. The all- important chapter on love was not so surprisingly, a whopping 100 pages.

Since I know that most readers are used to chapters in books a little more manageable in length, I split up this one chapter into three, in an attempt to allow for more typical breaks throughout this portion.

At one point, I finally came to a better understanding why I was directed to write on spirituality instead of holistic health. There are thousands of books available on most every health topic, and more being published each day. Although there certainly are many spiritual books as well, this is the information which we are *all* hungering for, whether we know it or not. Increasing our level of understanding in this area, *right now* couldn't be more important. So we need more books in this arena.

I know there are many powerful holistic health treatments available to help my patients heal, which I am able to facilitate, or direct into their lives. However, within a short time in practice, I noticed that there were many who would completely recover their health. And there were others who no matter how great the treatment, or my efforts would not heal fully.

It took several years of my learning and adding various new, improved techniques, or therapies to my practice to recognize that *still* about the same number of patients seemed to have a limited ability to recover. I finally realized what was missing: that cornerstone of *responsibility* we each have for ourselves. I finally grasped this important neglected piece for each of us.

We must first correct the *cause* of the physical health condition which involves consciously choosing health treatments such as Chiropractic, healthy diet, and nutritional supplementation to bring the physical body into balance. Next, we must practice to bring our own *thoughts, words, feelings* and *actions* into harmony to reflect the life we choose. Finally, we must move within ourselves to rediscover that vast potential we each have mostly forgotten.

Today, in addition to all of the other regular treatments in my clinic, I prescribe to each of my patients positive affirmations. It is my hope that this simple level of involvement will help give them a jump-start to become more pro-active, and realize their own responsibility for creating their own health.

I realized that this book really does fill in this important gap, which has been so ignored throughout the years. This book shows us step-by-step really how to take back the reigns of our own life again. The first portion of my title reflects this reality, *Love Yourself And Be Healed*. I have used this as an important message on all of my clinic brochures and advertising for the last few years. I have personally experienced this, and embrace this as the reality for us all. I know that *everyone* has the same opportunity to fully heal, and live a life of vitality and joy. It is my hopes that this book may be a bridge, which will allow as many who choose to *heal* and *grow* to the greatest heights beyond imagination.

Each different spiritual book has its own audience, and will reach and resonate with certain specific people. The group who embrace, learn, and grow from this book will be different than those attracted to another one. It is much the same as knowing that there are countless different roads which all will take us to the same place. So it is, when we realize that each of us really have the same goal, we simply need to find the road that most suits us, and then keep moving. *And* it is also beneficial to have as many different roads available as possible.

Once I was at a retreat with my Spiritual Teacher, Sai Maa. A woman stood and asked her for guidance, stating that she was completely confused. She said that she had attended a couple of retreats with Sai Maa, and also that of two other Spiritual Teachers. Now she was feeling really confused because each of them were teaching a little bit differently. Sai Maa told her that she simply needed to pick *one*, as one was all she needed, and then *do* what *that* teacher teaches. Likewise, we need to choose that path which most resonates with us, stay on it, and then *get moving*.

It is my greatest joy to share this most important aspect of my life with all who may be ready. It is my hope that you may find something within this book which serves your soul, and allows you to soar to the highest heights. I encourage each of you to join me, who have ever asked the question, *what else is there?* I invite you to boldly take those next steps to actively explore *all* that is available to us. May each of us continue in our journey together, and grow beyond our most magnificent dreams!

1

It's Time to Awaken!

Starting at about the age of four, a child starts to tell others she can't wait until she gets to go to kindergarten and can be with all of the other kids her age. She is excited that she will finally be like the "older kids," and even get to ride on the school bus. She arrives in kindergarten and is happy for the first month or two. Then she overhears at recess one of the first graders crooning," you are a bunch of babies 'cause you only go to school half a day!" So she now can't wait to *really* be like the big kids and go a full day of school. She gets to first grade, and soon discovers that the second graders are allowed to go on field trips to places like the zoo. She tells her parents that *now* she can't hardly wait to be in second grade.

She makes it into second grade and is happy to finally go onto her first field trip. Then her best friend tells her that she can't wait until they get to fourth grade, 'cause her older brother just got a real locker and gets to change classes and has several different teachers instead of just one. She agreed that would really be great, as it would be fun to decorate their lockers. She felt like fourth grade took forever to arrive and she thought it was cool to change classes and put a poster of Justin Bieber in her locker. Shortly thereafter, she finds out that the sixth graders get to have a spring dance. She and her friends giggled at the prospect of dancing with the boys, and started thinking about how much longer they would have to wait.

Two years later, the dance came and went, and next they wanted to hurry up and get to Junior high because then they could finally be out of grade school and be away from the "little kids." Junior high came, and she next couldn't wait to get to high school for the same reasons. Once she was in high school, she couldn't wait to drive a car and finally graduate so *then* she could *really* start her life and go to college. Once in college, she thought she would have freedom to get away from her parents. She arrived in college and found the freedom, but that it was a lot of hard work still being in school. She decided she would be happy once she graduated and *then* she could *really* get her life going. She graduated from college and found her first job.

She looked at her life after a few months in her new job, and felt like *something* still was missing. She finally contemplated that if she could buy a nicer car than the one she had been driving since her senior year in high school, and a house and maybe get married to her boyfriend, *that* would be the answer. Two years later she managed all three, but really felt like there still must be *something else*. A couple of her friends already had their first baby, maybe that was it, time to have children. She had two, and she found that she was absolutely correct that having children seemed to help her forget, most of the time whatever it was that seemed missing. She was busier than ever and no longer even had the time or energy to analyze any of that for a while. One year turned into two, and eventually several, and both of her kids were in school. Finally, two months before the youngest child is graduating from high school, she shudders to wonder what next? She notices *that feeling* starting to creep in again, just like the one she remembered nearly two decades ago, slowly slipping back up to the surface. She wonders, maybe after graduation, then *I* should go back to school? Maybe that's it. I just need to go back to school and change my career. On and on it goes, throughout all of the rest of her life.

During the last days of her lifetime, she finally has the time to reflect upon the past evaluating whether she truly accomplished everything. Once again, that feeling is there, only this time not nearly as subtle as it had been through the years before. As she realizes that her life is really nearly at the end, she feels more unsettled as her thoughts continue to search for the answers. Did I accomplish everything? Was there more? Did I miss something here? What was it? Her mind grapples with these attempting to capture the elusive answers. She wondered why she had never anticipated all of those years earlier, that these things were so important. Finally, all at once it comes to her. She takes a long and drawn breath, as if finally remembering a long lost secret. A tear begins to well up and then spills down the corner of her eye.

She awakens the following morning hearing soft whispers, and exchanges the last glimpses of her husband and children gathered at her bedside. A few moments later, she gently drifts away.

How many people would say, "That sounds like a pretty good life to me. Isn't that how we are *supposed* to live?" This is the mainstream way of thinking life should progress, but is this really why we are here? What is the purpose of life? Should we pause to ask this, or simply keep on moving in all of our busy-ness in the mainstream?

I remember distinctly when I was age eight sitting in my room, and praying in the hardest and most focused way my eight year young being could muster.

"God, please tell me the meaning of life. What's the purpose of life?" I paused quietly, hoping I might somehow receive an instant answer. I kept my eyes closed tightly, still listening with all of my might. I didn't hear the direct reply I expected. So I finally relented my effort for the night and went to sleep.

The following day I thought, the answer must be here *somewhere*. Maybe I need to go looking for it. So the next time my babysitter took my brother and I to the public library I went into the 'philosophy' aisle. I dragged several huge books off of the shelves, and carefully searched through them to select the books that had my answer. Since I could only check out up to six books at a time, I was meticulous and chose only the best ones. During our walk back home, the books were nearly too heavy for me to carry. Halfway back, my babysitter helped by carrying one of larger ones for me.

As soon as we were home I took the books straight to my room, and excitedly started flicking through the pages. Some of them were written by, and about historical people who lived hundreds of years ago having names like Aristotle, Plato and Socrates. A couple of the titles described *The History of Modern Philosophy* as well as *The Compendium of Early Philosophy*. I finally grabbed one of the books, and decided to start at the beginning.

Years ago my Mother divulged to me that when I took my first Iowa Basic Skills test in the fifth grade, my reading level was evaluated equivalent to that of an eleventh grader. That helped me to better understand why I always got into trouble with my teachers for reading ahead in the book. However, this occurred in the summer after I had only completed the third grade. So even though I was apparently an avid and advanced reader at an early age, at best my reading ability and comprehension at this time might have been at a fifth or sixth grade level.

I began to read the first page. I stopped at about every third or fourth word which was long and might as well had been in a foreign language. I couldn't comprehend anything. I threw aside that book and swiped up another. I flipped to the beginning. This time I attempted to read the first paragraph, second and third to see if I could somehow get it to make sense. I then rummaged to the middle of the book and tried again, thinking a different part of the book might be easier. I repeated the process in each different book thinking that I must be able to understand *at least* one of them. I was sure that the answer I needed was somehow contained in those books. I finally gave up for that day, and then tried again at least a couple of more times later.

The following week I schlepped those books back, and as I thumped them onto the counter the librarian peered over her half glasses giving me an amused smile. I am sure she was pretty tickled at me. I definitely figured if my answer was in any of those books, I might have to wait a few more years to find out.

I was fortunate to ask this question at an early age. Even though I didn't obtain the instantaneous answer I thought, this did definitively start me on my path. The answers started to come. They came in a way that I could understand at the age of eight, then again at the age of nine, at ten, eleven, at thirty, at forty and every other day of my life. I learned that when we ask, we get that which we can understand in our particular viewpoint. If I had been given every answer to my questions at the age of eight, then there would be nothing left to discover in my journey. Where is the fun and adventure of that? All of the perfect situations, people, relationships, and spiritual teachers each show up at precisely the right time and place.

What is unfortunate, is that so many people meander through life and never ask these important questions.

Instead of recognizing there is more, and grasping for it, countless people simply move through the daily motions blindly. The journey can be much longer and arduous, when we are caught in the blinding web of the outer world. Hopefully there comes an event or time which shakes our routine, and causes us to first question, and then seek out this other *something*.

What is That *Something* Which is Missing?

Congratulate yourself, for if you are reading this book at sometime during your life, you must have asked yourself some of the big questions in life. Most people at some point ask themselves these, but often these are pushed to the back burner. Often we think, yes I'd like to someday take the time to look into that, but right now I'm too busy with....(fill in anything).

What's the meaning of life? Why are we here? What's our purpose here? Where did we come from before coming here? Where will we go after we leave here? What's *really* the point of our living here from day to day? Why do some people live longer than others? Why are some people's lives easier(harder) than others? Is there *really* a God out there who decides and runs everything here? Why do things happen in the world(our lives) the way they happen? Are we *truly* the only inhabited planet in the universe? These are the kind of inquiries that a four year old will often ask the adults, but within only a few years later will become distracted and no longer ask.

Recently I attended a meditation group. After finishing up the evening, people were slowly coming back to the outer world and giving each other the routine good-bye hugs. One woman who had started attending within the last few months blurted out," I just have to say, that I am just *so* grateful that I have found this…this church, community, just everything!" She choked back the emotion in her throat," I can't get over that I have been just sitting with my beliefs doing *nothing,* and staying in the same place for years! For years!" she cried out," Now, for the first time in *years* I feel like I am *really* growing again!" She choked back a couple of tears as a grand wave of gratitude washed completely over her.

It is so rewarding to witness someone who is overcome with joy in the realization that they are back on their journey of awakening. That time in a person's life, when they have finally realized that there is *something* we might be here to find in our life, which has nothing to do with the typical day to day outer world activities. This is the time I am sure there are unseen ones rejoicing in other realms, as yet one more being on this planet has finally started the process of *awakening.*

That one elusive *something* which countless people grasp towards often in all of the wrong places throughout their whole life, is simply to *awaken.* Yet there are still many who may state, "Why do I need to *awaken* and what purpose would that serve?" There are quite a few who might argue, "But I am happy, I have a good job and a great family. I even grew up in a church where I learned everything I need to know. I have good values, and I follow all of the rules. *Sometimes* I still attend church and think of my beliefs at times. I think this *should* be plenty!"

The problem with this way of thinking is this is all we have ever been taught that we should strive for in this life. Many people have been led to believe that there is a stopping point in life. Where it is okay to reach out, and then once attaining that seemingly safe "comfort zone," that is our arriving place. This is the place in which many feel they have accomplished everything they were told was important in life, and can pretty much coast from there forward. This seeming "comfort zone," is really the place where most all of the possible spiritual growth and journey has come to a rest or may even completely stop.

It is important that we stop and really take a look at our life, and examine it closely at a window of about the previous five years. We need to ask ourselves questions such as: What kind of growth has occurred for me during this time? What are some of the events which have caused me to grow, and in what way? Can I name at least two or three important life lessons I have learned, and how has it caused me to become a better person? Am I able to notice clear signs in my life that I am experiencing spiritual growth? What are they? Have I actively pursued learning anything which has fed my soul? What kinds of transformative changes can I see in myself as a result? How have the patterns in my relationships with others changed and improved?

If we ask ourselves these questions and find that we can't really identify much that has changed during the previous five years, or if the only changes we can identify come from material things such as "bought a different house," then we need to recognize that we have come to rest in our "comfort zone." We may feel really content here, yet there is really little or no growth occurring in ourself.

We must realize, everything is always percolating just under the surface. Even as one settles in after acquiring the next better job, the next bigger house, or the next fancier car, we are never quite satisfied for long and are looking for that *something* else. That *something* which is always there and patiently waiting. It is persistent in its wait, and is timeless. It is that tiny whisper that pushes you onto the next search, to figure out if *this time* it will be different and you'll find that which will really satisfy you.

What is that elusive *something* that will fulfill the deep yearnings of humanity? It is ever-present, always waiting and eternal. It is for us to *awaken* to the true nature of ourselves. It is for us to re-member that which is our true essence, our own divinity. It is only when we *actively* pursue the understanding and experience of our own divinity, that we can finally move towards a sense of greater satisfaction and fulfillment in our lives. Every other outer world pursuit will always fall short, and feel empty compared to our own progressive journey toward *awakening.*

My beloved Spiritual Teacher, Her Holiness Sai Maa has repeated many times to her students: *Do you choose to take the slow way, or take the fast route? I can appreciate those who wish to go slow, but I am here for you who choose to go fast.* Many times throughout the years I have watched her working with different students during our retreats. Often times one of us might stand before her relating one of our issues in life. Sai Maa will guide us and help us to see whatever it is we need to approach differently. Occasionally, whatever direction Sai Maa has given will seem like an unexpected, or uncomfortable action to the student. Sai Maa will patiently attempt to redirect and explain some of the reasoning, and yet still there are times the student continues to resist Sai Maa's suggestion. After a certain point, if the student has built a strong wall of resistance and is unwilling to be open to any suggestions, Sai Maa will state: That's okay if you don't want to do the work now, then you may choose to do it during your next lifetime.

There are a few who may initially think this seems a little harsh, but this is the reality of it. Sai Maa has also related to us that her job as our Spiritual Teacher is to push us. One time she stroked her face into a giddy statue-like smile demonstrating: Going through life saying everything is fine, I'm fine, my family is fine, it's all fine, fine, fine. She shook her head back into a serious posture. When you are living your life in this way you are *not* growing. This is *why* I push you."

So we can relate that one of the typical by-products of *awakening* might include being uncomfortable at times. Although this may seem like it is a requirement, it does not mean that we need to live a life filled with suffering or pain. There are those who experience much of this throughout life, and *still* do not recognize the lesson or message which is there for one to learn.

Also, there is a difference between allowing ourselves to be open to *awakening,* and pursuing the experiences which will bring us new growth, versus permitting ourselves to be buffeted hither and yonder experiencing painful or disharmonious situations. How do we know which of these are occurring in our life?

Think about how you feel from day to day, and week to week. You most likely are in your journey of *awakening,* if you can examine a certain measure of time, and the majority of it feels peaceful or a sense of inner harmony. There is a distinct feeling of being on purpose most of the time and almost an inner knowledge that you are moving forward. This doesn't imply that there will not be times of difficult events which will cause an upset. However, these incidents come and are hurdled relatively quickly and then one gets back on purpose again.

You are most likely stagnant and *not* very actively in the process of *awakening* if you examine a certain measure of time and a good portion of it feels discordant, or in a state of upheaval. During this time you may more often have a feeling of being scattered, and may feel frustration because deep down you have a sense that you are off purpose. More often you may feel like you are in a rut, and not sure how it happened or how to move out of it. Many people sometimes become so used to moving from one disharmonious situation to another, that they believe eventually that this is simply normal, and how life is supposed to be lived. When difficult events occur, it seems to take a long time to recover, and the same situations have a tendency to recur over and over. If this continues long enough, a person may notice a moderate to high degree of emotional upset on and off which may show up eventually as depression.

It is also possible for us to have certain periods of our life in which for a few years we were experiencing growth, and then we become stagnant for awhile.

Sometimes one or more challenges may come, and we may simply get off track for awhile.

The important thing to remember is that it doesn't matter whether we are in the *awakening* process and experiencing rapid growth, or are stuck for a bit working to get out of the muckedy-muck of outer world sludge. Regardless of which we are doing, there is really no right or wrong way. *All* are destined regardless, to eventually fully *awaken.* This is that *something* everyone either presently seeks in our life, or eventually will try to find. The best part is that everyone *will* eventually arrive. We must ask ourselves, do I wish to move slowly, or quickly?

Awakening is every person's destiny here, regardless of if we are aware of it or not. It doesn't matter whether the religious teachings we learned as a child agrees with this concept. It doesn't matter if our family and friends think it is nonsense. None of this matters because it is our birthright. We know it is anchored in truth as it is *timeless* and *changeless.*

Truth vs. Be*lie*f

Sai Maa explained once how to determine if a concept is founded in truth or not. That which is truth is always *changeless.* That which is a be*lie*f always *changes.* Also, look what is in the center of the word be*lie*f. So that which is rooted in truth is so today, was the same 5000 years ago and still will be the same in 10,000 years from now. We can also take this teaching to the next step to recognize that truth is also *timeless.* A be*lie*f, on the other hand, might be one thing today, different 200 years ago and will change again in 500 years from now.

One example of an old be*lie*f system in science is that it was thought prior to the 1900's that all of the continents on the planet were static and never moved. However, during the early 1900's geologists first theorized that maybe the continents drift somewhat. Later it was determined that the theory was correct, and this drifting occurred over subterranean *plates.* Today the scientists call this phenomenon *plate tectonics.* This is the best explanation geologists understand right now. But in reality, it is possible that in another 50 more years with greater and more sensitive technology, scientists may understand there is *something else* which affects and causes the drift and may rename it yet again differently. So this demonstrates a concept, or be*lie*f which clearly has changed over time. Although this exemplifies a scientific be*lie*f, we could find numerous examples based in philosophy, religion, spirituality, health and more.

It is not as simple to choose an example of something which the vast majority of people would agree is the truth, and is completely changeless. This is where *only* firsthand experience can allow one to recognize that which is *changeless* and *timeless.* If I stated that a truth is that the essence or soul of each person is eternal, having no beginning and no ending, there are some who would agree and then those who would disagree. So the *only* way to *really* know that which is true, is to have encountered it directly. If we simply accept another person or group's opinion as our own, this falls back into the category of be*lie*f. Everything which is established in truth, can be experienced by us directly. It is only through our *own* personal experience that we have the ability to discern that which is actually a truth. Once we have the direct knowledge, it will never leave us. It might be similar to the first time a small child sees an airplane flying in the sky. She is told that people can fly in a plane from one place to another within a couple of hours, much faster than what it normally takes in a full day to drive. She is filled with awe and asks what it is like to fly. Her parents may attempt to describe what it is like to board the plane and take off, what the clouds look like and all that can be seen from above, and what it is like to land. She listens to all that she has been told by others who have flown in planes, and tries to imagine the feeling. Years later, she finally gets to ride in a plane and finds her experience to seem completely different from all that she has been told before. She finds that it is even better than she ever had expected. Until she had her own *individual experience,* no amount of description by another person could ever have helped her to *really* know. If anyone ever asks her if she knows about flying, she will always sound a resilient *yes,* and will be able to speak to others from her own experience.

This is what it takes to be on the path of *awakening*. It is having the thirst to actively pursue that which is *changeless* and *timeless*. It is having the desire like a child ready to take his first airplane flight to fully experience and know the truth.

Our journey of *awakening* has many similarities to taking a flight on an airplane. We may choose to book a plane on any one or more combinations of flights which can go to countless destinations. Some flights may be long, some short. Some flights may have one or more connecting flights, or be very short and direct. Each flight we take has a unique group of other people all riding with us. Some we may find are going to the same planned destination as us, and others may exit the plane at an earlier destination to go elsewhere. If we pay attention to the others on board with us we may also notice that there are those whom we have a lot in common, and others that seem very different from us. Finally, if we look around us and notice the experience the others are having compared to ours, we will see that everyone is undergoing a completely unique event based upon his own perspective.

One man may sit completely engrossed in utilizing all of his time on the flight to perform work on his electronic computer. He ignores all of the activity surrounding him, and speaks only to his flight attendant to specify his drink. A woman may be very uncomfortable after eating food earlier which has upset her intestinal tract. She has kept most of her focus upon going to and from the bathroom, and shifting in her seat to become more comfortable. Another man is sitting deliberately distracting himself by wearing earphones playing music and keeping his eyes tightly closed. He knows he is afraid of flying, and feels if he can divert his attention away from seeing out of the window and pretend he isn't really on an airplane, he can maybe get through it. Two rows away from him there is a woman who has announced to everyone near her that her son bought her plane ticket to come see him for her 60th birthday, and this is her first time getting to fly. Someone switched seats with her so she could sit right next to the window. She spent the whole flight gasping and marveling at what it was like to see the cities from above- buildings, lakes, and even cars driving down the roads. As the aircraft coasted into its first set of clouds, her smile widened like the delight of a child being told she could play in the middle of a mud puddle. Later into the flight as the clouds became instead of white and fluffy, much darker and dense the plane was jostled roughly about. She exclaimed,"What is this?!" A couple of people explained to her it is what is called *turbulence.* She continued on," Wow! Isn't this a lot of fun, like a rollercoaster!" Although a couple of people near her chuckled at her giddiness, the man two rows away closed his eyes tighter and turned his music up louder to keep his thoughts away from the thrashing of the plane. The man busy with his work let out a disgruntled sigh, as he was having trouble continuing to type on his keyboard. The woman at the back of the plane was told she needed to take her seat for a bit until the turbulence stopped. She sat hoping she could keep her nausea at bay by stuffing a couple of pretzels into her mouth.

    Finally, the aircraft lands and each passenger slowly files up the aisle to walk off of the plane. The flight attendant smiles at each passenger, thanking each of them for choosing to fly with their airline. Each person exits, and although this flight started at the same place and arrived at the same eventual destination for everyone, there are no two people who will describe their experience to another the same. Everyone rode in the same plane, had the same staff assisting, the same food choices, the same scenery, and same length of flight. However, each person later will most likely be asked," How did you like your flight?" Even if 85 people boarded the plane and exited at exactly the same time, there would be 85 completely different answers. Each one of them would relate a completely unique experience, although most all of the circumstances were nearly identical.

The man preoccupied in his work may relate, that it was a great flight as he accomplished a lot of his work up until the turbulence. Then he just wanted to hurry up and arrive, so he could get busy and be productive again. The woman who spent much of her time in and out of the bathroom, relates to others it was a lousy flight as she was sick the whole time. Her perception was the attendants didn't seem to care much about her, and even made her go back to her seat. The man who was afraid throughout the flight simply was relieved to be on solid ground. If anyone asked him about it he would avoid answering, and simply say it was fine. The woman who savored her first flight will meet her son and speak nonstop for the first hour. She will likely relate to him every detail she can remember gleefully, and thank him for such a wonderful trip.

This is precisely the way we each spend our life journey. We might be experiencing nearly identical circumstances as another, yet our focus, perception and response to all that is occurring to us are completely different. These people each exemplify a few of the major ways we may decide to travel through our life. One may be self-absorbed, and driven to live mostly through working. Ignoring most everything surrounding oneself, and focusing mostly on career advancement and success is one pattern many may find themselves. Another group of people may spend much of the time during life in a state of fear or worry. They focus so much upon the possibility that something bad may happen. Much time is caught up in this battle of constant concern over things which most likely will rarely happen. Yet another group may have health issues which seemingly come up frequently throughout the life, and are often a moderate to serious distraction. Lastly, there are those progressing through life being fully in the experience much of the time. These people are the ones mostly engaged and enjoying most of their life. They tend to have a variety of interests, and are more balanced and tell others they love their jobs, their family, and seem genuinely happy.

Is there one of these groups we can identify ourself in either most of the time, or a portion of the time? If so, hopefully it is in the last group. It is when we actively pursue *awakening,* which allows us to mostly move out of the first three groups, or other less desirable group patterns into the last group. It is here where we can ultimately experience a greater sense of peace, balance, growth, and happiness during our life.

2

What is *Awakening*?

The dictionary definition of *awakening* is: The act of starting to understand something or feel something. The root of the word is *awaken* which means: Rouse from sleep; cause to stop sleeping. Simply by looking at this definition we might deduce that the opposite of being in a state of *awakening* would be instead a state of *sleeping*. How many people go throughout a whole lifetime completely asleep? Unfortunately, quite a few more than we would like to see.

Another way to describe this also is the level, or degree of *awareness* we have in our life. This defined is: the knowledge or perception of a situation or fact. So as we have already established, there are people going through life at all different levels of *awareness,* which is directly related to the degree in which a person is *awake.* We might ask in many different ways how to fully understand this concept. Once I witnessed the best explanation of this ever by Sai Maa.

When Sai Maa first came to the United States she travelled back and forth across the country. During this earlier time, smaller groups would attend her retreats. I heard she was going to be in Indianapolis just for a two-hour program on a Saturday night. So I drove up to see her. It was held in the Ebenezer Baptist Church, and all of the public were invited. She had finished leading us in a meditation, singing a chant, and began teaching. She began telling us that the *only* thing we each came here to do, is to become *fully enlightened.* That this is simply it, and there is really nothing else. Basically in just a few short sentences, she summed up the meaning of life I had asked years ago.

A man stood up and interrupted her saying," Well, I feel like I'm *already fully enlightened* and there isn't anything else I need to do." he jeered at her and continued, " A few years ago I gave my life to Christ and was saved and now I'm born again. There isn't anything else that I *need* to do now."

Sai Maa calmly explained, this that you describe is that you had a certain *spiritual experience.* This is different than being enlightened. A person may have a number of different experiences such as this throughout one's lifetime. But when a person becomes *fully enlightened,* this is a *state* of being. An individual afterwards is in this *constant state* of higher awareness.

The man sat down looking a little puzzled afterwards, but I understood and felt this was a great explanation. A *state of being.* The concept is very simple, but not necessarily so easy.

We came here to re-member that which we have forgotten through the process of *Awakening,* which eventually leads us to the continuous *state of being fully enlightened.* Whew! How long does it take us to figure this out? And do we really understand?

Throughout the years I have come to realize that there is truly never any end to our *awakening*. Even when an individual eventually moves into the realm of being *fully enlightened,* this is not where it ends. At this stage there is usually a greater level of responsibility, in fully living on purpose and helping others to accomplish the same. There is never an end point where we may rest on our laurels and state," I finally am there, and now there is nothing more to attain."

It is an infinite journey which never stops, no matter which level one has reached. A few years ago Sai Maa would speak about one of her personal assistants and tell others that she had reached, "baby enlightenment." She attempted to explain how there were varying levels. During this time I was still attempting to wrap my Westernized brain around its importance and how all of this *enlightenment* stuff worked.

A few years later I finally let go, deciding that maybe it was one of those concepts that it would be okay if I never fully understood. A little after this, I had a dream or vision which allowed me to finally "get" how this works in our lives. I found myself on what seemed like a platform. I knew I was on a break from my life. I was either between lifetimes, or simply taking a rest of some sort. There were a couple of other beings with me too. I seemed to know the other two who were there, and we were joyous to see each other, as if it had been quite a bit of time since we had seen each other. As we stood on this platform and walked about, there were about 15–16 identical television-like screens each showing the activities of one person on the planet. It showed exactly at that moment what activities each one was doing, and the whole scenario of their life on the screen. Each of us excitedly went from one to another watching each person and cheering them on. We seemed to know every one of them. Just above each screen there was a large red LED type display of numbers. Each person's number screen displayed different numbers. One read 374, another 414 and each one had other varying numbers. Suddenly there was a flicker as one person's numbers moved up a few digits higher. We all raced over to his screen, and watched what he was doing in his life, whooping and hollering so happy for him. We knew that whatever decision and action he had just taken in his life moved his number up a few points higher. This activity also indicated that his level of awareness had just increased. We marveled and watched intently for a moment to see what specific circumstances and actions he had just taken, hoping to see what we might learn from him. We then stopped at every other member's screen and we recognized and applauded those whose numbers had advanced higher since we had last seen them. Also, we noticed those numbers which hadn't moved up at all, and stopped to analyze their life scenario. We sent them loving thoughts filled with hope, that they would take action in their lives to start moving higher again. Later, I noticed that there were two different people's screens that were missing from the group whom I knew had previously been in our group. I asked what happened to them? I was told that the two had moved on to a different group, and a new level. Initially, I felt like I would miss them greatly, but then a feeling of joy washed over me as I knew they moved up in their awareness and went onward to have new experiences.

    I returned after this detailed vision feeling much more clarity. It impressed so much upon me, and has never faded with time. I experienced how much pure love we have for each other. There was no ego at all, and we truly wanted everyone to grow and expand in awareness. There was no competition, no hurry, simply learning. We cheered and encouraged each other, wanting everyone to progress and grow. I felt a hunger there to learn, grow and expand. I saw that we seem to stay in a particular group along with several others, as we continue to learn our lessons. When we finish growing all that we can at that particular level, then we move on to the next one. So it is here that I discovered with no uncertainty, that there is not any end place. We are infinite beings on an eternal adventure of encounters, and all of our possibilities of growth are limited only by whatever we can't imagine. Everything is possible and there are a never-ending number of possibilities.

I realized that *enlightenment* is not the final destination. Although it is a higher state of awareness than *un-enlightenment,* it doesn't matter whether we are there yet or not. What matters is that we are growing, learning, and progressing in our level of awareness, and not sitting stagnant. This increase in awareness and growth only occurs when we are open and actively seeking it. It is not enough for us to read a lot of books, or sit and think of a few theories or ideas now and then. It is when we put our feet to the pavement, and put all we learn into practice day to day, and *only* then we will be able to recognize and know that we are growing.

It is not that we love to be alone, but that we love to soar, and when we do soar, the company grows thinner and thinner until there is none at all. ...We are not the less to aim at the summits, though the multitude does not ascend them.
— Henry David Thoreau

Fortunately, throughout the history of this planet we have had several living examples of people who were able to fully step into mastery, or *full enlightenment* as many call it. Most of them lived a public enough life to attempt to lead others by being a model for the rest to follow. The Eastern portion of our world are more familiar with Gautama Buddha, who attained his mastery after sitting in the practice of meditation many years. He reached his full awareness finally after sitting many days under the Bodhi tree. His teachings and practices have been passed throughout the years and are essentially still mostly intact today in the religions of varying types of Buddhism.

Westerners are more familiar with the life of Jesus, the man who eventually became the Christ after several years of similar study and practice. His original teachings and practices have been passed throughout the years, but unfortunately are not as well intact today in the religions of varying types of Christianity.

The major thing for us to notice are that each of these people who moved into Mastery all had much in common. Each lived their life initially in the same types of circumstances as any other person, but then at an early age had the desire to know more. Each of them had the same hunger to learn, and then practiced all which they learned vigilantly. They were dedicated and determined to fully understand, and experience the truth. Neither would stop practicing, nor allow themselves to become sidetracked. Both were able to accomplish on this planet that continuous state of being *fully awakened,* or *enlightened.* After they accomplished this for themselves, they reached out to others to teach them how to do the same in their lives.

It is unfortunate that over the centuries many of the original practices which Jesus taught to his disciples during his life have become watered down, at the least. This is why at this date there are at least 41,000 different Christian religious denominations. Each one of these have a differing be*lie*f system, which is from slightly to vastly different from the other. The variety of Christian dogmas run the whole spectrum, such as those who be*lie*ve Jesus taught that one might die and burn in hell if one doesn't live just right. Others be*lie*ve that a person dies and stays in the grave, and only certain ones of the "chosen few" will be resurrected someday when Jesus returns. This is one be*lie*f that it seems at least a portion of the Christian denominations agree with each other in some form. Most agree that there will be a *Second Coming of Christ.* This is that Jesus will someday return to our planet, and in some shape or fashion save either some, or all of the people here in some way. These limitless number of differences in Christian denominations are so great, it almost looks comedy-like if we lined them all up side by side to each other. But it is a serious subject, as this means that the actual *changeless* truth Jesus attempted to teach others has split off into at least 41,000 different variations. All of these variations do not stand up to our method of measuring the truth. They do not meet the qualifications of truth, because they are not *timeless* and *changeless*. Even a minimally adept analytical person might see, that if his actual teachings had continued untainted throughout the years, there would be only one Christian Religion today.

There are two great errors which have been passed down through the generations that many Christians have embraced. Sai Maa mentions these usually once at nearly every event of hers. She will explain this to everyone just in case there are those still caught up in the web of these Western be*lie*fs.

She will scan the room intently pointing upwards, you *must* know there is no God *out there* sitting watching you, and waiting to do things to you if you are bad. She next moves her hand over her heart, this is it *right here*. You have *everything* here. You must *know* this.

Later, in a lighter mood, Sai Maa explains, don't be thinking that Jesus plans to come back to this planet. He *already* came here and there are those who think he is coming again. Why would he even *want* to come back here anyway? So the people here could kill him again? Jesus is off doing many other things now, and is much too busy to come back here. Her amusement dissipates and she pauses with urgency. *You* are the ones you have been waiting for, *you* are the second coming of Christ. It is time for *you* to wake up and re-member you are that. You are *everything*!

3

Establishing The Framework

Anytime we wish to create a shift of awareness and move actively into the process of *awakening*, there are a few foundational concepts we must first embrace. I have found that there are three concepts which in my life have given the framework to help understand, and to put everything into perspective.

The first of the three was introduced to me years ago while I was stationed in the Army in Germany. It was about three years after I had given up my self-appointed task to find the "one correct Christian religion." After visiting at least 20 or more different churches throughout a year, I decided there wasn't any *one correct* church or religion and had stopped trying to look for anything. During these three years I had simply given up, and was no longer actively studying or pursuing anything religious at all.

Then I was introduced to a wonderful woman twice my age, who would sit and teach two of us for a couple of hours at a time about *reincarnation* and *karma*. I had heard of the words, but had never been exposed to anyone who might explain them. I knew these were understood more in the Eastern part of the world, but nothing more than this. She patiently answered all of my questions, and eventually recommended that I read a book about Edgar Cayce. I read the book as she advised, and this lead me to many more books. I think of her fondly as my first spiritual teacher. Another important thing she taught was the important phrase, *when the student is ready, the teacher will appear*. Our paths crossed in the same part of the world for nearly two years. She set me back onto my path of at least actively pursuing knowledge. Hereafter, instead of thinking I was simply off of any religious path, I realized that I was now on a spiritual path and there is a definite difference.

The most difficult concept for me, and I am sure for most other traditionally trained Westerners was understanding *reincarnation*. I know I had the greatest number of questions surrounding this idea.

The East Teaches the West

Reality is merely an illusion, albeit a very persistent one.

– Albert Einstein

I find it amusing that throughout the years there has been such of a division between the Eastern side and Western side of our planet. Just as the geography has separated these two regions, so has the primary thinking of her people within these two areas.

Growing up in the West from a traditional Christian-Judeo be*lief* system fosters in most of us a fairly restricted and sheltered way of looking at life. My background was similar to this, and even during college I remember for my liberal arts degree our advisors did not recommend such classes as philosophy or religion beyond possibly taking a single new testament or old testament class. I remember one student choosing to major in philosophy being chastised by the rest, telling him nobody would wish to hire him later with that type of degree.

I feel that education then and now in the West has a tendency to compartmentalize everything. We tend to separate our courses of study into each specific isolated, and focused areas. I remember having quite a heated discussion on this topic with a friend of mine during my freshman year in college. He was very aggravated that we were required to take general education classes for our degree. He felt that since he was majoring in biology, it made no sense why he needed to take any other courses which were not science related. We argued on this matter several times. He could not see the necessity that he needed any courses outside of science. None of the other classes seemed useful(to him) as he planned to have a future profession in science. The last time I heard, he is currently serving as the Department Head Professor of the biology department in a large university.

There are some aspects of our way of education being so specialized like this which are beneficial, but there are other times it is not. When we have so many people who only know one area or have a single specialty, we each seemingly become our own separate island. This creates a society which has several different fields, each focused upon trying to serve its own interests, and often-times ignoring the rest. This also has a tendency to foster an *us vs. them* type of mentality.

Everywhere we look today we witness this. Whether we specialize as an Engineer for GM, Hospital Administrator, Farmer caring for 3000 acres, Computer Analyst, Artist, Maintenance Technician, Heavy Equipment Operator, Politician, Production Worker, or Librarian, we each tend to know only about our own sector or corner of the world. We have a tendency to isolate our attention and concerns surrounding the well-being of the planet from our separated portion. For example, the Hospital Administrator is concerned about the upcoming Medicare cuts and rising costs to replace outdated equipment, while the farmer most likely is not. Likewise, the farmer is working to problem solve how to get his corn to produce more in the middle of a drought, and the Hospital Administrator is mostly unaware of farming issues. The production worker who assembles parts for a large automotive manufacturer may be keenly aware of the changes of specifications in a brake system which has been recently recalled in a vehicle, but hasn't any awareness of the work required by computer analysts to check a software program being updated to perform this year's tax returns.

Because of this way in which we have been so encouraged throughout our years of education in life to focus our energy, time, understanding and talents into mostly one area, we have a tendency to lose the big picture. We each worry mostly about what is happening in our own world and within our own corner, that we somewhat ignore all of the rest. Day to day we usually keep to ourselves, focusing on our own individual itinerary, or "to do" list. Especially today, it is easy to see that our focus may extend mostly to only immediate family, such as our partner, children, and other family members. During the "daily grind" of life, this is about the extent that the average person concerns oneself with on most days.

It would be ideal if at some point in the typical Westerner's education, that someone might stop and ask us some important questions. How does each of these areas(Health, Manufacturing, Environment, Computer Science, Art, Education, Etc.) affect another? How can they work together? How can we bring these together to better serve humanity as an interwoven team, working towards the greater good of all? Obviously, it is not only in the West that this attitude of separateness has become so inherent. However, it is rare for a person during the years of standard education to search for, and elaborate upon these greater meanings of life, and how everything we do in our day to day lives may be affecting others.

I know for myself, when I first had been given the two Eastern concepts of *Reincarnation* and *Karma*, these gave me a new lens in which to witness the world. I was amazed that so many people outside of the Western side of the planet grew up having been taught these philosophical concepts, and these were simply an accepted part of life for many of them. I was also upset that I hadn't taken any Eastern philosophy courses in college, which would have introduced me to these views a few years sooner.

If we can truly grasp and understand the meaning of *Karma* and *Reincarnation*, then we are truly on our way of understanding how every living being on this planet are interconnected. This can become our own natural response to move into a higher overview of life here. Rather than taking the approach of *my separate corner* and *my own needs*, we may begin to approach life here as *our connected needs* and eventually such ideas as *our greater good*. We can then begin to take a greater responsibility for our own actions and their effects on everyone. Instead of thinking day to day, *how may I serve myself and my family?* This shifts, and becomes *how may I best serve the needs of us all?*

And Justice for Us All

Throughout the years I have come to understand *Karma* to be that which truly is the equalizer. It is really that which makes the playing field for everyone truly level. *Karma* is simply the law of cause and effect. Everything that we *think, say, feel, speak and act upon* has a creative energy which we may call the *cause*. And the *degree* or *quality* of the energetic level which is behind the thoughts, words, feelings and actions are that which determines the eventual outcome, or *effect*.

This concept is also contained in most of the Western Christian *Bibles* and is stated 36 times in a variety of ways. It states in Galatians 6:7:....*for whatever a man sows, this he shall also reap.* Then 2 Corinthians 9:6 states: *Remember this: Whoever sows sparingly will also reap sparingly, and whoever sows generously will also reap generously.* It is apparent this is the same concept as *Karma,* and similarly describes the act of *sowing* as the same as the *cause* and *reaping* is the same as the *effect.*

A few years ago this law was a little more difficult to see and visualize in our daily lives, as the *effects* were slower to be noticed and occurred over a longer period of time. Today due to the fact that everything is going so much faster, we can see this law manifesting much more quickly in our day to day lives. This law may affect us in either smaller ways, or in very large ways depending upon in what way we are creating in our lives using these energetic potentials.

Most of us have experienced a day when we notice generally everything seems to be going wrong. It may start with one simple event, such as arriving at work and finding out you have a mandatory meeting that you must attend, and realizing that you are completely unprepared. Then your emotions begin to race, and you maybe become angry at yourself for forgetting and quickly you begin to throw together everything you should have done one or two days earlier. Later that morning, one of your co-workers suddenly makes a couple of sarcastic remarks as though she is upset at you about something. This catches you completely off guard as well. Your day becomes so busy that you don't have enough time to make any preparations for your meeting. You decide to take a shorter lunch so you have more time to get ready. Just before lunch you are given an insurance form that must be filled out that day for a patient coming back to pick it up that afternoon. After you return back to work, after lunch you notice that someone had hit your right front bumper on your car. You finally take a long deep breath and think, "What in the world am I doing to bring on all of this?" This is an example of how very quickly our thoughts and feelings about even one single event can draw a whole set of lower energetic situations right to us.

On the other hand, hopefully most of us have had days when we awaken and just feel awake, alert and happy. Perhaps the evening before we had some good quality time with our loved ones and were able to talk and have some fun. We start our morning smiling thinking about incidents from the previous night. Maybe we start singing in the shower and, smile as we notice that our version of a popular song sounds almost like the original artist's. We go to work that day, and just feel like we are *in the flow.* Everything we do just feels right. During the day we think about how much we love our work, and all of the people we are able to serve. That same co-worker you had trouble with a couple of weeks ago opens up to you, and both of you are able to talk out your differences and greatly improve your relationship with each other. Later in the day you receive a couple of compliments. That evening you stop off at the store which is really busy, and you are able to find a parking spot open close to the front door. During this day our higher feelings and thoughts of joy, and love brought the situations which most closely match that energetic level to us.

This law of *Karma* is constantly working in our lives whether we are aware of it or not. This is much like the law of *gravity*. This law works in our day to day lives and is ever present on this planet, and is similar to *Karma* in that it is an unseen energy. *Gravity* and *Karma* are also alike in that both of these laws are continuously working whether one be*lie*ves in them or not.

As a child I remember the Superman cartoon being everyone's favorite. Every boy(and some of the girls) wanted to be just like Superman. I can remember one very valiant boy getting a Superman costume for his birthday. The first day he proudly dawned his costume for all of the kids in the neighborhood to see. He ran throughout our yards and the street, seemingly as if his new outfit gave him all of the powers of Superman. At one moment, he was so convinced of his newly found abilities that he climbed a ladder onto the roof of his garage. We watched him announce one last time, "I am Superman, and I can leap the largest buildings and can fly!" His feet clambered quickly and sure across the shingles on the roof of his garage, his right arm flung straight out in a perfect fist fitting for Superman himself. As he reached the edge of the roof and took a giant leap, he didn't fly. He fell straight down onto the ground, and fortunately only broke his arm. All of his strongest be*lief* still could not take away the effects of the law of *gravity*.

Similar to this, our be*lief*s no matter what they may be cannot take away the effects of the law of *karma*. A person may choose to disregard that *karma* plays a huge role in each one's life, and continue to live a life having a point of view of ignorance. Or we can decide to embrace and understand how it is that we are creating our own reality each day in our lives. We must come to a place of understanding, that our lives are not simply a large pool of willy-nilly circumstances which are all random. Instead, we must recognize that everything is not all simply "accidental" occurrences, but we have our own control which allows us to move into a place of empowerment. Only then will we be able to see our lives in a way that puts each of us in the true management of our own destiny as an individual, and as our own interconnectedness to all of the world.

Karma, when properly understood, is just the mechanics through which consciousness manifests.

-Deepak Chopra

Let's Play It Again

The other major concept that many people on the planet(except in the West) simply accept as true is that of *Reincarnation*. If we truly wish to understand our highest greatest purpose, and comprehend the *how* and *why* of the law of *Karma,* we must be able to acknowledge and truly understand just how *reincarnation* works.

Reincarnation defined by the dictionary is: that an individual has a rebirth into another body after death. Those who accept this concept acknowledge that we are eternal beings, rather than thinking a person is born, lives a single life, then after death may or may not have some sort of afterlife on another plane of existence. It is the premise that each person is definitely eternal. It acknowledges that each individual has experienced many previous lifetimes in a variety of differing circumstances. The ultimate purpose of these experiences is to grow in our awareness and is also a vehicle for each of us to potentially "cleanse," or clear away some of this past *Karma*.

Reincarnation occurs because we decide that we haven't learned enough lessons.
                              -Sylvia Browne

It never made sense to me that certain Western religions teach that a person comes and lives one life, dies and then is simply finished. I wondered how one could make sense of why one person is born into extreme poverty and dies of starvation before reaching the age of two, and another is born into extreme wealth and receives every advantage and lives a long and lavish life. Then there are those who be*lie*ve that there is an afterlife; but it consists of a place which is either hell, a place where the person suffers for all of eternity, or heaven, a place the person lives in perfection and peace for all of eternity. Even as a child this never made any sense to me. And what purpose might this possibly serve, and how could any of this justly be decided? It all seemed to be a flimsy view to me even before I reached a full age of reasoning.

However, if we think of the idea that we have multiple lifetimes, then this makes everything have so much more sense. This allows us to see that the universe is truly fair. Everyone has the same opportunities to evolve, grow and experience as another.

As an example, during one lifetime maybe one lived a life in the Army during a war in which he was in charge of taking care of prisoners of war, and treated his prisoners badly. Although he had plenty of rations to adequately feed his prisoners, instead he sold them off keeping the profits for himself. Most of them eventually perish due to a lack of food, living a life of abuse and suffering. During his next lifetime, this person through the law of *Karma*, is born into a family with one of her parents being an alcoholic. The father uses all of the money from the family to buy alcohol for himself, and doesn't care about his wife or children. She lives all of her childhood being hungry from a lack of food and essential care. Occasionally, her father abuses her physically. Finally, at the age of 12 based upon a school complaint that she had been absent from school for a few days, the police come to the house to discover the girl locked in a room and severely emaciated from near starvation. The girl is placed in a foster home where she recovers mostly physically, yet spends the rest of her life experiencing the left-over emotional scars from her father's abuse. This is an example of how *reincarnation* and *karma* work together, and what one might experience from an accumulation of extreme lower vibrational energies during a previous lifetime.

On the other hand, one can experience similar effects during subsequent lifetimes from the accrual of higher vibrational *karma*. An example of this might be that one has lived a life in which she successfully raised four children, and while living on the Ohio river assisted in being part of the underground railroad. She secretly assisted a group of nine other people dig out and maintain an underground tunnel on her property, which helped slave families get from the Southern Kentucky side of the river to the Northern side of the river in Indiana to obtain their freedom. She risked the well-being of herself and her family for over fifteen years, until the Civil War finally ended. She assisted over 250 slave families to safely cross the river and gain their freedom. During her next life, she was born into a large and wealthy family in Europe. She went to Oxford University for her education and eventually rose to become crowned the Queen of her country. During this lifetime, she again grows and has the opportunity to touch many lives through her service. Although she still faces challenges during her life as may be expected, she is adored and respected by her whole country and leads a healthy, happy and love-filled life.

These are theoretical examples of the way in which *reincarnation* and *karma* become the means which allow fairness and balance of these laws to occur in each person's life. As mentioned, this gives us the ability to see that truly every event, and every circumstance in our life has been created by ourselves, and not by some outside happen-stance luck of the draw.

Where's The Proof?

Dr. Ian Stevenson previously researched and documented over 2500 cases of *reincarnation* throughout his 40 plus year career as a psychiatrist. His research shows that he has verifiable cases of young children, typically first beginning between the ages of three to five remembering details of their most recent past life. The child may remember all types of details, such as location of the previous home, the previous spouse's name, children, siblings and often may even remember the cause of the previous death. Dr. Stevenson was very meticulous in his method of researching each possible case. He typically would interview the child, and obtain as many possible details. Next, he would search and attempt to find the location and family to verify if the information the child has provided seemed to match. Only after he had diligently confirmed all of the specifics of the case, he would arrange for the child to go to the location and meet the family. Typically the child would astonish everyone present with the ability to recall and identify various family members, names and incidents only *that* particular deceased family member might know.

Dr. Stevenson had published several books and articles throughout the years detailing specific cases, and all of the usual patterns he had noticed which seemed to be consistent with his verified cases. Some of his later studies included the correlations between the children during their current lifetimes having particular birthmarks. He found that these birthmarks seemed to match the same location of certain health conditions or incidents of trauma which occurred during the previous lifetime.

One case he wrote about in his book, *Twenty Cases Suggestive of Reincarnation* was called "Sweet Swarnlata's Story." Typical of many of Dr. Stevenson's cases, Swarnlata first began recalling details of her previous lifetime starting at the age of three. She was able to give Dr. Stevenson over 50 specific facts of her previous lifetime. This enabled him to locate the family of the deceased person she remembered, and he was able to subsequently verify all of the details she had given him.

Swarnlata was born into a prosperous family in Pradesh in India in 1948. At the age of three while traveling past the city of Katni more than 100 miles from her home, she pointed suddenly and told the driver to turn down a road to "my house." She further suggested that they could get a better cup of tea there than on the road. Soon after this incident, Swarnlata began to relate more details of her life in Katni, which her father began to write down. She told him her name was Biya Pathak, and she had two sons. She continued to give a specific description of the house she lived in, and that her family owned a motor car(a rarity for a family in India during this time, and especially before the 1950's). She related that Biya died of a "pain in her throat," and gave details of the name of the doctor whom had treated her. In the spring of 1959, one of Dr. Stephenson's colleagues first learned of Swarnlata's case, and informed him of her when she was ten years old. He first met with her father and took the notes from him, and was easily able to find the home based upon the detailed description of the girl. He met and interviewed the Pathak family living in the home. They were a wealthy and prominent family, who verified that Biya Pathak had died in 1939 leaving behind a grieving husband, two young sons and many younger brothers. The Pathak family had no idea about Swarnlata's family, nor did Swarnlata's family know anything about the Pathak's, as both families lived over 100 miles away from each other.

Next, during the Summer of 1959 Biya's husband, son, and eldest brother journeyed to the town where Swarnlata was living to test her memory. They did not announce their identities or purpose to others in town, but requested nine other people to accompany them to Swarnlata's home where they arrived unannounced. The ten-year-old immediately recognized her brother and called him "Babu," Biya's pet name for him. She then went around the room looking at each man. Some she identified that she knew from town, and others she identified as strangers. When she came to her former husband, Swarnlata lowered her eyes as was customary for Hindu wives to do during that time, and called him by name. She also correctly identified her son, named Murli, who was 13 years old when she died. Swarnlata even reminded her former husband of a box containing 1200 rupees. He admitted that only he and his wife had known of this, and had kept this fact private from the rest of the family.

A few weeks later Swarnlata's father took her to Katni to visit the home and town where Biya lived and died. She correctly described the décor and layout of the home, and trees in the yard during the time she had lived there in 1939. She correctly identified Biya's room and the room in the house where she died. She identified correctly her other son, several of her brothers, a sister-in-law, cousins, a midwife, a former house servant and even the family cow herder.

The Pathak family were convinced that Swarnlata had been Biya in her previous lifetime. They accepted her warmly, and she continued throughout the years to visit and maintain contact with her former family. Dr. Stevenson continued to remain in communication with Swarnlata for at least another ten years. She lived her life normally, eventually marrying and completing an advanced degree in Botany.

Dr. Stevenson's extensive work and diligence with each of his cases, demonstrates to even the most skeptic that *reincarnation* is not simply a far-fetched theory. He dedicated most of his life to *verifying* and *proving* that this concept truly does exist.

On the other hand, Delores Cannon, a past life regression hypnotherapist, has dedicated her life to understanding the *how's* and *why's* behind *reincarnation*. Delores Cannon has been a hypnotherapist over 40 years, and initially similar to many Westerners did not be*lie*ve in *reincarnation*. She describes herself during the 1960's as a "conservative and typical happily married woman." Initially, she became trained in hypnotherapy hoping that she might be able to help some people to quit smoking or to lose weight, the typical applications of hypnotherapy. Then one day she had regressed one of her clients back to her childhood during a hypnosis session, and then quite unexpectedly, her client went further before her birth. She reported in great details her decision to take birth "again," and the lessons she was coming here to learn which she had struggled learning in her previous lifetime. Ms.

Cannon was really surprised at this revelation, and soon after began to hear similar accounts from many of her clients during their sessions. She noticed even though her clients didn't know each other, they were relating the same types of descriptions during their hypnotherapy sessions. She noticed that it didn't matter what the person's religious be*lie*fs were, as many described a vivid previous lifetime to her. Each were reporting what aspects were successful and which things were still left to learn. They even saw how they died, and most described a resting period afterwards, and how they actively made the decision to take birth again into their present embodiment.

When she first started witnessing her clients experiencing these "past lives," Ms. Cannon began keeping scrupulous recordings and notes from the sessions. She began to notice that certain topics came up over and over by different people during their sessions, and she was able to group them into different categories. Ms. Cannon out of "her own curiosity" started researching, and finding as much information as possible on the periods of history and various subjects which her clients were describing. Nevertheless, she found that all of the accounts each person had recounted during the session seemed to not only verify various periods of history she had researched, but also seemed to fill in the gaps and elaborate more on areas not described in any of the documented sources. She found that the information seemed to be impeccably consistent from person to person.

Throughout the years Ms. Cannon has been honored with several of the highest awards for the advancement in research of psychic phenomenon. As of today, she has written and published at least 16 different books, each categorizing these accounts from her clients into different subjects. She has one which details our common experiences after death and before the next birth, another of those people detailing a lifetime being with Jesus, one book details people describing previous lives on other planets, and yet another describing how there are three waves of "volunteers" who have come to help the planet earth. Ms. Cannon warns those who read her books, that this new information causes the mind "to bend like a pretzel" into a new shape from contemplating all of these incredible realizations about our lives, and the universe in which we are living.

It is apparent that no matter how much one's upbringing has caused one to become cemented into a be*lie*f that each person gets a single shot at a life on earth, and there is little responsibility required here, all of the evidence from multiple sources shows the contrary. Clearly we can see that our life *is* infinite, and everything we do does create our own reality and has purpose and meaning. Now it is time for us each to decide whether we wish to continue to take the easy way, avoiding taking responsibilities for our own lives and actions, or if we will step up and acknowledge that there is a higher purpose which we each must realize. These concepts have been taught for hundreds, if not thousands of years in many of the Eastern portions of the world. If we truly wish to understand *who* we are, and *how* to live our life more fully, enabling us to learn to heal at all levels, we must allow ourselves to embrace these concepts, grow and become *awakened.*

My beloved Sai Maa often during our spiritual retreats will often tell us: I am here for those of you who want to do the work and go fast. I fully respect the ones who choose to go slower, I have no problem if that's what you wish. She gives us a huge smile and snaps her fingers rhythmically into the air, but you know how I am, I like to do *everything* fast!

There always comes a place in our lives where we must make a decision. Do we plan to take the fast track? Or continue to move about the same as always. The fast track always involves us taking action. The slower way always involves us avoiding taking active steps in our life.

The term *ignorance* is defined from the dictionary as: The state or fact of being ignorant: lack of knowledge, education, or awareness. I feel that there are two types of ignorance. There is the type of ignorance wherein the person truly has a lack of knowledge or awareness as described in a certain area or topic. Then there is another type of ignorance where one truly is aware of a concept or truth, and chooses to *ignore* it. Rather than embracing the concept, it gets pushed to the back burner, thinking if we *ignore* looking at it completely, maybe this will be easier. However, this merely puts it off until later, and at some time it will *have* to be faced.

The doorstep to the temple of wisdom is a knowledge of our own ignorance.

-Benjamin Franklin

So once we are informed, and have been given the framework of certain laws and truths to move forward and take action in our lives, what is our choice? What actions will we take? Or will we not do anything? Whether we assertively *take control* and move forward, or passively stand by and *ignore* or *resist* everything, these are each decisions. These alone determine whether we are propelled forward on the faster journey of *awakening*, or stay rooted in the same slower safe pattern of *simply existing* and doing the same thing over and over. Those taking the safer and slower route may expect to spend much more time being born again and again recycling here through many more incarnations, until finally choosing to *awaken*, and reaching to learn all of the needed lessons through taking full action.

4

The Glue That Unites Us

Are We Harmonizing?

I remember growing up there was one of the kids in my neighborhood who I always seemed to have many conflicts, arguments, and eventually fights. As the only girl growing up in an all-boy neighborhood, this one boy was always stirring up trouble with me and I would never back down from him. Commonly we would chant at each other," Sticks and stones may break my bones, but words will never hurt me!"

During those turbulent years living on my street, I had been taught to say these words and did just that over and over again. As I continued to grow up and eventually moved away from this harsh conflict, this be*lief* seemed to stay attached to my way of thinking. Even during high school and college I recall discussing this with my friends. We all mostly agreed that it was okay to think anything you want, say anything, and as long as you took no action it was all fine.

Often we pick up these kinds of notions early in life, and may carry them with us for a very long time unless we finally get woke up by the unexpected "bend in the road." I reached my "bend" when I was introduced to my first spiritual teacher while I was stationed in Germany.

After she introduced me to the concepts of *karma* and *reincarnation*, it was then I first began to realize that not only our actions, but our *thoughts and words* do really matter. These are what create the reality we are living in our life.

At this stage of my understanding, I first realized there was a distinction in what *negative* thoughts, words, and actions would create later in my life from the *positive* thoughts, words and actions. Several years later I learned that our emotional feelings are also included in this mix, and is the main driver behind all of these.

Today I find it better to think differently, instead of *positive* and *negative* in relating to thoughts, words, feelings and actions. Having these as our two categories requires us to make harsh judgments of everything, and categorize the world surrounding us as either black or white. I have found this seems to create more separation in our lives. When we look at everything we see and place them into one of these two categories, this causes us to treat them more like things. Unfortunately, this is how the majority of people look at everything in the world most of the time. Another dualist category used by many are *right* and *wrong*. This simply leads us into further judgments such as *good* and *bad*, and *truth* vs. *false*. Taking this approach fosters each person to attempt to categorize each thought, word, feeling, and action of ourself, and that of those surrounding us into one of these categories.

Some examples of this judgemental duality we see today here in the U.S. are that of the Democratic Party and Republican Party. Many Americans feel one side is right and the other side is wrong, and a few may even think that one is good and the other bad. Each major political issue seems to be split into two sides. Another great example is Religion. Many have tendencies to attempt to categorize once again, into right and wrong, good and bad thoughts, words, feelings, and actions of specific religious groups.

Of course, we see this emanate throughout the day in our relationships with ourself, our partner, children, parents, relatives, friends and co-workers. We are continuously analyzing every aspect of these relationships. It might be, "My Mother and I argue about how I am raising my children, and I feel that she is *wrong*." Or, "My boss keeps showering me with compliments and that makes me feel *great*." Or lastly, "This is the third time this week I messed up, and this time I ruined the mower when I ran over the rake in our yard. I can't do anything *right*!" Continually, most of us are evaluating everything in our day to day lives just like this.

At least a portion of the population have no idea that in these day to day situations, we are continuously creating our own reality in our life. Whether we are experiencing a life filled with conflict, or a life of peace is dependent each day upon the *quality* of our thoughts, feelings, words and actions.

The Miracle on 34th Street

When I look back at those tough years as a child, today I am able to see that we had it completely wrong. We were told and be*lie*ved that all we might say to another, think or feel about others carried no power. We were completely off the mark, as portrayed in the following two contrasting incidents during my childhood.

I had one last blow-out with that same kid just before my family moved out of that neighborhood. I was in the sixth grade, and by then all of us kids knew all of the rules, such as we weren't supposed to fight, etc. I was walking home from school late one day(yes, I grew up in the era when most kids didn't ride a bus) after basketball practice. The boy I usually had trouble with was out in the side of his yard with one of his friends as I was walking past on the sidewalk. He lived about four houses down from ours on 34th street. They both stopped passing the football to each other and one hollered," You need to get off of *my* sidewalk!"

Stubbornly, I stopped and shouted back," This is a public sidewalk, and I have every right to be here!"

He puffed up and demanded," If you don't leave my sidewalk *now*, I'll just have to *make* you move."

"Oh yeah? I guess you'll just have to *make* me then," I was belligerent and unbending.

He turned to his friend and said," Go ahead and throw rocks at her." He stood behind his friend with a satisfied grin as he watched on as several rocks were hurled at me. Four or five rocks came sailing toward me, none coming too close to his mark. As I witnessed his devious chuckle of pleasure, I felt the swelling of anger within me. I knew I wasn't supposed to throw rocks, but I thought to myself, *maybe it would be okay to just throw one.* I picked up a rock and hesitated just a moment still deliberating, and then pitched it the same as if I were throwing a baseball. (I had a pretty good arm, and could throw as hard as all of the boys my age and even some older) The one who was throwing at me ducked to the ground just in the nick of time as it sailed across his head. I heard a solid thud as it made contact just below the other boy's right eye. His laugh and giggle stopped abruptly as he touched his face with his hand to find blood, and then started crying and went into his house. As soon as I and the other boy realized he was hurt and bleeding, we knew we were both in big trouble and ran home.

I went into our house and slumped down into a chair in the living room. I knew I was in trouble, yet had no idea what to do. I felt bad, because I knew better and yet realized I couldn't undo anything now. A few minutes later there was a pounding on our front door. My Mom answered the door, and shortly thereafter was out on our front lawn with his Mother. Years of these kind of arguments which often seemed to lead to fights, now culminated into our two parents in my front yard hashing out everything.

"Your daughter just threw a rock at my son and nearly put his eye out!!"

" There was the time your *little angel* deliberately pushed her off the neighbor's glacier rock, and we had to have her head stitched!"

"Well your *little darling* one time hit him and blackened his eye…"

"And did he tell you that it was *because* he was strangling a little boy half of his age?!"

"How about the time the neighbor *paid* your *little angel* to paint her garage and he threw grapes at it right afterwards and blamed it on her. Did he tell you about that?"

It went on and on seemingly for an eternity. Several years of my facing the neighborhood bully created all of this. I was only brave enough to look out of the corner of the window once, and saw both women in a tirade of furious finger pointing, yelling loudly enough that I was sure the neighbors were out on their lawns to see what was happening. When it finally ended, my Mom came back into the house slamming our solid oak door so hard that the walls shook. She flew back into the kitchen, and I skulked down into my chair attempting to make myself as small as possible. I was surprised that she didn't say a word to me, and I actually didn't get into any trouble. Being a witness to all of that probably was torture enough. That was my last fight with any neighborhood kids.

Although this is an example of a juvenile situation, it works the same for any situation. We might start out thinking a certain way, which leads us to use our words. Once we begin to speak our words, these can become emotionally charged with our feelings. Once our feelings become activated with heated emotion, it is easy for these to escalate into actions which may possibly become really harmful.

A few months after this my family moved, and I found myself in a completely different environment. I managed to make several new friends in the neighborhood, and the dynamics of my day to day life morphed into nearly the opposite of my previous experience. There were kids on our street ranging from ages 6 to 15. There wasn't any fighting amongst us. Those of us who were a little older watched out for the younger ones. We played together, helped each other do outdoor chores and gardening, and if there ever were arguments they were always short-lived and reconciled nearly immediately.

Then it finally happened that all of this harmony was challenged. I was about to enter high school, and we had an exchange student about my age come stay with us for a month in the summer. Delia seemed very charismatic and was able to get along with my friends right away. She was quite a story-teller and captivated the others as she described her typical home life. She enamored others about the lavish-sounding lifestyle of hers with having lots of clothes, and parents giving her everything. She also claimed to have at least two different boyfriends back home. I eventually began to wonder about some of the stories, as some seemed almost too good to be true.

Nevertheless, after about three weeks into her stay, everything started to go a little sour. She began telling my different friends a variety of hurtful things about each of them, which she insisted I had shared with her in confidence. I was oblivious to what she was doing. One by one, each of my friends stopped wanting to see me as she systematically continued to drive a wedge between us. Within a few days nobody on my street wanted to have anything to do with me, and I was completely clueless. She finally returned to her home, and I felt like all of my once great friends had abandoned me.

Slowly, one by one each of my friends came to me, and asked me directly if anything she had told them was the truth. After openly answering all of their questions and explaining that all of it was simply made up by her, they decided mostly as a group that I just couldn't be like she had told them. Within a few short weeks, we became the close-knit group of friends just as we had been before.

Here is another example of a group of young people which demonstrates these principles. Everyone mostly had thoughts, feelings and words toward each other that came from a place of cooperation, kindness, respect and love towards each other. So this created a group of kids being in harmony with each other, and those surrounding us. Even when one person came from outside attempting to highjack this peacefulness through misleading words and actions, the group was able to eventually see through the disruption. They were able to return very quickly back to a place of support for each other again. Whether we are looking at the experiences of children or adults, the dynamics of what is occurring is all the same.

Today, I am able to look at both of these nearly opposite living situations during my youth, and see that these experiences helped me to learn first-hand early in my life about the two types of energy. Obviously, when I lived on 34th Street this demonstrated that if we allow ourselves to be in an environment filled with lower energies such as jealousy, pride, and anger, it is difficult to avoid getting caught into this web with others. The more we are in these lower situations, the more we become this way. But if we are surrounded with others who mostly live from the higher energies such as love, cooperation, and kindness then this is what we reflect back toward others and become.

The miracle is being able to have this discernment from these two contrasting experiences, and deciding to turn away from those lower energetic situations and people. This allows us to look at life from yet another perspective. If we can start to look at everything in terms of energy, we may begin to see ourselves and the world around us as though we have replaced our glasses with a new set of lenses. As we are able to do this, there becomes less conflict and a greater ability to have peace in our lives.

Our New Paradigm

This newer paradigm is simply that everything is energy. The dictionary defines *energy* as: a fundamental entity of nature that is transferred between parts of a system in the production of physical change within the system, and usually regarded as the capacity for doing work. Energy is that invisible "stuff" that science at times can measure, but most of the time cannot. It is found in everything, everywhere and is essentially the responsible catalyst for all we can see and that which we cannot. These "newer energies" we are more recently recognizing are those which mostly are the ones science has difficulty measuring. The field of quantum science are witnessing the effects of these, but are still at a loss to completely understand them, as they do not follow the typical rules used in the standard scientific method.

Further, if we look at these esoteric energies instead of from the more limited thinking such as *good* and *bad*, *right* and *wrong*, *positive* and *negative* and instead use the two categories of *high energy* and *low energy*, these actually fit better and open us up to a whole new realm of possibilities.

When our thoughts, words, feelings, and actions are a higher energy, they carry a higher vibration or frequency. These are those which typically create expansion, openness, and freedom. Those which carry a lower vibration or frequency typically will manifest contraction, a feeling of isolation or restriction in our lives. The higher energies typically are uplifting, and the lower energies generally deflate or depress us.

One of our simple technologies we have had at least one hundred years illustrates this concept easily. If we look at the blades of an oscillating fan while it is turned off, we can see there are four of them- all solid, gray colored, and metal. The blades of this fan are an example of a lower vibration. They are tangible, solid and can be seen. If we turn the switch of the fan on to high, within a few seconds we no longer see the blades of the fan. They no longer can be seen, nor determined whether they are solid, or any color. This demonstrates a higher vibration, or frequency. Just as the blades of the fan are now spinning fast enough that we can't see them, yet they are still there. We have the evidence from the cool breeze they create, yet we cannot see the blades which are too fast. Just as it is possible for the blades of a fan to oscillate at such a high enough rate of speed that we don't see them, the same is true for the vast sea of invisible energies swimming all around us. Similary, most of these energies are unable to be seen with our outer eyes.

Analysis Of The Invisible

During the 1960's Dr. George Goodheart, a Doctor of Chiropractic, was the first to determine that the physical body can be strengthened or weakened by unseen energies. Dr. Goodheart founded, and developed his findings into an elaborate technique based upon this simple premise. It is presently called *Applied Kinesiology,* and is today one of several Chiropractic techniques frequently used by a significant portion of the Chiropractic profession. During the more recent years, it has been picked up and used somewhat by other health professionals.

When Dr. Goodheart first was developing this technique, many Doctors were initially resistant and even skeptic to the idea that there could be unseen and unmeasurable energies affecting the body. Furthermore, he determined that it was possible to find specific areas in the body which are weakened, then treat these in a certain way which would allow the body to become stronger and function at a higher level.

The basic method of Applied Kinesiology is that the Doctor, or Practitioner first isolates a specific muscle or muscle group in the body to test, usually in the arm. It is then tested using a firm pressure by the Doctor. The patient is told to resist this pressure. Once it is determined that it is initially a strong muscle, then this muscle group is used as an *indicator muscle.* Either the Doctor or the or patient can touch other specific areas of the body, and the strength of the same indicator muscle gets tested again. If the muscle stays strong, that indicates the area which was touched of the body is strong. If the previously strong muscle becomes weak instead, this indicates there is a weakness in that related area. Once a particular area of the body has been isolated and found weak, a variety of treatments may be utilized such as specific Chiropractic adjustments, nutrition and others. After these treatments are administered, the Doctor retests the same previously weakened area. If the treatment(s) which were given strengthen the previously localized weakened area, we will find that the previously weakened indicator muscle test will now test strong again.

Many Doctors throughout the years have built highly successful practices using Applied Kinesiology in their clinics as their major technique to help people heal. Many of their patients will come to them after having had all types of other traditional medical lab testing and treatments with minimal success. Often by using Applied Kinesiology the Doctor may find one or more specific weakened areas, or organ systems of the body which were not indicated during lab testing which may then be treated. These findings in the body are what is called *subclinical.* This means we are able to find an underlying weakness in the body much earlier than it will typically show up in traditional lab testing. Once these areas are found and treated holistically, this helps to prevent these imbalances from developing into major health conditions.

Much has been accomplished throughout the years as several Doctors have expanded the use of Applied Kinesiology. Today it is used not only as a tool to help facilitate healing the physical body, but also is used to assist patients improve their emotional well-being.

We had a breakthrough during the late 1990's which shook up and surprised even the Holistic Health Community. Dr. David Hawkins, A Doctor of Medicine specializing in Psychiatry, published his first book of several. This book was a synopsis of his years of clinical study. He constructed an elaborate numerical system using Applied Kinesiology to measure the energetic levels of specific thoughts, words, feelings, and actions of each person.

He tested these over a period of years on well over one thousand people, and found that every person reacted consistently the same. He was able to determine that higher energy thoughts, feelings, words, and actions *always* in each and every person strengthened them in a tested *indicator muscle,* and every person was weakened by lower energy thoughts, words, feelings, and actions. Dr. Hawkins found consistently which of these are lower and higher, and more importantly, that every person he tested were either strengthened or weakened by the same ones. His system describes a total of seventeen different energetic levels. Each of them have its own relative position and qualities on the numerical scale.

The first and lowest energetic level on his scale is *shame* (calibrating on his numeric scale at 20), then the next higher is *guilt* (30), followed by *apathy* (50). The next is *grief* (75), then *fear* (100) followed by *desire* (125), next *anger* (150) and finally *pride* (175). Each of these energetic levels are shown to weaken a previously strong tested indicator muscle. The first energetic level which maintains the strength of a strong tested indicator muscle, and he considers the lowest of the higher energy levels is *courage* (which calibrates at 200). The next higher energetic level is *neutrality* (250), then *willingness* (310), *acceptance* (350), then *reason* (400). The highest energetic levels he determined were *love* (500), then *joy* (540), and *peace* (600) and lastly, the highest possible energetic level he determined is *enlightenment* (700-1000).

This seemed to be quite a turning point for us. It was the first time that a well-respected Doctor and researcher articulated in such a detailed and consistent manner that *everything* a person may *think, feel* and *speak* carries a measurable and demonstrable energetic level. These range from the lowest possible state, all the way to the greatest known energetic state. Another component of his research also indicates that people as individuals, people as groups, and even particular actions or events can be calibrated numerically. Once doing so, it can be determined which one of the above seventeen listed energetic levels it most closely matches in its resonance.

During 2001 I attended a large Chiropractic conference in Las Vegas. Dr. Deepak Chopra and Dr. Wayne Dyer both participated as speakers. Both of them were enthusiastic and elaborated on Dr. Hawkins's new book appropriately named, *Power vs. Force.* They were excited to get the word out, and I shared their enthusiasm after reading his book. There were many of us feeling elated that a whole new door of possibility and understanding had just been flung wide open.

Not only did his work open a completely new area for all Health Professionals to investigate, but this seemed to undeniably show that these energetic levels truly exist. So not only may we correlate that these different energetic levels are connected to the health and well-being of each person, but his research shows these are also related to particular levels of human consciousness.

His work is monumental in allowing us to truly recognize that there is a hierarchy of incremental energetic levels, we are continuously creating in our day to day lives. The way in which these energies become manifest are through our *thoughts, words, feelings,* and *actions* which either are serving our highest and greatest well-being, or are serving to disempower us.

Simplifying The Science

It is important for us to look at all of these elaborate distinctions of energetic levels and to make them easier for us to understand. All of the Great Spiritual Masters have been teaching always that there are really only two types of energetic types on this planet which are *Love* and *Fear*.

Interestingly, even with Dr. Hawkins's breakdown of his seventeen different levels, it is possible to place each of these into either that which *strengthens* founded in *Love,* or that which *weakens* based in *Fear*. If we list every possible energy that a human being can experience, it will fall into one of these two categories. So *Enlightenment, Peace, Joy, Love, Reason* and *Acceptance* are all founded in *Love. Pride, Anger, Desire, Fear, Grief, Apathy, Guilt* and *Shame* are each rooted in *Fear.*

Any *feelings, words, thoughts,* and *actions* we may experience can easily be placed into one of these two categories. Everything which has a foundation centered in *Love* will feel uplifting, create expansion, higher growth and awareness in our life. All which is centered in *Fear* will feel more contracted, create diminished capacities, and lower awareness in our life.

A few examples which emanate from the position of *Love* might include: stopping to help someone pick up the groceries she just dropped onto the ground. Reading a book to a two- year old child. Sitting for 30 minutes in meditation and experiencing the stillness. *Really* listening for a few minutes as a friend tells you she is struggling in her recent divorce, and encouraging her that it is okay to love herself and take care of her own needs. Taking a walk in the woods and sending a silent blessing to two deer in the distance, and feeling how grateful you are for the trees, grass, wildflowers and wonderful fragrance of spring you enjoy.

Likewise, we can determine if our feelings or actions are out of *Fear*. Examples are: telling yourself the recent end of a relationship probably wouldn't have happened if you were a better person. Treating a co-worker poorly because he recently was selected for a promotion you had hoped to receive. Yelling at a child who just ran over your newly planted flowers on her bicycle. Avoiding looking at a homeless couple holding a sign near the road as you drive past thinking, "They should get jobs." Laying on your horn at the driver in front of you who sat through most of a green signal, because you didn't make it through the light.

The differences of these two groups at first may not be the most obvious, and may take a bit of discernment to distinguish for some people. The first step is to become aware. Even a few may wonder, why in the world is this so important? Why do we want to be able to place everything we might think, feel, say, or take action upon into a certain category? How might this serve us?

The importance is that this understanding is key to enabling us to move ourselves to a greater level of awareness. When we move throughout our life clinging to our old *fear-* based consciousness, we not only do not, but cannot move into a greater level of awareness. A higher state of awareness not only includes being at an elevated energetic state involving our spiritual levels, but also encompasses all aspects of our physical and mental well-being. If we work to spend the majority of our time focused on *love*-centered vibrations, this is a huge key to assist the body to heal at every level.

My Spiritual Teacher, Sai Maa, for years has been teaching these concepts. I recall her instructing us that as we first become aware of our thoughts and feelings, and attempt to shift our thinking from *fear*-based to *love*-based, that we should try to be easy on ourselves. Maybe as we first begin, we might have 200 thoughts each week based in *fear*. As we start to become more aware and make changes, maybe the following week it is reduced down to 160 during the week. Possibly the next week it drops to only 120. As we continue to be diligent in our practice, it may gradually drop to as few as 20 or so of these types of thoughts during the week. Sooner or later, these lower energies will lose their grip, and instead mostly the *love*-rooted energy is what will propel our life forward. This is *the* foundation to healing. Absolutely no healing may occur without *love* being present. The greater amount of *love* we experience day to day directly correlates to the health and well-being of *all* of the aspects in one's life.

Sai Maa gives us the analogy that it is similar to us having two plants in our life. One plant represents *love* and the other *fear*. Everyday we are watering either one or the other. Each time we think, feel, speak, or take a lower action, we are moving to the *fear* plant and giving it water. If we continue to do this, obviously our life will become a well-rooted plant of *fear*. If we spend our day moving over to the *love* plant and pour water on it throughout our day, then conversely our life will have this elaborate-rooted plant of *love*. When we quit making trips over to water the *fear* plant, it will eventually shrivel and die away. Our life would certainly improve in all of its aspects, if its foundation is based upon *love*. Once again, it is a very simple concept, but not always the easiest to bring about into our life. It requires that we are persistent in our efforts, and are patient with ourselves.

During the 1960's *The Beatles* returned after spending a period of time in India. They reportedly had similar realizations after learning from a Spiritual Master, or Guru. Shortly after returning from this experience, the group was inspired to write several songs placing *love* as the central theme. All of these songs moved very quickly up the charts, and became legendary including the blockbuster hit, *All You Need is Love*. Some Westerners during this time thought the group had somehow fallen away from reality for awhile, and had become somewhat brainwashed by this simplistic new concept they seemed to embrace. The reality was that the lyrics in these songs were right on the mark, although maybe a few decades ahead of the typical American thinking.

5

Elevating Our Love Experience

There are four major areas or components we must focus upon developing in our life when we choose to actively pursue *Awakening* in our life. Much like the four legs of a chair, all four are required for a chair to be fully functional. If any one of the legs of a chair are either weaker than the rest or non-existent, then the chair is not useful. Likewise, if we ignore any one or more of these areas we can expect much less progress or advancement in our Spiritual Journey.

The four essentials are: *Love, Power, Discipline* and *Wisdom.* Each of these are inter-connected with each other, and also have its own unique dynamics.

First, we will examine *love.* If we only practiced this exclusively, and ignored all of the other areas, we would have great transformations in our life. *Love* is of the utmost importance, yet each of these other components are needed as well.

Feeding The Tree Of Love

There seems to be three keys to becoming able to fully understand and practice shifting into a *love*-based life. The *first* is that we need to fully understand that there are the two energies that each person every day we spend our day feeding. We are either making trips to water the *love* tree, or the *fear* tree.

Secondly, we must learn to develop what is called *discernment*. This means: "The ability to see and understand people, things, or situations clearly and intelligently." This also is when we are able to perceive subtle, and sometimes not so subtle differences and distinctions in our daily activities. I feel this is the greatest challenge for us no matter how long we have been practicing. Even when we fully understand about these energies, it can be difficult to *discern* whether we are watering the *love* or *fear* tree. When we are in the middle of some sort of conflict or situation, it can be tough to recognize our own feelings. The best way for us to determine this is to ask ourselves if the way in which we are responding allows us to feel comfortable, light, and uplifted, if this is so, then most likely we are on the *love* side. However, if we notice our experience has feelings of heaviness, discomfort, or in any way irritation, then we are most likely watering the tree of *fear*. The greatest portion of the solution comes simply by being able to recognize when we are reacting in a situation out of a feeling of *fear*.

Lastly, in the cases where we determine that we are handling certain circumstances in our life from a place of *fear*, it is best to fully recognize how we are feeling. Often during our lives we will try to avoid something which is painful, pushing it away in an attempt to ignore that it exists.

This is similar to a person attempting to walk down a street having a small barking dog constantly nipping at your pant-legs. Try as you might to push it away from you, it keeps coming back and digging its teeth back into the hem of your jeans. You attempt to ignore the scruffy little dog, thinking maybe if you don't look at him he might eventually wear out and stop. No matter how much you disregard him, he clings and tugs on you consistently and you can't get away from him. The only way you may hope to get this dog to leave you alone, you first must quit ignoring him and acknowledge that he is there. Then you might need to call out to the people in the neighborhood in hopes to find the owner of the dog. Once the dog's owner comes and can call him away from you, only then will you be able to walk in peace again.

Often this is just what happens to us. There may be an adverse situation in our life which seems to show up on and off throughout our life. We can choose to do one of two different things. We might decide to ignore it, possibly even denying that it exists at all. Or we may instead face it fully and recognize it. Simply by taking this action we might be able to *discern* how this has become a noticeable pattern in our life. Once we have the ability to recognize that it is impacting our life, we can take the next step to reduce or neutralize its effects upon us.

Once again, we must understand how energy works. When we move a lower vibrational energy into a place of higher vibration, it has no choice but to move towards resonating at the level of the higher vibration. Otherwise, energies based in *fear* will dissipate and dissolve when we move them into the higher frequency of *love*.

Dr. David Hawkins determined in his research, for every individual on this planet who has a consciousness level which calibrates at the higher energetic levels, these higher level energies neutralize those who have lower awareness levels. So anything less than a 200 calibration on his scale are associated with the lower vibrational frequencies. A calibration level of 200 or greater indicate the higher resonance frequencies. He states in his book

Power vs. Force, that during the time he wrote this in the 1990's only 15% of the population on the planet are above the critical consciousness level of 200. This means the other 85% are at the lower levels of awareness.

He ascertained that one person at the level of 300(Willingness) counterbalances 90,000 individuals below 200. One person at the level of 400(Reason) counterbalances 400,000 individuals below 200. One person at the level of 500(Love) counterbalances 750,000 individuals below 200. One person at the level of 600(Peace) counterbalances 10,000,000 individuals below 200. One person at the level of 700(Enlightenment) counterbalances 70,000,000 individuals below 200.

Dr. Hawkins states that during this time there were 12 people on the planet who calibrate at the 700 level. He indicates that all the individuals who have attained these higher levels are responsible for helping to maintain the balance of the planet.

His work also reveals that the average individual throughout an entire lifetime will only increase in consciousness by about 5 points. However, he gives hope for us all by affirming,"…it is possible for isolated individuals to make sudden positive jumps, even of hundreds of points. If one can truly escape the egocentric entrainment of sub-200 attractor fields (*fear*-based energies)…higher levels can certainly be attained…"

So this certainly indicates if we make the effort, we are able to make great strides in our awareness. So how can we *escape* from the lower *fear*-based energies and move into a state of *love* vibrations?

Just A Heartbeat Away

There is a whole organization presently dedicated exclusively to the study of the energy related to the heart in the human body. It is called *The Institute of HeartMath,* and has been extensively researching every aspect of the relationship between the Heart, Brain and Human

Emotional States since 1991. One of their key findings states:

The Institute of HeartMath's research has shown that generating sustained positive emotions facilitates a body-wide shift to a specific, scientifically measurable state. This state is termed *Psychophysiological Coherence,* because it is characterized by increased order and harmony in both our psychological (mental and emotional) and physiological (bodily) processes. *Psychophysiological coherence* is [a] state of optimal function. Research shows that when we activate this state, our physiological systems function more efficiently, we experience greater emotional stability, and we also have increased mental clarity and improved cognitive function. Simply stated, our body and brain work better, we feel better, and we perform better.

So they have coined this newer term, "Psychophysiological Coherence." All of their research shows that when we live in this higher energetic state that it allows us to experience, "a state of optimal function...our body and brain work better, we feel better, and we perform better." Thus, this equates to a higher degree of health. One of the other key findings these researchers have found is that the heart in the body disseminates an unseen, yet powerful and measurable energetic field surrounding the human body. They have demonstrated that this field projects several feet around the body, and even appears to communicate with each other person's "heart-field" who comes within close proximity.

This information becomes significant in allowing us to become aware that science is beginning to validate the esoteric teachings which have been taught by all of Great Masters throughout time. The heart is the powerful energetic center of the body and this "heart-center" continuously radiates a high vibrational field surrounding the body.

Sai Maa teaches that the heart energetically has two components, or compartments. The first of which is the center of *human love.* This is the energetic love in which many people mistaken through life for *love.* Actually, this is of a lower vibration than *love* in its purer form. This *human love* is usually *conditional.*

This is demonstrated when a person sends out the feeling, "I love this (person or thing) because s(he)/it gives me (something) in return. The person with this type of love will send only what one be*lie*ves to be love, thinking that most likely one will get something in return.

One example of this is," I agreed to help my husband to host a superbowl party this year at our house with all of his friends. But little does he know, that since I helped him, I expect him to help me when I plan my family reunion this year." Another might be heard in the divorce court," When I married you, I thought you agreed to stop spending so much money. I can't stay with/love someone who won't listen to me and is such a spendthrift." Or, "Hmm, we gave *nearly double* to our favorite charity than we did last year, and they didn't list our name in the annual report as a major donor." Finally,"I gave our daughter permission to start learning to play soccer with a couple of her friends, but only if she mows the grass and does all of the yard work every Saturday."

Each of the above examples show a situation in which one person is willing to give to another, but with certain strings attached. The first example shows the wife willing to allow her husband to have his friends over for the superbowl, but has the expectation that he must return the "favor" by helping with her family reunion. The next example as a marriage is ending, there was an apparent earlier promise from one spouse to change the spending habits. Apparently after some time the spouse realized that this wouldn't change, and this was unacceptable behavior to endure in a relationship. This exemplifies a conditional marriage. The third example shows a couple giving to a certain charity thinking that they would receive some type of acknowledgement in return. This action reflects how these people are giving to a cause, but wish to be publically acknowledged for their generosity. The last example shows a parent allowing her daughter to go learn and play in a new sport, but only if she works most of her Saturday performing yard work. Again, this is an example of giving a loving action to another with certain conditions attached.

The second compartment of the heart houses *divine love.* This is the energetic love which carries the highest vibration. This type of love is *unconditional.* Divine love is demonstrated *when the person loves someone or something, simply for the sake of loving.* One does not expect to receive anything in return, and the love is ever-present regardless of the situation or actions involved.

One example of this is, "I noticed my wife was up past midnight last night studying for her exams, so I made her breakfast thinking she could sleep a little later." Another might be," I saw someone homeless curled up on a park bench and he looked cold. I went back to my car and walked back to give him my emergency blanket, and I also gave my change I normally keep for toll roads." Another is, "I go up to visit my Mother in the nursing home every night after I get home from work. She has been there now for at least two years, and doesn't recognize us anymore. I go anyway so she can tell others she has a visitor every day, and somehow I know she realizes that she is loved." Also, pay attention to your pet dog or cat. Everyday they show us affection. It matters not the day, your pet will come running to greet you at the door. They are full of wagging tail excitement, or purring happiness as your ankles are rubbed up by your feline. Your pets always gives you the warmest and most loving greeting no matter if you or they had a lousy day. I am convinced their major purpose here is to teach us through bathing us with *unconditional love.*

The first example shows a genuine act out of concern which comes from the higher levels of love. The spouse thoughtfully cooks breakfast to help her have more time to sleep. There isn't anything expected in return, simply a wish to help, fueled by love and concern. The second example illustrates a high level of generosity without any expected return. Assisting a person who appears to be homeless and without enough essential clothing or blankets to stay warm is an act of pure compassion and love for another person. The third example displays the same type of higher love again simply for the sake of loving. Going everyday to see your Mother in the nursing home, is purely unconditional love at its best. The last example of our beloved pets are the greatest example for us to learn to imitate. If we can embody the level of love and devotion our furry best friends harbor for us, we would certainly evolve beyond the need for any further studies or practice. Unfortunately, most of us have quite a way to go yet, but we can still watch and learn much from them.

Unconditional love really exists in each of us. It is part of our deep inner being. It is not so much an active emotion, as a state of being. It's not 'I love you' for this reason or that reason, not 'I love you if you love me.' It's love for no reason, love for no object.

-Ram Dass

Once again, *human love always* has an outright or underlying expectation, and *divine love never* has any expectations. An attribute about the heart-center is that this higher level *divine love* radiates from here and is ever-present. It is *divine love* only, which will transform and neutralize any lower frequency energies(fear-based).

Taming The Beast Within

Now we have come to understand that there are higher vibrational energies founded in *love,* and lower vibrational energies founded in *fear*. How do we defuse these *fear-based* situations from grabbing ahold of us in our lives?

The *first* step is to use our *discernment* that we are reacting to a situation in our life from a place of *fear*. Again, the best way to determine this is to check in with how our body is feeling. If it feels in any way contracted, agitated, or upset, then it is a *fear* based situation.

The *second* step is to fully allow ourself to face what we are feeling. Do not deny the feeling or push it away. If we feel anger, allow ourself to fully be angry and acknowledge how we feel. Other examples of emotions we may feel include jealousy, worry, anxiety, blame, regret, guilt, fear or shame. If we are able to identify whatever we feel, we simply allow that feeling to come.

Third, find a quiet place to sit where you won't be disturbed and close your eyes. Continue to allow yourself to think about the situation and let the feelings to arise within you. Permit yourself to fully be in whatever emotions that surface. If tears come, don't fight them back. Just allow them to wash over you. At this point you will most likely feel these feelings causing discomfort in your abdominal region near the umbilicus or "belly button." Give yourself permission to fully face these emotions for about 2 – 3 minutes.

Next, take your hands and place them both face up with the palm of one hand touching the bottom of the other. Position both of your hands "cupped together" like this against the front of your body, and just under the location of your "belly button." Both palms should still be facing up creating a scoop with your hands. Now slowly move your hands straight up the front of your body, imagining that you are moving those lower energies up until your hands are just in front of your "heart-center." This is where the sternum, or "breastbone" is located. *Now* slowly move your cupped hands up and over "scooping" the energies directly into your *heart-center*. Your hands are now both palms forward touching your body directly over the middle of your heart. *Finally,* continue to sit and remain silent for a couple of minutes, keeping your hands touching your *heart-center.* Whenever you feel ready, gently open your eyes.

You will most likely notice an immediate shift in yourself. If you attempt to think about the situation again, you will notice there has been a change. There will be a difference in the way you now perceive the situation. You will notice how it has lost its grasp on you. *Any* lower energy cannot continue when it is moved to the *heart-center* where there is *divine love.* This is yet another life-altering teaching by Sai Maa.

There may be those of you who may perform this once, and have an experience such as, "I didn't seem to notice anything." This is completely okay. Not every person is immediately sensitive to these subtler energies. I have had many people throughout the years tell me," I typically only notice something once it hits me over the head like a hammer." There are many people who are simply not as sensitive, and this doesn't mean that nothing is happening.

Dr. Elaine N. Aron in 1996 first coined the term from her research a "Highly Sensitive Person." Her research seems to show that about 15-20% of humans have a nervous system that is more sensitive to subtleties and has a higher degree of discrimination. This means that typical sensory information is processed, analyzed and perceived to a greater extent in this portion of the population than the rest.

This enables us to understand how 80-85% of those who first use this tool may not readily sense the changes. However, regardless if you are one who is sensitive to these energies or not, this doesn't matter. When you use this incredible tool, transformations *are* occurring in your life. As with any tool, rather than trying the teaching once and then tossing it aside into the corner to gather rust, it must be used regularly to see the results and gain a shift in one's life. It also doesn't mean there won't be similar challenges which arise periodically. At times a new situation will most likely arise that seems almost identical to one you thought had been resolved. It is easy to be tempted to think that you are not really making any progress, because this thing is happening once again. If we look at the new situation, most often we will see that it may have other slightly different nuances. Also, it is interesting to note, that oftentimes we may notice that we seemed to handle the situation easier and faster than the last time. This in itself means that we are growing, and ultimately spending more of our time watering our *love* plant than before.

Practicing In The Trenches

How may we use this in our life? One example may be, we have a sister in our family in which each time we see her there is a lot of friction. At family gatherings she will bring up things from the past, such as how she feels that your parents always gave you everything because you were the youngest. She reminds you that she did all of the household chores growing up, and you were just spoiled. At other times, she brings up her perception that you weren't a very good Mother to your child because you spoiled her in the same way while you were raising her. She adds, "That's why your daughter as a grown up now can't seem to keep a job anywhere."

So the first hurdle with this situation is to recognize whether or not we are engaging, and doing battle with our sister every time she brings these things up to us. When we are in the middle of something like this, it can be very difficult to see through the smoke from the battlefield. Hopefully we can recognize that in this situation: everytime these things from the past are brought up to me, I become engaged in an argument. The very first step is for us to realize that there is this pattern. Many people go throughout their whole life unable to see that these types of patterns even exist. Once we are capable to recognize this is present, then we have taken our initial step. In this case it is: *everytime my sister brings up these things from the past, I become engaged in an argument.*

The next step is *discernment,* realizing that each time this occurs we are moving over to water the *fear* tree. This is the greatest step we can take to move towards the resolution.

Next try to identify what is the actual feeling, or emotion being invoked within us. There may be a couple of different feelings we may identify. We may notice that every time our sister says these things we become defensive, and feel the need to justify our life and decisions. Take a moment to really identify which emotions which are triggering your response. It may be that we notice there are feelings of guilt or shame which lead into anger. Perhaps the actual situation was that you were several years younger than your sister, and were too young to be given any major chores at home. During the time she lived at home this was her perception, and actually after she moved out of the house you assumed all of her responsibilities. The actual events of this back story doesn't really matter at all. There is never any *right* or *wrong.* There are only the emotional triggers from these events which we carry as baggage, and are lower energies ready and waiting for us to clear them.

Now that we have acknowledged these feelings and put some sort of name on them, tell yourself," It is okay for me to have feelings like this in this situation." You may even continue," I have feelings of *anger* at my sister, and am feeling *guilty* that maybe I was treated differently than her in the past." Next, be sure to sit in a quiet place and simply sit with these for a couple of minutes. Be sure to allow whatever thoughts and feelings that swell up inside to percolate. Close your eyes and think of your sister and this situation. The focus now is to simply allow our emotions to emerge. There may be some new ones which you didn't notice before. Do not analyze, or make any judgments of who is right or wrong. Allow tears to come and flow. Now notice that there is a tightness in the lower portion of the abdomen. You may notice other physical symptoms present such as slight nausea or other discomfort.

Now we place our hands on top of each other both facing up against our body, just below our "belly button." Slowly we cup and cradle these energies and feelings, slowly moving them up the body until our hands reach the heart center at the middle of the chest. We move our hands gently toward our body until they are resting palms down on the center of the "breastbone." Allowing our hands to rest at this place for a couple of minutes, we continue to let the tears to stream freely. After a couple of minutes, we may open our eyes and take in a couple of deep breaths.

We may choose to think about our sister now. Whether we notice it immediately or not, the dynamics of the quality of the feelings and emotions in that situation has shifted. The next time we see our sister, although she may still bring up similar things from the past, there will be a change. Possibly the change is, this time you are able to recognize that going back to the battlefield again doesn't really serve you. Maybe this time you still go there, but it feels different. This time you don't stay there quite as long, and even your sister is surprised that for the first time ever, you disengage from her. This may be the only thing you notice that has changed at first. Do not let yourself think that you have failed to make any progress. This is a victory, as this work has helped to initiate the change. So, we use this tool again and go through everything step by step again doing the same work on this situation with our sister.

During the next holiday gathering our sister dawns her armor to go back into the arena with you again. This time you notice that you don't seem as angry as before. This day you look at her instead with compassion, wondering how difficult it must be for her to spend so much of her time thinking about the past and focusing on you. Today you think and realize that you forgot that you really do *love* her. Amazingly, you notice that she seems to be losing steam with her argument, realizing that you don't seem to be engaging back with her.

A few more times like this using this tool with the situation surrounding your sister, and it is most likely that you will have shifted away from the lower *fear*-based emotions, and find there is more harmony and *love* moving into that relationship. A year later you notice that your sister has seemingly stopped bringing these things up from the past, and the relationship seems to be easier than you can ever remember. This is one way we can bring great transformations into our life.

So what has shifted? Did our actions in this case cause our sister to change? No, we jumped to a newer level of awareness as our thoughts and feelings within ourself moved to a higher vibrational level. As a result of this, as verified by *The Institute of HeartMath,* the energetic level surrounding our heart-center when we are near our sister has been gradually raised to a higher level of *love*-based frequencies. Because we raised our own energetic levels so we no longer are reactive to our sister, the communication between her heart-field and ours become modified. The interactions of the two heart-centers are able to move to a higher level of more harmony.

There will always be events in our lives or relationships which are difficult. It is the way in which we react to these which indicates whether we are living our lives grounded in a place of *love* or not. Even when these lower energies poke their head out at us from time to time as they sometimes do, with practice it is possible for us to learn how to identify them, and move through them faster and faster.

Another example might not necessarily be a difficult relationship, but a particular event which has occurred in our life. Maybe years ago something traumatic happened which we just can't let go. Twenty years earlier you were

18 and were driving with two other friends in your car, and racing against another car up one of the main streets in your city. A large truck pulls out into your path, and when you swerve to miss it your car strikes a parked vehicle. At 70 miles per hour this launches your friend in the passenger side out of the front window, since he didn't have on his seatbelt and airbags were not invented yet. You and your friend in the backseat survive the impact having cuts, abrasions, and whiplash as both of you were wearing your seatbelt. However, your other friend loses his life.

It would be very easy to spend the rest of your lifetime after such an incident being merciless and blaming yourself for everything. We may use this tool exactly in the same way as before. First of all, we must recognize that this event is still affecting our life. Next, we use our ability to *discern* that we still are experiencing many lower feelings from this. This might be showing up in our life in a variety of different ways. We might spend much of our life having a feeling of unworthiness. Perhaps we planned to attend the same college with our other friends after graduation, and at the last minute stayed home and took a job working in a local factory. After a few years at the factory, when your supervisor encouraged you to go take company training to help you move into a higher position, you turn down the opportunity. When some of your previous friends from high school return from college and start their lives back in your city, you avoid reconnecting with them. You deliberately cut yourself off from everyone in your past. It might be that you notice there are certain triggers that really bring up many feelings in yourself. The anniversary date of the accident may be one.

Next, try to identify some of the feelings. These are most likely grief, guilt, resentment and still maybe some anger. Allow yourself to remember the event for a couple of minutes and allow these emotions to surface. Again, it is important to be as gentle as possible with ourselves, yet being fully in our feelings. Now we close our eyes and same as before, move these lower energies from our abdominal area slowly up to our heart-center. We sit for a few minutes and take a couple of deep breaths.

The results may be noticed more gradually in this situation. You will wish to do this practice even daily at first for at least four or five days, and then occasionally if you notice that any of these feelings become triggered again.

After the first practice, you may notice that the intensity of the feelings seem the same when they get triggered, but this time instead of feeling upset for a full day you notice that you only stay upset for part of a day. Then maybe the next time you do notice that the feelings seem a little less intense. As you continue to periodically go through the steps again, you may notice that there are fewer "triggers" than before. A couple of months later you notice that you feel less stress at work, and decide to speak to your supervisor about applying for a higher paying position. A year later you think about the accident, and for the first time ever you are able to look at yourself, and realize how young you were and have learned so much from all of it. Eighteen months later you run into an old friend from school, and this time instead of hurrying away and avoiding him, you have a real conversation and find out more about his life. Three years later you notice that your life seems much different. You still remember the accident, but now look at yourself with real *love* and *compassion*, knowing that you deserve to have a life, and have finally forgiven yourself the same as you would any other young person. You no longer feel like you are carrying such a burden, and now know that you are free to live your life again more fully.

Once again, we didn't do anything to change the situation which occurred in our life. This still was a major traumatic event from our past. Gradually we altered our perception about it, and we simply *became the change.* When we continue to use this tool, over time this practice allows us to bring more *love* and harmony into our lives. We are bringing the high vibration of *love* deliberately, and directly to the lower *fear* energies which allow them to gradually dissipate and clear out of our lives. As we continue to regularly practice this in our lives, then we look back and think about the way we had a certain level of reactivity to the people and events in our life noticing there is less, then we know there is has been a shift in our life. This shows us how when we *love* ourselves we are healed.

Finally, we are able to understand that all of our thoughts, words, feelings, and actions each carry energies, and these are affecting our own well-being depending upon whether they are rooted in *fear* or *love*. As our ability to become more aware increases, this in turn allows us to be more open to fully embrace and understand *divine love*. As we deliberately move more of this into our life, this is what permits us to be *truly* healed.

Is Love In The Air?

Now we have come to understand that we have energies which lie at the opposite ends of the spectrum, from *love* to *fear,* and we have *conditional love* and *divine love,* which also are at different energetic levels. It is time to now focus on exclusively that which serves us the greatest in our life.

Divine love is that which every human being on this planet is seeking whether we know it or not. Sai Maa really helped me to grasp this concept several years ago. We know that darkness is simply an absence of light. Many people spend their whole lives working to analyze what is creating the darkness in their lives. There are many who attempt to quantify all of the different variants of darkness and the underlying reasons. A similar analogy is how modern medicine attempts to quantify all of the different variants of lack of health in the body. These variants are named as different diseases. People have similarly named these varieties of darkness as things such as evil, sin, depression, fear, guilt, jealousy, and so forth.

Once again, darkness is simply *an absence of light*. As Sai Maa teaches, imagine a room which has been closed up for many years sitting with no light able to penetrate. Then finally we are able to open the door to the room and the light starts to go in a little bit. Then we take a bright flashlight and shine it into the room. What will we see? We will be able to see the dust which has collected for so many years. So then we have to go in and start cleaning away all of the collected dust. This is what happens when we first open ourselves up. There is *no need* to come up with names for what we see in the room, nor to make comments on, "Wow, there sure is a lot more dust over in this corner over here!" We simply need to allow the light in, and this will allow us to see what needs to be cleared away. This is merely us beginning to *Awaken*.

What happens as we allow the light to shine greater and greater into the previously darkened room? Eventually there is no more darkness. This is what we are here to do. What beam of light will illuminate our room? *Divine Love.*

As it is with anything, we must fully understand before we can expect to use it. *Divine love* is again completely *unconditional* and *pure* in nature and can be expressed to ourselves or towards others.

We can better comprehend how to practice this in our day to day lives, if we move it from being so idealistic and esoteric into being broken down into its interlocking major components. We may think of each of these as a strand which is braided amongst the others, as though we were creating a really strong rope. If each of these are present, we can expect to have the strongest tensile-strength rope. If any are absent or weak, we can expect that our rope will not hold our weight nearly as well. If we choose to develop the optimal level of *divine love* in our lives, it is important that we fully understand each of these interlocking strands in our rope.

Interlocking Components of Divine Love

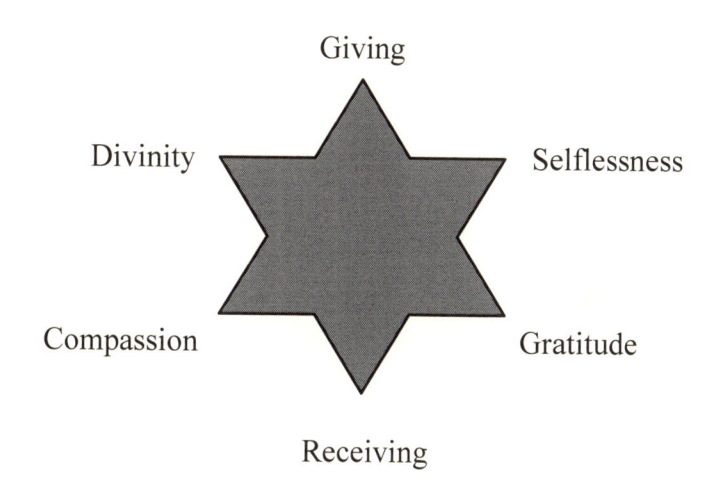

```
                    Giving

       Divinity              Selflessness



       Compassion            Gratitude

                   Receiving
```

We could attempt to describe the numerous attributes of *divine love,* and create a complete encyclopedia which might take eons to sift through and completely understand. Instead, it is easier to focus in on the six key elements. Once we fully grasp and begin to deliberately incorporate these into our lives, then we can truly be on our way moving into *awakening.*

The six keys to unlocking our own ability to more fully experience *divine love* in our lives are giving, receiving, compassion, selflessness, gratitude and divinity. Our goal is to first completely grasp each of these concepts, and then to learn how to bring these into our life each day through active practice.

Living Without Conditions

Probably one of the greatest hurdles most of us face every day in moving into the state of *divine love,* is letting go of our expectations. When we first arrive here, we are little *divine love* beings to the core. As a baby, we know nothing except the joy and thrill of exploring this wonderful new world we newly have joined.

Watching any nine month old crawling and making happy, "ma ma ma or da da da," sounds as she jabs the corner of her furry bear's ear into her mouth, shows the delight and pure bliss of simply being. She has no cares and is fully happy when she gets enough sleep, a diaper change, and some food every few hours. She smiles at her older brother when he walks close to her, and takes the brown bear from her grasp while giving her in exchange a red building block. Her brother, merely one year her senior swipes her bear and announces," That's mine!" He hurries over to place it on the couch, arranged with his collection of storybooks and other assembled toys. His sister, simply smiles at him and then looks at the block and grabs it continuing happily in her rhythmic chatter.

So at nine months we have absolutely no cares, no worries and for many of us are experiencing the most joyous, and loving state of our life. Then something happens somewhere during the next year or so of our life. During that very short time frame we begin to be*lie*ve that certain things belong to us. We seem to start thinking that we own certain things in our lives and we don't really wish to share them with others. Although this attitude begins at such of a young age with seemingly simple toys, it does tend to follow us throughout our life.

Most children are taught that they should share with each other, in theory. But often many different distinctions are made to the idea of sharing. As I was growing up I was taught that certain things should be shared, and some things were not to be shared. I recall when I was a young child, I was taught about sharing my toys with others. However, as I got a little older I was told there were "certain things" that I shouldn't share with the other kids. We were all told that we should only ride our own bicycle, and never allow anyone else to do so. We should not loan any books of ours to our friends, nor let anyone borrow any of your clothes. A few years later it was, "don't let anyone drive your car." After that, the message seems to have become fairly well embedded for all of us. We eventually get to a place where the undercurrent of what we have picked up in our life is, "It is okay in *certain circumstances* to give freely to others, but there are other times when it is best to safeguard that which is *yours*." This idea gets eventually ingrained into the way in which we see the world surrounding us. As a result, we have this tendency to make sure that our own needs are completely satisfied first and only later do we think of others.

Not only do we seem to place conditions upon allowing others to use *things* or *objects* which "belong" to us, but place similar conditions upon our *actions* with others. Another aspect of this which becomes hardwired into us starting at an early age, is that we get rewarded by certain actions.

Many families start giving their children at an early age a monetary weekly allowance for doing certain chores around the home. Kids participate in all sorts of contests to see who can be the best and win a prize. It might be for selling the greatest amount of Girl Scout cookies, or for winning a race event at a track meet for school. During high school those who make the best grades may expect to be rewarded with scholarships to college. Those who work hard in a large corporation may be awarded annual bonuses, or expect eventual promotions. What we can easily see is that very often throughout the average person's life, one gets certain types of rewards for various type of actions.

Because this seems to become so embedded into every aspect of school, careers, and every other organization, we then seem to allow this to automatically spill over into all of the rest of our lives. We develop this same *expectation* into our relationships with our families, friends, and even ourselves.

We think to ourselves, "If I take care of my brother's dog while he's out of town for a week, then he will *owe* me. When I go away next month for two weeks, I can ask him to mow my lawn while I'm gone." This is a simple example of how oftentimes in our relationships, we either consciously, or even subconsciously are "keeping score."

Several years back I recall being in a relationship which was quickly racing towards its finish line. Both of us during this time were caught up into a heated argument over who was doing more household chores than the other. The battle culminated in my partner drawing up a list of tasks including,"wash dishes, cook dinner, wash laundry, clean house, mow lawn,etc." These were written on a paper, and were posted on the refrigerator for the next couple of weeks. We were each supposed to keep a strict record of who did which chore each day. At the end of the couple of weeks my partner tallied up the results, and then we ensued into a new dispute over whether it was really uneven or not. Obviously, this relationship was finished within just a couple of short months later.

Other ways this can show up in our relationships are at a more emotional level. This might appear in a way in which we are often completely unaware. There are times during intimate relationships that one person may feel like there is an emotional imbalance. One states," I am open and tell you[my partner] my deepest thoughts and feelings in my life, but you only seem to share with me the more surface things." The one who has shared more thoughts and feelings may eventually at a deeper level, feel short-changed and that the partner is not giving back as much in this relationship. This person may eventually decide to move on and seek a different relationship which is more balanced in the giving and receiving. Sometimes we may go throughout our whole life attempting to find a relationship in which we feel the other person is giving back to us as much as we are giving, yet never find it.

Other times I have witnessed within families the perception of favoritism between different family members. This can result in long-term disputes which may start during childhood, and continue well throughout the adult lives of two or more people. Sometimes this might be a more subtle undercurrent which is able to take root within the family, and the parents may or may not reinforce it. It also can be more outright such as, "Look at how much more time grandma spends with me than you. I am her favorite and she loves me more than you!"

"Yes, but do you notice that dad takes me with him to go fishing and you stay at home, and he says *I'm his best buddy*." This type of bantering, if it is allowed to continue within a family either overtly or covertly, reinforces the attitude that *love* has many conditions. It also reinforces the idea and be*lief* which will follow these people throughout their lives; that *love* somehow needs to be earned, and can be measured based upon the apparent actions of others.

All of these show us examples of *human love,* or *conditional love*. We might even state that each of these examples display a certain level of *selfishness,* or *self-centeredness*. As we can see, there are many of us who have lived our whole lives swimming through a seemingly endless sea of this. Now it is time for us after recognizing how these often show up in our lives, to learn how to move ourselves into the opposite direction. The opposite of this, and one of the major requirements for *divine love* is *selflessness.*

Selflessness is exactly as it seems, it is when we are focusing upon other people's needs first without thinking about ourselves. Although there are many examples of this in humans, we will first look at a couple of excellent examples we all have witnessed within the animal kingdom.

Our Furry Friends Are The Wayshowers

Every person unless they have lived in a cave in Tibet, has either had a pet dog or cat within her family or at the very least in a friend's family. Cats and dogs are here as teachers for us. They are here to teach us *unconditional love* and they perfectly show us *selflessness* most all of the time. Another role they play here are to help balance the energies on the planet.

Many people have a tendency to identify greater with one or the other. It is not unusual for us to announce to others, "Oh, yes, I am a cat person." Or, "No, I am *really* more of a dog person."

I am definitely more of a "cat person," and my partner is undeniably a self-proclaimed "dog person." We were out on a walk together on a path at the riverfront which are frequented with many people out walking their dogs. One little black terrier mix was tugging away on his leash scuttling his little feet excitedly trying to come see my partner.

"Awww, he just is sooo happy to see everyone!" He continued blinking his black eyes moving long strands of hair with each blink and now started pulling feverishly with little whimpers to get to my partner. He finally gets close enough to get a few hard earned pats on his head and his chin rubbed.

" He is *soo* cute, and what a sweet dog!" The couple smiled and nodded moving on, pulling their reluctant puppy along the path.

We continue on our walk and later a black cat looks up a distance away and sees me. Without further ado, she makes a beeline straight for me bouncing quickly with an excited, "Mow, mow, meow," with each breath, finally arriving she rubs into my pant legs. I squat down and reach for her as she pushes her fuzzy head into my hand. She allows me to stroke her head and the left side of her body a couple of times. Then as she hurries away I notice her battered tail, ruffled fur and lack of a collar evidencing a strictly outdoor life. My partner now announces in dismay, "That's a feral cat!" I seem to ignore the comment as I am focused on her bounding away, and moving between several rose bushes.

" I think that's a wild cat!"

I finally answer," It doesn't matter, she *knows* I am a cat person."

About a month earlier on just such of a walk, two-approximately four month old kittens came bounding up to me and we quickly became friends. They played and romped loving every bit of attention I gave them as I caressed their calico chins. After a few minutes we continued to walk home, and they started to follow me. Both of them seemed very healthy, and each wore a little collar. We knew they had a home *somewhere*. Nevertheless, as I walked them back to the yard they had been near, as I walked away they both scampered up the road following behind me again. I finally gave up after multiple attempts to get them to go back, and had to walk back to our house. Once we were home the pair stayed on our front porch. My partner was distraught as we didn't really need any additional pets besides our present dog and cat. I figured after a little bit the two would wander back home. An hour passed, and I looked out the window to see them curled up next to each other patiently waiting. Two hours passed and it started to get dark, and they were still on our porch. After three hours, I finally knew I had to get these two little ones back to their home. I filled a small plastic sandwich bag bulging full with cat food. I came out of the house and they both aroused excited to see me. I quickly walked up the road with the two merrily following behind me. I finally approached the place we three initially met. The house there looked dark as though nobody was home. I knew that it must be close enough to their home, so that they would find it. I picked a safe spot in the yard, and emptied the baggy of food for them. They devoured into the food, and at least for a few minutes they forgot all about me. I gave them each one last head pat, and very quickly walked and then ran back home. A couple of weeks later on one of our walks I spotted the two off in a distant yard playing, and my partner firmly said, "You're not allowed to pet those kittens," and hurried me along so they wouldn't see me.

Dogs and cats are a perfect example of *selflessness*. As I mentioned before, they are definitely here to help and to teach us. If we watch them and their relationships to the humans in their lives we can see a display very often of *unconditional* love. Cats and dogs come here with no agendas. They do not keep score, only giving love and affection to others when they think it has been "earned." They are constant and consistent in loving always no matter what the circumstances. There have been many examples showing this trait of theirs throughout time.

A famous example of this occurred many years ago in Japan. Professor Ueno Elizaburo in 1925 walked every day from his home to take the train to his work, during this time it was the Tokyo University. He had an Akita dog named Hachiko who would accompany him every morning until he boarded his train. Of course, Hachiko could not go on the train with him to work, but would patiently wait at the gate for him at 3:00 each day for the Professor to come home. It mattered not the weather, as Hachiko always waited for his master every time.

On May 21st of this same year, Professor Elizaburo died of a stroke suddenly at work. Hachiko was at the station that day waiting for him patiently, as usual. When he saw that his beloved master did not arrive at 3:00, he continued to wait and wait for him. Finally the station closed up. The next day Hachiko again came to the station at 3:00 and waited patiently again until the station closed. He continued to go to the station daily at 3:00. Everyday for nearly ten years Hachiko went to the Shibuya station at 3:00, and sat waiting for his beloved Professor. The Professor's gardener and the stationmaster understood what Hachiko was doing, and gave him food and shelter. Soon the word started to spread about this dog. People started travelling to come see him, hoping to feed him or touch him for good luck. The Japanese people during this time felt that Hachiko was a prime example of what humans should aspire to become in their own lives.

On March 7, 1934 Hachiko was found having made his transition on the same platform in which he had waited faithfully for the Professor so many years. Regardless of his advanced age, and arthritic condition he had ceaselessly continued his love and devotion for the Professor everyday. Hachiko's death were in all of the newspapers nationwide in Japan, and there was an official day of mourning for him. Many of Hachiko's mourners contributed to make a statue of him, and it was placed in the exact place where he had sat at the station all of those years. During World War II the statue was taken and melted down for use in the war. After the war a new sculpture was created, and placed in the same place honoring Hachiko, where it remains today to inspire all who know his story.

Several years ago, I was living in a house with a boxer, two blue heelers and a Persian mix cat. One day a black cat came up to the back of my house. He looked terrible. I thought that he had been maybe hit by a car as his body looked like he was broken in the middle, and he was walking sideways with the outlines of his ribs rippling across his fur. If I tried to approach him, he would get scared and run sideways away from me. I had never seen anything like this before. He was definitely wild, and would not allow anyone to come close to him. I didn't know what else to do for him, other than to put a bowl of food and water out under my carport for him. While I was anywhere outside, he wouldn't go to the food dish. I finally gave up, knowing I had done everything possible for him. I noticed a day or so later the food bowl was empty, so I filled it again. A couple of days later I was out in my driveway washing my car, and I saw him walking up near my house. This time I was astonished to see that he no longer was walking sideways, or thin and broken-looking. It finally dawned on me, and I said to him, "Oh my, you were nearly *starved* to death!" This reality blindsided me like a cold hard punch. I couldn't imagine how it was possible that *any* cat in my neighborhood might nearly starve. I spoke to him and tried to coax him near me. This time he would come a little closer, within six feet or so. He wouldn't run away like he did before if I approached him, but he maintained a strict six foot perimeter. I respected this, and he seemed to simply watch me as I went back and finished washing my car. The following day he came back again for a visit, and I continued to speak to him and see if I could sweet-talk him to come closer. He would attentively watch me, and rub up against the tires of my car and bat his eyes at me lovingly, yet cautious to maintain now about a four foot distance. His daily visits continued, and finally one day he allowed me for the first time to stroke his head. Not much differently from Hachiko he started to recognize my daily routine. At least five days a week I went out to get into my car in the carport and he would be waiting to see me as I left for work. I would get home at about 6:30 each night, and he would be there to greet me as well. Finally, one day my partner's three year old niece aptly named him, "Valentine." As time continued, he blossomed into a friendly, and loving cat who would eventually allow a three-year-old to run up and play with him.

During most days my three dogs stayed in my fenced in backyard, which had a separate runway from the carport to the back door of the house. One evening I came home from work, and Valentine had decided to get into the back yard with the dogs, and seemingly was getting along well playing with them. One evening after coming home as I opened the back door to let the dogs in, Valentine ran into the house along with them. He had apparently determined on this day, this might become his home too. He wandered around from room to room in the house and settled in really easily.

Many evenings he would find his place in my lap while I was sitting in my easy chair. His rhythmic motor would wind up, and vibrate across my lap as I stroked his coat. He would pad his paws into a pillow, his pink tongue protruding slightly in a heavenly, slightly drooling bliss.

My other cat,"Wilma,"seemed to accept his presence in the house just the same as she did the dogs. I had chosen Wilma about a year earlier from a friend's litter of kittens, which magically appeared out of a woodpile. She had always been a skittish kind of cat. Try as I would to get close to her, she kept her distance from everyone. She wouldn't get too close to any of the dogs, myself, or my partner. If a visitor came into the house, she would hide in the basement and not be seen at all. Most of the time if the house was relatively quiet(which wasn't so often), she might come sit across the room from me. If I attempted to go near her, she might allow me to stroke her head once, and then she would run away.

I was so happy that Valentine was such of a ham for my attention and a "lap cat." One might never have known that he had been previously completely wild and untouchable. He and I seemed to have a great routine. Each morning when I left for work, I let Valentine out of the house for the day. When I got home Valentine would be waiting for me, and I would let him back into the house for the night.

This continued for several months until one day I was driving up my road, and about to pull into my driveway. Lying in the road right next to my driveway was my beloved Valentine. It seemed he was on his way home to see me, and didn't make it into the driveway before getting hit. Of course, I was devastated to lose him. I called my newly-former partner right away, to come help me put him into his final place of rest. Afterwards, I returned into my house. Just a few weeks prior to this time my partner and I had split up, and the dogs were no longer living in my home.

The house was completely quiet, and my new grief and realization that Valentine was now gone started to wash over me. I plopped down into my reclining chair where Valentine had spent so much time with me. I sat with the tears streaming down my face feeling so full of heartache just hoping that he hadn't suffered. I rubbed my eyes and noticed that my cat, Wilma, had come to the edge of the living room and was sitting watching me.

I looked at her and sobbed," Valentine is gone...he got hit in the street today, and now he's gone." I continued painfully telling her over and over, caught up in my own misery.

Wilma sat and listened to me and watched me for another minute or two. Then she came over to me and for the first time, jumped up into my lap. She curled up with me and allowed me to stroke her head. She studied me intently as I shifted nearly immediately from feeling overwhelmed with loss, to tears of joy at her coming to comfort me.

She sat with me and eventually started to purr as I settled down and became more calm. She continued to stay in my lap with me for about five minutes this first time, but it seemed like an eternity. I was in shock and overwhelmed that Wilma seemed to simply *know* that at this moment, I simply needed to be consoled. I realized that she understood all that I had said to her, and she stepped in to help me in the way that only these wonderful little beings are able to do.

Every evening from that day forward, Wilma would come sit with me while I was in my chair. Each time it gradually became a little bit longer, until there were times we both might fall asleep together for a nap on a Saturday afternoon. Although I still grieved the loss of Valentine, Wilma's loving presence certainly made everything much easier.

I have experienced first-hand the gift these furry companions are to us. They truly help to keep our planet balanced and assist us to understand unconditional love. Dogs have the job of reflecting and are reflectors; Cats have the job of absorbing and are absorbers.

It is not by accident that we notice dogs tend to look a lot like their owners. Their job here is to display continuous love and affection, and also to be a reflector. It is interesting to notice how some people feel that dogs have "more" personality than cats. This is simply because dogs are mirroring back the personality of his primary master. They over time become a direct reflection of us. Whatever we are projecting from our personality and emotional being, the dog will reflect this in his manner of being right back to us.

Everyone has seen extreme examples of this. All have seen a woman who's personality is to dress flamboyantly in heavy makeup, elaborate fashionable clothing, and expensive shoes. She will be sporting a tiny shiatsu dressed like a doll with the pink ribbon on its head, glittery pink collar, pampered with the latest doggie coif. It will be easy to notice that not only has her owner taken great strides for her dog to reflect herself, but the dog also will display certain actions as to mimic those of her owner. As an example, the dog might be real particular, and eat only a "certain brand" of dog food which must be served only in a "particular bowl."

Another such example of the opposite extreme is the larger gruff man who is loud and wears mostly jeans and sweatshirts. His personality is boisterous and he likes "hanging out with the guys" at the local pub shooting pool, and having a "couple brewskies." He has been known to overindulge at times, which can lead to getting into a scuffle with others outside of the bar. His dog of choice is a bulldog. During the winter he stretches a dingy red "dog sweatshirt" over him. The dog not only resembles him in his looks, but typically barks loudly almost all of the time. He also has had trouble in the neighborhood being aggressive to smaller dogs, starting a couple of fights. His owner simply tells the neighbors, "*They* need to keep *their* dogs away if they don't want any trouble."

These are both extreme examples and most of us fall somewhere in between with our dogs. If we look at the dog, Hachiko and his Professor, I am sure that Hachiko had developed and reflected many of the character traits of his beloved Professor. It is likely if we travelled back in time, those who knew the Professor most likely would report that he was very dedicated, disciplined, and loyal to his position teaching at the University. Similarly, Hachiko displayed these very traits as he daily sat and waited at the train station each day. He was truly being dedicated, and a true reflector of his master.

Recently, I was out for a hike at a local state park. There was a husband and wife couple walking on the same trail with their dog. She was a very well-fed, and sturdy black Boston Terrier. It was in the middle of the day, and in the heat of July. The man and woman passed me on the trail walking a fairly fast pace, with the dog trailing behind them at least 25 or more feet. She swayed along as quickly as her four short feet could move, with her pink drippy-tongue hanging as far out as possible. She seemed to be smiling taking her time to merrily splash through every ditch filled with even a little water, until she was dripping with mud-soaked water. She started falling further behind the couple. The woman turned and snapped at her," Come on, and hurry up."

The dog continued at her slower, waddling pace. As everyone continued hiking on the trail, the woman started to get more agitated. Once again, she started yelling at her dog saying, "Get over here, hurry up!"

She continued to get even more distressed that her dog wasn't keeping up with them. She came back to her dog and snapped her leash back onto her again. The woman walked forward briskly. Her dog walked a few steps, and stopped. She brought her happy tongue back into her mouth, and instead of a smile she clenched her teeth and became a statuesque pose of determination. The woman kept walking and all of the leash was finally tight and tugging the dog. She dug her paws into the ground becoming dead weight, until the leash had pulled and rolled the harness up from her shoulders to over her neck, and nearly past her head. The woman finally looked back, and now angrily came back and worked for quite awhile to untangle her harness.

The woman whisked off again, and her dog slowly walked three steps and stopped, still posing like a solid statue with her teeth gritted together stubbornly planting herself. She continued this throughout the remainder of the trail, to walk a few steps, and stopping repeatedly in defiance. Her face told the whole story, with her black bulging, yet alert eyes, pink lips, and gums pressed together with head cocked to the side, glaring at her master, and poised in the ultimate show-down. I now was doing everything possible to stop myself from laughing, and wishing I had my video camera. This scene would have easily been on *America's Funniest Home Videos.*

At nearly the end of the trail, the path split off. Instead of following the pair, she decided to take the other path and keep going straight.By this time I wasn't a bit surprised, and I was silently cheering for her.

It didn't take me long afterwards to recognize that this dog was simply doing her job. She was literally reflecting back everything to this woman that she was putting out. As the three of them walked in the woods, it was apparent that the woman felt that they should take a fast walk. When her dog didn't keep up with them as she felt she should, she became really rigid. As the woman continued to become more inflexible, her dog simply reflected back to her the same degree of stubbornness.

We can easily see in every situation that a dog is echoing back to us that which we are sending out. Every major aspect of us is displayed by them. It is hopeful that we are able to see our own reflection in them, and can eventually learn from this.

Interestingly, a recent study was performed on dogs in which MRI's were used to determine and measure the dog's specific brain activity, when they were exposed to certain sounds. They tested the dog's response to 200 different sounds, measuring the brain activity, and including the portion of the brain which was stimulated. Many of the sounds included certain words spoken by humans. They determined that the same auditory portion of the brain which is activated in humans, is also activated in the dogs. They also found that when certain words or phrases being spoken were charged emotionally, the same portion of the dog's brain was stimulated as the human brain for emotions.

This appeared to shock the scientific world, as this was the first study of its type to show such a similarity between the human brain, and another non-primate mammal. So, this fairly well confirms that whatever words or sounds we utter, which are or are not emotionally charged, activates the same areas of the brain in our furry dog-friends. It is then reasonable to deduce that if we are using any words which are emotionally charged, then our dog is sensitive and picking up that same emotion, and will display it right back to us.

Cats do not have the same job as dogs to reflect back to us. Their job here is to absorb, and neutralize the discordant energies in their surroundings.

This was exactly what my cat, Wilma, displayed for me so many years ago. Immediately after I lost my cat, Valentine, she came and sat on my lap to console me. I was filled with grief, and within just a few minutes later, she was sitting in my lap. I shifted from feelings of sadness, to joy and love. She helped to lighten the grip of these lower emotions I was emitting, over to the higher levels. As I look back on that event, I notice that she stayed next to me just as long as was necessary, to help me move from a lower emotional energetic state of sorrow, to a higher state of love and joy.

Another excellent example which any cat person has witnessed, is when a couple of friends stop by at your house. Often if there is one person who says," I don't really like cats," it is almost guaranteed, your cat is going to go rub right up against and try to get as close to that person as possible. One time Valentine was in the house, and a friend of mine stopped in the house for a visit. She announced that she "really wasn't too crazy about cats." Instantly, Valentine was up onto the couch and trying to get onto her lap. She at first politely got up and moved into the loveseat, and Valentine followed her and jumped onto the arm of that chair. He tentatively looked at her, and stretched one of his paws out onto her lap to try to get onto her lap, yet again. He, of course, wasn't listening to any of my calls for him to get away. She next stood up and moved across the room from him, and this time stayed standing. He jumped off of the chair and ran over to meow at her, and bat his head lovingly into her legs. It was nearly comical to watch her anxiously moving away from my cat, and him being as determined as ever to stay as close to her as possible. I finally had to scoop him up, and ban him into my separate piano room and close the door. During the next ten minutes Valentine stood near the door, vocalizing to us his dismay of getting exiled with some sporadic and very vocally disheartened, "meow...mooowrr...moooorowww's!" Shortly thereafter, my friends abruptly decided to leave, probably at least a bit sooner than they had planned.

Looking at this behavior exemplifies once again, how a cat is simply attempting to serve his purpose here. Valentine wasn't simply chasing my friend around my living room because she didn't like cats. He most likely sensed that she was experiencing fear and anxiety, and he simply was trying to get near her to help absorb some of that so she may become calm, and alleviate this stress.

All of these examples emulate the characteristic of *selflessness,* and are direct inspiration for us to strive to emulate these qualities in our lives. As we move to become more *selfless* in our lives, we are focusing upon bringing an important component of *divine love* into our life. It is important to ask ourselves. Am I displaying *selflessness* in my daily life? In what way? What are some ways I might increase *selflessness* towards others?

6

Regain Compassion and Giving

The next characteristic, which is a component of divine love is *compassion*. The definition of *compassion* is: the sympathetic consciousness of other's distress together with the desire to alleviate it. If we break down the word *compassion* further into its two components, there is the prefix *com-* and the word *passion.* The prefix *com-* means "with" or "together." The word *passion* is: a strong feeling of enthusiasm or excitement for doing something or about something. *Compassion* is witnessing or experiencing something, in another living being, and having a great desire to take action to assist. This is *divine love* in its pure essence.

"We Can Do Small Things With Great Love"

There are many examples of famous people throughout history who have displayed great levels of compassion towards others. However, one single person who constantly displayed this attribute ceaselessly throughout her whole life is that of Mother Teresa. Her devoted compassion towards others melted through all of the barriers of humanity.

She was born the youngest child in 1910 in Albania into a Catholic family. Her Father died unexpectedly when she was at the age of eight. This launched her family into financial struggles, yet her Mother provided her children with a firm and loving home. As a child, she became extensively involved in her local parish, until at the age of eighteen she was moved with the desire to become a missionary.

She left her home in 1928 to move to Ireland, and join the *Institute of the Blessed Virgin Mary* known as the *Sisters of Loreto*. It is here she received the name Sister Mary Teresa after St. Therese of Lisieux. She was sent to Calcutta, India in 1929 and assigned to be a teacher at the *St. Mary's School for Girls*. During 1937 she took her final vows, and forever-more was known as Mother Teresa. She continued teaching at St. Mary's until becoming the school's principal in 1944. During these years she was well noted for her charity, unselfishness, courage, and her capacity for hard work. Many also remarked that she had a natural talent for organization.

One day she was taking a train ride to Darjeeling for her annual retreat in 1946. During this ride she heard a new, "call within the call." She was never able to explain to others how Jesus' thirst for love so penetrated her heart, that the desire to satiate His thirst became the driving force for her life. During the course of the next few weeks, Mother Teresa received various visions and inner promptings with Jesus revealing to her the desire of his heart to "Radiate His love on Souls." He communicated his discontent at the neglect of the poor, and encouraged her to "come be my light." He asked her to establish a religious community dedicated to serving "the poorest of the poor." Two years later after more discernment and testing, she was given permission to begin.

It was August 17, 1948 she dressed for the first time in a white sari with blue borders, and passed through the gates of her beloved Loreto Convent to serve the world of the poor. After studying a short medical course, she started her work. December 21, 1948 was the first day she went into the slums of Calcutta. She visited families, washed the sores on some children, cared for an old man lying sick on the road, and nursed a woman dying of hunger and tuberculosis.

She started each day communing with Jesus first, and then went out into the community, rosary in hand to find and serve Him in "the unwanted, the unloved, and the uncared for." After several months, many of her former students began to join her.

The new congregation of *Missionaries of Charity* was officially established by the Archdiocese of Calcutta in 1950. During the early 1960's Mother Teresa began sending her Sisters to other cities in India. She established a house in Venezuela in 1965, and next in Rome, and Tanzania. Shortly thereafter, there were foundations in every continent. Starting in 1980 and into the 1990's Mother Teresa opened houses in nearly every communist country, including the former Soviet Union, Albania and Cuba.

Mother Teresa was given the Nobel Peace Prize in 1979. When she received the Nobel Prize, she was dressed in the same trademark sari with blue edges, she wore in the streets. She convinced the committee to cancel the dinner in her honor, using the money instead to "feed 400 poor children for a year in India." Her description of the mission of *The Missionaries of Charity* when accepting the peace prize was: "to care for the hungry, the naked, the homeless, the crippled, the blind, the lepers, all those people who feel unwanted, unloved, uncared for throughout society, people that have become a burden to the society and are shunned by everyone."

Mother Teresa tirelessly continued her mission and duties heading her organization despite her health challenges up until the last few months before her death. At the time of her transition in September 1997, her society numbered over 4000 and was established in 610 foundations within 123 different countries.

I never look at the masses as my responsibility; I look at the individual. I can only love one person at a time - just one, one, one. So you begin. I began - I picked up one person. Maybe if I didn't pick up that one person, I wouldn't have picked up forty-two thousand....The same thing goes for you, the same thing in your family, the same thing in your church, your community. Just begin - one, one, one."

-Mother Teresa

Mother Teresa displayed continuous *compassion* to those who were downtrodden within her community. Her efforts started by tending to one man lying sick in the street, then a child wandering alone and hungry, then another, and another. Soon the word spread of what she was doing, and others came to help.

This is a great example of how the passion of one being on purpose, and called to action inspires others to do the same. During this writing, the *Missionaries of Charity* have over 4500 members located throughout 133 countries throughout the world.

Mother Teresa is a famous example of living a life of compassion in a very large way. Certainly there are numerous opportunities for us each to practice compassion in our own lives, without the need to leave our home and become a missionary. We can perform acts of compassion to our own family, friends, neighbors, and strangers.

It can be something big or small. It might be as simple as sitting up with a child in her room, when she is sure there are monsters under the bed, and reading her a story with her until she falls asleep. Or it might be something bigger such as being a foster parent, and taking in a child of special needs who was given up by his natural parents. There are simply countless occasions for us to show our compassion to others.

First Day on the Street

Many years ago I served as a police officer in Arlington, Virginia. A new officer on the street moved from being a "rookie" to a seasoned officer very quickly in that community.

It was my very first day after graduating from the police academy of actually going to work on the street. We were required to ride along with a Field Training Officer for six weeks, until we had been fully checked out and trained to work alone. My first morning out, there were three of us who were fresh from the academy riding with our FTO's and we had a homicide call. Our FTO's decided it would be good for us to get our feet wet, and dropped us off at the crime scene.

It turned out that it was actually a rape and murder, which had occurred in the stairwell of a four floor apartment complex. The crime scene in the stairwell had been secured on the floor in which it occurred. However, they assigned the new officers each on post at the other three floors to keep people from entering the stairwell.

As the other officers processed the crime scene during the next nine hours, one of the supervisors on the scene decided that the new officers should get as much of the full impact as possible. It was usual during this time that several polaroid photos would be taken documenting every angle of the body, complete scene, and any evidence. The supervisor came to the floor where I was on my post. He fanned out about six or seven polaroid's for me to see.

He stated, "We cannot take you directly into the area, but we wanted you to get the full impact of what you will be doing when you are on your own soon. Look at them good, because this is what you'll be working in just a few short weeks. And the pictures are nowhere close to what it is like in person."

I looked at the images and saw a thin, small brown-skinned woman with black hair and a rope wound around her neck, tied to a fire extinguisher which was attached to the wall. Half of her clothing was missing from the waist down, and her body was an ugly bloody mess. There were puddles of blood surrounding her, and smears of footprints all over the floor. As I worked to swallow back my emotions, he continued," It looks like she was stabbed at least nine times. So far, we don't have any clear suspect." He turned his head toward the opposite end of the hallway, where I could see that one of the apartment doors was open having several people milling around in the hallway," Oh, and you probably should know that the victim has an identical twin sister that lives on this floor over there." He nodded again in the same direction. " She and the rest of her family have been informed." He walked away and I resumed standing my lone post.

It was usual on a homicide in an apartment building such as this, at least a few officers would go to every apartment in the building asking if anyone heard anything, or saw anything unusual. If someone has witnessed anything, the officer will get a brief detailed description, and then turn the individual over to homicide detectives for an in-depth interview. Fairly quickly after such an event, most everyone within the apartment complex knows that the police are there investigating a murder. I could see that there was quite a bit going on at the other end of the hall, but was glad that it was quiet at my end next to the door of the stairwell.

Now that it was a couple of hours into my "guard duty," the original adrenaline rush of "working a homicide" was starting to wear off. I suddenly realized I was in for a long day, and wished I had a book or something to help pass the time. Then just a couple of moments later I saw a single lone figure walking up the hallway towards me, leaving everyone else in the distance.

She was at least a head and a half shorter than I, having thin, long stick-like arms and legs. Her large brown eyes and silky hair pleasantly accented her bronze complexion. As she timidly approached me, I suddenly recognized her, and instantly knew. It was almost like someone had suddenly knocked the breath out of me as I thought," Oh my God, this is her *identical twin!*"

She carefully looked at me and said calmly," Is it true, my sister is gone?" her accent was of a thick Ethiopian descent, yet clear.

I got caught up in the reality of being official and doing my job, and how delicate this situation had just become. My mind was racing, as I had thought my supervisor told me that the family knew. Yet she seemed to act right now as if she had no idea.

I finally looked into her eyes that were so determined looking straight into me for her answer. My breath seemed to become just as shallow as hers, and I finally replied," I am so sorry, but your sister is gone."

She continued to look right into me for a few moments, as if she was searching for something. I saw tears well up into her eyes, and her tiny shoulders started to shake as she allowed herself to shudder and cry. She asked again, "My sister is *really* gone?"

I nodded and again said, "Yes, I am so sorry."

She slowly turned from me with her head down sobbing, and started to shuffle slowly back down the hallway. Within a few minutes she seemed safely back down with her family.

I took a deep breath, and then quivered as I thought about the pain and shock she must be experiencing and disbelief. Ten minutes later, I saw a tiny figure walking back up the hallway. She continued until she was squared up facing right in front of me, this time not as shy as before.

She looked square into my eyes and said, "May I go see my sister?"

I looked into her eyes again and said, "No, again I'm sorry, but you can't right now."

She continued becoming tearful and asking yet again, "She is gone?"

This time I simply nodded. She folded her arms around herself and waivered up the hallway again.

About an hour later all of the officers working at the scene were brought sub sandwiches. I was glad to be off of my feet and sit on the floor to eat in peace for a few minutes.

Dutifully, I stood back up again to see a small, slumping form shuffling towards me once more. She again fixed her gaze into my eyes," I wish to go see my sister now." After her announcement, she moved wearily in a mild attempt to move past me to the door.

I took a slight half-step in that same direction and planted my feet firmly into the floor. I affirmed," I can't allow you into the stairwell."

She looked up at me and winced," *Please* allow me to see her…"

At that moment, I dropped all of my previous six months of Police training and my seven years of Army training. I felt her loss and grief. I reached out and cupped my hand over her unsteady shoulder and was silent. Although it was only for a few seconds, her whole being seemed to shift, the tears seemed to slow, and she looked back into my eyes again. This time she knew. It was as if she had just become a little bit stronger, as for at least a moment she knew that I really could feel the trauma of her experience. There was only silence as she turned and moved back down the hallway.

At least every twenty minutes throughout the remainder of the day this beautiful human being came to me again, over and over. Each time I simply listened, and learned as she shared a little more with me each time.

The next time she announced, "My sister was a good person," pausing to study the reaction on my face, "and she was my best friend."

"I am sure that the two of you really were close."

Every time she came back to speak to me she was always by herself. I thought how uncanny it seemed, that the rest of her family simply allowed her to keep coming down the hall by herself to keep talking with me.

"We just moved here three months ago from Ethiopia. You know we were planning to open up a restaurant here," she swiped the fresh tears away from her water stained cheeks.

I spent my whole day listening, and continuously available to another deeply wounded human being. I shared in her feelings of pain and bewilderment.

The day finally finished with another officer coming to get me, as the coroners were preparing to move the body. About half a dozen of us surrounded the gurney as *her sister* was wheeled in her black bag through the lobby. Two different news video cameras had bright lights glaring towards us. One reporter shoved a microphone up towards me asking me something, in which I muttered, "there is no comment."

I noticed that a couple of her other family members stepped off of the elevator to follow us, and the reporters pointed the cameras greedily in their direction. I stepped away from *her sister* for a moment, and thrust my hand in front of one of the camera lens.

I puffed up stating, "They need their privacy." The other officers looked at me seemingly surprised at my assertiveness. Later that night I saw myself on the ten o' clock news, and was astonished too.

Looking back on that "first day" on the street, I know that I learned alot. Today I realize that when we have a responsibility which is "part of the job," we can still really help others during their time of need by responding with *compassion*. During this situation, the turning point seemed to occur when I reached out to her, and she recognized that I *really* understood. After this she shared more and kept coming back to speak with me. This shows that when we have *compassion*, this enables us to truly experience our connectedness with each other.

This event occurred over 20 years ago, and I didn't understand many things nearly as well as I do today. It seemingly was by the luck of the draw, that I was assigned to guard that stairwell door on the same floor in which the victim's family was living.

Several years ago Sai Maa taught us, that we must understand that there are truly *no accidents* in our lives. Absolutely nothing occurs in our life simply as a coincidence. This is really one of the deeper and enhanced ways of understanding *karma*. Every incident, occurrence, situation, person, or event which happens to us has come for a reason. We have drawn the person, or situation to ourselves for any number of reasons and nothing about it is simply by happen-stance. It might be that the energetic level of our previous thoughts, feelings, words, and actions have drawn the situation to us. It may also be that we have an opportunity to learn a much needed lesson from a particular situation.

Today I can see that because I was assigned to the same floor where this woman lived, it allowed me to have the chance to be fully present for another person during her time of need. I was able to learn how to connect to someone, and be *compassionate* in a way which I otherwise might never have experienced in my life.

During the next three and a half years I continued to serve as an Arlington County Police Officer, working as the primary officer and assisting officer on many more homicide calls. Never again did I have another experience such as this, in which my whole day I was available to serve the desperate needs of one other in this great of a capacity. Everything happens in just the way it does for a divine reason. Whenever we find *compassion,* this allows us to connect with each other.

If you want others to be happy, practice compassion. If you want to be happy, practice compassion.

-The Dalai Lama

We have many occasions to find *compassion* for others in situations which have nothing to do with our career. A couple of years after I had worked as a police officer on the street, it was sometimes a struggle to keep from becoming calloused and judgmental about people and certain situations. When I was first hired on the department, the detectives in charge of the hiring were so diligent in finding candidates, who were completely free of prejudices about certain groups of people. I know that this was one of my strong qualities when I was first hired. But after a couple of years of continuously witnessing the same crimes and behaviors over and over again being committed by certain common groups of people, it was hard to not get caught into this type of judgmental thinking.

One such group that was highly prevalent within the county where I lived and worked were the homeless people. Every day we were answering calls for one or more of them causing some type of disturbance. Many during this time were typically alcoholics, and might cause some sort of ruckus if under the influence. After only a few months on the job, I knew all of the troublemakers, and had arrested each of them many times. However, not all were this way. Quite a few people lived in the wooded areas and parks, and were Vietnam Era veterans who stayed mostly secluded from others.

One day I was off duty and driving to the grocery store. At the corner of the street near the entrance of the store, I saw a leather faced man holding a cardboard sign. His sign written in black marker stated, "Will work for food." I slowed and took a better look as I passed, realizing that I had never seen him before. He had dark, oily strings of hair with lighter sun baked strands in between. He wore scuffed brown leather boots which matched his sunbaked skin, grungy blue dickie pants, and a solid tan smeared t-shirt which hung loosely around his lean frame.

As each car passed by him he leaned forward holding his sign gravely, hoping for someone to do something. As I passed by him I looked directly into his eyes. He raised himself up taller and looked right back at me. His blue eyes were open wide, and I could see the wild desperation written all over his face.

I drove on to the store, wondering if I might have been the only one passing him who had made eye contact with him that day. As I marked the items off of my grocery list, I worked on another list. I was a little aggravated that it took me so long to figure out the best foods for a person with no refrigerator and no stove. I finally compiled everything and got checked out.

I found a spot to park my car within a couple hundred feet of his corner in a parking lot. The blacktop was scorching from the 90 plus degree heat. I grabbed three bags and slowly carried them over to him, feeling the weight of them stretching the plastic out and nearly scraping the pavement. I was happy to see he hadn't left the corner yet, and hoped I had chosen the best food for him. I thought he probably needed electrolytes, something to eat right now, and things to eat later. So I had three extra-large bottles of Gatorade, a fresh deli-made turkey sandwich, a couple of boxes of crackers, and a couple dozen cans of tuna, chicken, vegetables and chili.

I approached him and plopped the bags down onto the sidewalk stating, "This is for you."

His eyes flashed me a moment of silent gratitude, and then he quickly snatched one of the bottles of Gatorade out of the bag and sat it onto the blistering cement. He ran over inside of the McDonald's on this same corner. I wiped the sweat from starting to trickle into my eyes, and began to walk back to my car. I glanced back and saw he now had a large cup of ice he had sat onto the ground, in which he was carefully pouring the Gatorade. I saw him very cautiously replace the cap. Next he stood and leaned his head back and started to gulp his drink so quickly, I could see some of it escaping down the sides of his face and dripping off his whiskery chin. His super-size cup was empty within about twenty seconds. Once I got into my car and passed by him on the corner, I saw he was on his second cup of Gatorade. He looked up at me, and this time I saw in his eyes at least a little less despair. He gazed over at me for a moment and waved. I waved back. During the next few years that I lived and worked in Arlington, I never saw him again.

I think back to this time in the early 1990's, and can't recall whether there was a regular soup kitchen or other food charity in our community. During this time I wasn't aware of one at all. As a police officer, we were kept informed in most of the available resources within the community to refer those in need. I know that during this time, the people living on the street were highly visible everywhere. Although I no longer live in Arlington, I am sure that as awareness has increased now there are many more services available than there were previously.

Sai Maa tells us over and over about the importance of helping to feed others. She says there is no greater service we can give to others. She pleads on their behalf, telling us how it is not possible to grow and remember your spirituality when you are hungry. You cannot focus upon meditation when you are hungry. There is no greater gift you can give another human being than to fill an empty stomach. I agree with her on all of this, and add that if we were to measure *compassionate* actions on a graded scale, feeding a hungry person would be at the top of the list.

It is very much like the following story. There was a woman walking on the beach at the ocean. As the tide washed in each time, she noticed that thousands of starfish were getting stranded onto the beach. Each time the tide came in there were more and more. She stopped and busied herself with picking up the starfish and throwing them back into the water, each time the water receded. She continued to work diligently.

A few minutes later a man approached her and said,"There must be at least a thousand starfish washed up onto the shore. Do you really think that it is possible for you to save all of these starfish?"

She bent over and picked up another starfish and held it carefully in the center of her palm, and held it up for the man to see. Then she threw it into the ocean at the moment the tide pulled back from the shore.

"I made a difference for that one, didn't I?" She reached down to pick up another.

There are times that we could easily take this man's attitude. We might think that there are so many that need help, and what difference can one person make? Or where does one start when there are so many? Yet this is the exact approach that Mother Teresa took when she stepped out into the streets of Calcutta to help others. She said,".... *one person at a time - just one, one, one. So you begin. I began ......The same thing goes for you, the same thing in your family, the same thing in your church, your community. Just begin - one, one, one."*

Compassion, it is what we are here to learn and practice, and we will grow as a result. It is one of the essentials of *divine love.* Just begin.

Heart-Centered Giving

One may begin to notice as we look at all of the components of *divine love,* that each are inter-connected and related to each other. The next major factor is *giving*. Many of us would relate," I already understand and know all I need to know about *giving*, and already do this regularly in my life."

However, I invite each of us to really look at this in our life. *Giving* is closely related to *compassion* and *selflessness*, yet needs its own category. This is an area we each need to closely examine in our lives.

There are some important questions we must ask ourselves. First of all, do we give? What different ways am I giving? How do we feel when we give? What are the reasons behind why we give? Do we give enough? Or, do we give too much? Is it possible for me to give too much? How do I determine any of this?

A minister of the *Unity New Thought Spiritual Movement*, Rev. Stretton Smith, developed a program called the *4T prosperity program* in 1988. This program, and it's teachings have become widely embraced throughout the Unity Movement. The core concept of Rev. Smith's program is that when we *give* to others our *time, talents, treasures, and tithes,* this action of *giving* will in turn tend to manifest a greater level of abundance in our life. Although our major reason for *giving* to others is not simply to receive back abundance in our life, it certainly can become a side-benefit. Looking at the 4 T's, *time, talents, treasures* and *tithing,* are an excellent way to fully examine all of the ways we may give to others.

The first way we might give of ourself is our *time*. Where am I giving my time to others? The second is we may give of our *talents*. How do I give to others through the use of my talents? Otherwise, how do I use my own unique abilities to help serve others? Third, we may give our *treasures*. This is giving of money, or our financial wealth or other possessions to others. How do I give my treasures to benefit others? Lastly, we may give our *tithes*. This is financially helping to support the organization which spiritually feeds us. How do I financially support my spiritual home or community?

Giving is the most fun you can ever have, I highly recommend it.

- Oprah Winfrey

Having The Time Of Your Life

I must admit that it was only after first meeting my Spiritual Teacher, Sai Maa many years ago that I was directly taught the importance as well as the full meaning of *giving*. The common term for this used in India in Sanskrit is *seva,* or *selfless service*. We can also relate that the term, *seva,* also is simply equivalent to *time,* and is one of the four T's of giving.

Whenever Sai Maa has a spiritual retreat she has spoken many times on the importance of volunteering to do *seva* during the retreat. During one of her events, a person can choose from being on a team to set up the hall, to take down and pack up the hall after the event, cutting and arranging flowers, working at the registration tables, cleaning the hall in between sessions, assisting at any number of different booths, helping with the audio-visual, be on the security team, or even be a microphone runner during the event. There is literally something suitable for everyone.

Often when new people first come to an event with Sai Maa, this concept may seem a little strange due to our western upbringing. Sai Maa once again tells us that it is important to perform *selfless service*, which is giving simply for the sake of giving. Again, this is simply giving of our *time* to others, by supporting an event, or organization. Another side benefit she mentions is that when we are performing *seva,* we are working also with other people. It is during this *time* we spend working with others, that often old unresolved issues we may have with our ego and relating with others may come to the surface. She tells us that this gives us the opportunity to see these old patterns we may still carry, and to work towards transforming these in our lives.

Several years ago I made the decision to move to Colorado as during this time Sai Maa's headquarters and most of her events were being held there. I was so excited to live and participate in nearly every event that was held in or near Boulder. I was really happy to become part of a large spiritual community.

My partner and I after getting settled, started attending the weekly *satsang,* or spiritual gathering every week at the spiritual center. It was usual that Sai Maa travelled most of the time world-wide and was away much of the time, but would return and lead events and retreats locally about every three months. During the rest of the time when she was out of town, these were led by other members of the community.

After first moving into the community, my partner and I were so excited to begin attending the weekly two hour long *satsang.* During this time we would be led by one of the appointed members of the community in various types of meditation, chanting, or maybe a *kirtan.* This is when a small group of musicians would play various instruments and lead us in songs. It was typical on these evenings that between 30-50 people would be in attendance.

We were excited to be in community with so many other like-minded people. At the end of these evenings, it was usual that everyone would congregate afterwards for another 10-15 minutes visiting with each other. When we first started attending these, we noticed that we seemed to have a difficult time meeting the other people in the community. Both of us seemed to experience that many of the people seemed to keep a palpable distance, and were difficult to speak with after the programs. After the first few weeks of these types of encounters, we decided on a game plan. We decided each week that we would team up together, and approach at least one or two new people and deliberately go speak with them together. Every week we worked this plan diligently, with at least some success hoping to eventually meet and get to know everyone.

The first time Sai Maa came after we had moved there a few months later, she asked me how I was enjoying being in my new spiritual community. I complained somewhat," I'm having a difficult time getting to know many of the other people. I had some fairly major conflict while performing *seva* with one other person. Otherwise, it was going okay."

I was able to see that wasn't the response Sai Maa had expected, or wanted to hear from me. I thought that Sai Maa might be a little sympathetic and wish to hear about my previous efforts. At the time I thought that she might even wish to hear my side of the story, and maybe even buy into the idea that I had done everything possible in this situation. My *expectation* at the time was that she would listen to my *story* and tell me something like," Yes, you poor dear. You have been treated terribly. I am sure you were right, and this person was wrong. We'll just have to have a talk with the two of you, and we will get this straightened out."

Instead, she firmly instructed me to go get her CD recording teaching on *community,* and to go listen to it three times, and put this into practice.

She directed me to listen to her teaching on this matter. I did as she directed, and learned that *I* needed to change *my* thoughts, *my* feelings and no matter what the other person or circumstances revealed, stay in the state of love. I started focusing upon myself in this way, and soon after I witnessed my relationships with others in my spiritual home change drastically for the better.

All types of situations may arise either involving the people we know, or those who are strangers. I have learned that each situation, even those that seem adverse at the time are really giving us the opportunity to practice staying heart centered.

An example of this occurred to me only a couple of months after I had been practicing the teachings from Sai

Maa's *community* CD. I was driving home from the store, and my partner told me to take a different road back home that was faster through a residential neighborhood. I had never driven down this road. We approached an intersection which was a four way stop. I simply didn't know, and didn't see my stop sign and drove right through the intersection. There was a car stopped at the intersection on the opposite road. My partner hollered after I sailed through the intersection, "That was a four way stop, didn't you know to stop?"

I answered," I didn't know, and didn't see the sign. I've never been on this road."

I continued driving and now noticed that the same adjacent car was following behind us. Every turn I took closer to home, the other car took as well. The other car followed us the remaining five minute drive it took us to get home.

I finally pulled my car up at our home. The car pulled up and abruptly stopped in front of my yard. A woman jumped out of her car, and bolted across our yard towards me stopping about three feet from me as I turned to fully face her.

I attempted to speak and she furiously interrupted,"You blatantly ran through that four way stop. You could have hit someone!"

I deliberately lowered my voice about an octave lower than hers, and kept myself peaceful answering," Yes, I did run that sign, and I apologize. That was my first time down that road, and I simply didn't see the sign."

She continued still flushed in fury," What if I had a child in my car! You could have easily ran right into us!" She moved her finger at me in pointed sharp motions, as if trying to send invisible darts at me.

I calmly replied again," Yes, I apologize, and I made a mistake. Once again, I didn't see the sign," starting to warmly smile at her, I caught myself. I decided it might be better in this heated situation, to send loving thoughts without the smile.

She bent over to examine my license plate, noticing that it was an out of state tag continuing," Well, I don't know what the laws are like in the state of *Indiana*, but here in *Colorado,* we *stop* when there is a stop sign!"

I once again lowered my voice, "I made a mistake, and now I know that is a four way stop."

Turning from my car to look at me she declared, "Well, I guess since you aren't *from* here, I guess I'll give you a break *this* time!"

Still nearly as angry as after arriving she marched straight back to her car, got in and sped off. I sent a silent blessing for a moment to her, and this time allowed myself to smile.

Then I looked over to my partner, and took a breath of relief and said," Wow." About a minute later I was unloading groceries from the car, and everything was back to normal again for me, almost as if it never happened.

It is in times such as this that we have the opportunity to decide what words, thoughts, feelings and actions we will give to others in a stressful situation. It also allows us to practice being heart-centered, and giving to others higher vibrational energies even when it may be amidst a difficult situation. Also, when these types of incidents occur, do we allow them to disturb our own peace? Or are we able to maintain our own sense of harmony, no matter what the behaviors may be of others.

Often when we think of *giving,* we think of only tangible things such as money, items, and service to others. The areas most do not think of in terms of giving include our thoughts, words, and feelings. What thoughts am I sending out and *giving* to others? What feelings are radiating from me that I am *giving* others? What are my words that I am sending and *giving* others? Whether we realize it or not, we are *giving* these to all of the other people we contact. Are these of the high *love* vibration, or do these resonate more with *fear?*

Particularly when we are actively seeking our spiritual growth, we will be given many opportunities in various situations to test our level of readiness. If we are able to recognize this and direct our thoughts, words, feelings, and actions towards others with divine love, we eventually will find much less conflict. Then we may notice that we seem to sail through similar situations much easier than before. It does not mean that all types of circumstances will not show up in our lives, which may seem to test us. If we stay consciously aware, we increase our ability to quickly master ourselves, and stay in the vibration of love no matter what are our surrounding conditions. This is another aspect of *giving* which every one of us do every day, regardless if we are aware of it or not.

Our Gifts To The World

The next of the important T's which are a component of giving are our *talents*. A talent is: A special ability that allows someone to do something well. It also was used during ancient times as: A unit of value equal to the value of a talent of gold or silver.

I recall as a child studying the bible, and really enjoying the parable about the talents. I embraced this story, and took it to heart recalling and reciting it whenever the time seemed appropriate to help guide myself and others. I referred to it as a teenager, young adult and throughout the years whenever I needed insights in any of my major life decisions. A funny thing happened only a couple of years ago. One day I was reciting my now favorite teaching from the bible to my partner, who then and presently is a Unity ministerial student. She informed me that I had interpreted the talents incorrectly. As a child, I only thought that a *talent* was our special ability, or that which we have as a gift we are to use to benefit others. She advised me that during the time of the story, it was a type of money. Amazingly, I decided that the story worked just as well, regardless of how I was interpreting it. The awareness we can gain from this can serve us well.

The Parable Of The Talents

[14] "For it will be like a man going on a journey, who called his servants and entrusted to them his property. [15] To one he gave five talents, to another two, to another one, to each according to his ability. Then he went away. [16] He who had received the five talents went at once and traded with them, and he made five talents more. [17] So also he who had the two talents made two talents more. [18] But he who had received the one talent went and dug in the ground and hid his master's money. [19] Now after a long time the master of those servants came and settled accounts with them. [20] And he who had received the five talents came forward, bringing five talents more, saying, 'Master, you delivered to me five talents; here I have made five talents more.' [21] His master said to him, 'Well done, good and faithful servant. You have been faithful over a little; I will set you over much. Enter into the joy of your master.' [22] And he also who had the two talents came forward, saying, 'Master, you delivered to me two talents; here I have made two talents more.' [23] His master said to him, 'Well done, good and faithful servant. You have been faithful over a little; I will set you over much. Enter into the joy of your master.' [24] He also who had received the one talent came forward, saying, 'Master, I knew you to be a hard man, reaping where you did not sow, and gathering where you scattered no seed, [25] so I was afraid, and I went and hid your talent in the ground. Here you have what is yours.' [26] But his master answered him, 'You wicked and slothful servant! You knew that I reap where I have not sown and gather where I scattered no seed? [27] Then you ought to have invested my money with the bankers, and at my coming I should have received what was my own with interest. [28] So take the talent from him

and give it to him who has the ten talents. ²⁹ For to everyone who has will more be given, and he will have an abundance. But from the one who has not, even what he has will be taken away. ³⁰ And cast the worthless servant into the outer darkness. In that place there will be weeping and gnashing of teeth.'

-Holy Bible, English Standard Version Matthew 25:14-30

As I read this modernized version, I know that the bible I read as a child was the King James Version and was not as plainly stated as it is here.

However, if we look at the first portion where it states it is similar to each person *going on a journey*. Each person is given *according to their abilities*. The first person is given five talents, the second is given two and the third is given one talent. The first man with five talents *went at once and traded with them and he made five talents more*. The man with two *made two talents more*. This shows that the first two over a period of time were able to double the original talents in which they were given.

The third man *who had received the one talent went and dug in the ground and hid his master's money*. Later when his master returns he admits to him, *"I was afraid, and I went and hid your talent into the ground. Here you have what is yours."*

His master becomes angry with him declaring," *You ought to have invested my money with the bankers, and at my coming I should have received what was my own with interest."*

The master takes away the talent from this man and gives it to the man who has ten talents.

He states," *To everyone who has will more be given, and he will have an abundance. But from the one who has not, even what he has will be taken away."* This shows how the person who has cowered away in fear, will eventually lose what he has.

Finally, the passage states *cast the worthless servant into the outer darkness. In that place there will be weeping and gnashing of teeth.'* This signifies that the person who eventually has his talent taken away will experience sorrow and suffering.

Whether we assign the *talent* as a unit of money or as our own special abilities, gifts or *talents,* this works the very same way in each of our lives. Each and every one of us on this planet has our own special skills or aptitudes in specific areas. Are we expressing these fully each day in our lives? One person may be most talented with teaching others, singing, and growing vegetables. Another person may possess strong abilities in mechanics, woodcarving, swimming, and story-telling. Do we readily share our talents with the rest of the world? This is yet another important aspect of giving.

This exemplifies if we readily take our own talents and gifts out and use them freely for ourselves and others, eventually even greater gifts and abilities will be given to us. If instead we take that which we have been given and squirrel it away in fear, over time it will be taken from us.

The Bulb Is Still Burning

I recently returned from vacationing in Florida. I went to Ft. Myers and visited Thomas Edison's winter home for the first time. I was so amazed and inspired by this man, that my partner had to nearly drag me away from the museum as they were getting ready to close.

I am sure that previously I was not any different than most, knowing that there was such a man as Thomas Edison who was an inventor, and made many different things we commonly use today. However, after perusing only a small portion of the audio tour of his winter home, I was hooked and quickly attempting to sponge up as many details as possible about him. During the few short hours I was able to spend on his previous stomping grounds, laboratory, and home, I was left amazed and newly inspired. Thomas Edison is a well-known historical example of the *parable of the talents* in real life.

Thomas Edison was born in 1847 in Ohio and the youngest of seven children. His father was an exiled political activist from Canada, and his mother was an accomplished school teacher. During his early years he had multiple ear infections and a bout with scarlet fever, which left him with difficulties hearing throughout the rest of his life.

At the age of seven, his family moved to Michigan where he was enrolled in public school. Edison attended school for 12 weeks. He was described as a hyperactive child, prone to distraction and was deemed "difficult" by his teacher. His mother quickly decided to pull him from school and taught him at home. By the age of 11, he showed a voracious appetite for knowledge, reading books on a wide range of subjects. In this wide-open curriculum Edison developed a process for self-education and learning independently, which would continue to serve him throughout his life.

At the age of 12, Edison set out to put much of his education to work. He convinced his parents to let him sell newspapers to passengers along the Grand Trunk Railroad line. Since he had access to the news bulletins teletyped to the station office each day, Thomas began publishing his own small newspaper called the *Grand Trunk Herald*. The up-to-date articles were a hit with passengers. This was the first of his long string of entrepreneurial ventures, where he saw a need and created the opportunity.

Edison used his access to the railroad to conduct chemical experiments in a small laboratory he set up in a train baggage car. During one of his experiments, a chemical fire started, and the whole car caught fire. The conductor rushed in and struck Thomas on the side of the head, probably furthering some of his hearing loss. He was kicked off of the train, and instead was forced to sell his newspapers at the various stations along the route.

One day Edison saved a 3-year-old from being run over by a wayward train. The child's father was so grateful, that he rewarded him by teaching him to operate a telegraph. By age 15, he had learned enough to become employed as a telegraph operator. During the next five years Edison traveled throughout the Midwest, subbing for the telegraph operators who had gone to the Civil War. During his spare time, he read widely, studied, and experimented with telegraph technology, and became familiar with the science of electricity.

At age 19, Edison moved to Louisville, Kentucky and worked for *The Associated Press*. Working the night shift allowed him to spend most of his time reading and experimenting. Edison excelled at his telegraph job because early morse code was inscribed on a piece of paper, and Edison's partial deafness was not a handicap. As the technology advanced, receivers were increasingly equipped with a sounding key requiring the telegraphers to "read" messages by listening to the sound of the clicks. Eventually Edison was disadvantaged due to his impaired hearing, leaving him with fewer opportunities for employment.

At age 21 Edison returned home to discover his beloved mother was falling into mental illness, and his father was out of work. His family was almost destitute. Upon the suggestion of a friend he ventured to Boston, and landed a job for the Western Union Company. During his spare time, he designed and patented an electronic voting recorder for quickly tallying votes in the legislature. However, Massachusetts lawmakers were not interested. They explained that most legislators didn't want votes tallied quickly. They wanted the extra time to change the minds of fellow legislators.

A year later Edison moved to New York City and developed his first invention, an improved stock ticker which synchronized several stock tickers' transactions. The Gold and Stock Telegraph Company was so impressed, they paid him $40,000 for the rights. At the age of 22, he quit his work as a telegrapher to devote himself full-time to inventing.

At age 23, Thomas Edison set up his first small laboratory and manufacturing facility in Newark, New Jersey, and employed several machinists. He formed numerous partnerships, and developed his products for the highest bidder. He devised for Western Union the quadruplex telegraph, capable of transmitting two signals in two different directions on the same wire.

A year later he married one of his employees and they eventually have 3 children together.

After only six years he outgrows his first facility, and moves his expanding operations to Menlo Park, New Jersey, building an independent industrial research facility incorporating machine shops and laboratory. During December of 1877, Edison developed a method for recording sound we know as the phonograph. This invention brought him worldwide fame.

The 1880s found Edison becoming busier and busier. After being granted a patent for the light bulb in January 1880, Edison set out to develop a company that would deliver the electricity to power and light the cities of the world. That year Edison also founded the Edison Illuminating Company, the first investor-owned electric utility. It later became the General Electric Corporation. In 1881, he expanded yet again to establish facilities in several cities where electrical systems were being installed.

Edison's first wife dies in 1884 after thirteen years of marriage of a probable brain tumor. He remarries again in 1886.

Edison spends much of his time during these years supervising the development of lighting technology and power systems. He also perfected the phonograph, developed the motion picture camera, and the alkaline storage battery. He created the first talking doll, and also was the first to establish the use of a production line in his factories to be able to more efficiently produce his products for the public. This same concept was copied by all of the other manufacturing companies and is still used today.

During the 1890s, he built a magnetic iron-ore processing plant in New Jersey that proved to be a failure. Eventually, he was able to salvage the process into a better method for producing cement. On April 23, 1896 Edison became the first person to project a motion picture, holding the world's first motion picture screening in New York City.

Edison worked on developing a viable storage battery that could power an electric car. Though the gasoline engine eventually prevailed, Edison designed a battery for the self-starter on the Model T for friend and admirer Henry Ford in 1912. This system was used extensively in the auto industry for decades.

During World War I the government asked Thomas Edison to head the Naval Consulting Board, examining inventions submitted for military use. Edison worked on several projects which included submarine detectors, and gun location techniques. Since Edison had an aversion toward violence, he specified that he would work only on defensive weapons. Later he noted, "I am proud of the fact that I never invented weapons to kill."

In 1915 Thomas Edison and three of his famous friends began a series of annual summer trips lasting two to three weeks. Every summer he and Henry Ford, Harvey Firestone, and John Burroughs took camping trips to various locations to relax, and become inspired with new ideas for developing their businesses. They continued these annual trips until 1924, when their notoriety made it difficult to travel and remain inconspicuous. It was during these trips and era of time, that a couple of photographs were released showing him taking his famous "cat-naps." He related to others that he routinely would think about any problem he was working on just before taking one of his *cat-naps,* and often after he would awaken, he reported seeming to have either a solution, or new idea to pursue.

During the end of the 1920s Thomas Edison was in his 80s and he applied for the last of his 1,093 U.S. patents, for an apparatus for holding objects during the electroplating process. Edison and his second wife spent part of their time at their winter retreat in Fort Myers, Florida, where his friendship with automobile industrialist Henry Ford flourished. He continued to work on several projects, ranging from electric trains to finding a domestic source for natural rubber. Thomas Edison died of complications of diabetes in 1931 in his home at the age of 84.

As I looked at this man's life, I saw someone who definitely well used his apportioned *talents* to the fullest. Instead of hiding them under a rock, he nurtured them to eventually share with all of the world.

How many children are there today with our "better educational system" than over 150 years ago who might be labeled as a "difficult" child in school? At the age of seven he actually received 12 weeks of formal education, and left school for a few years of "home schooling." Then at the age of 12, with a whopping five years of education under the belt, set off and started his first job. He sold newspapers and then soon after determined he could write his own.

As we continue to examine Edison's life, the common thread that weaves throughout the fabric, is that at every single moment he used his *talent* to the greatest of his ability. Every single instance brought even larger opportunities for him to expand them even more.

As I walked through Edison's winter home in Ft. Myers marveling at the countless displays, there were two that impressed upon me the most. The first were several vintage 1880's light bulbs, each were hanging throughout his home over the dining room table, and in the center of the living room. Each of them were larger and more round than the standard ones we use today, and had clear glass with the filaments burning a reddish glow of light. All of the bulbs were original, made by him and still burning today each in its own glory over 130 years later. Unlike the light bulbs produced today, he designed them with the intent that they would not burn out.

The second item which captivated me on display was one of his original phonographs. It was encased in an ornate, solid oak cabinet. Looking at one corner of the wood cabinet-closest to the side where the needle contacts the spinning portion of the phonograph, there was a distinct, well-worn divot into the wood. Since he had even more difficulty hearing as the years passed, these were his teeth marks into the cabinet of the phonograph. He stated that he couldn't rely on others to hear for him, and to distinguish whether each piece on his phonograph was adjusted just right. He gripped his teeth into the wooden portion of the phonograph, so he could feel the conduction of the sound through the bones of his teeth, as it played so he could "hear" and fine-tune his instrument perfectly.

There might be those in these same type of circumstances who might stop and get caught up in the idea of limitation. One could think, maybe I am not educated enough. There are some who might have quit experimenting after the lab caught fire, and being thrown off of the train. Another might have attempted the first invention for the vote tallying machine, and after it was rejected by others decide to quit. Or choose to give up because the iron ore processing factory was a failure. Yet others might get caught up in the notion that there are certain things a mostly deaf person simply can't accomplish.

There was never any of this with Thomas Edison. He never doubted what he could accomplish. His life exemplifies what is possible when a person embraces *all* of the *talents* one has been given fully. There truly are no limits to what any of us can accomplish.

If we are *fully* using our own talents, and sharing them with others, we will be in the flow of life. We will know that we are completely unstoppable, and more and greater opportunities will unfold themselves to us every day. When we are fully expressing our true talents, there will soon follow a side benefit of financial abundance. These two are undeniably and automatically connected to each other. If anyone of us during life is experiencing any kind of lack in any financial areas, the absolute underlying cause is because we aren't using our underlying talents *completely*. It is imperative that we each identify our own *talents* and develop them as much as possible. This is the elusive truth so many struggle to understand and manifest into life. These are also our *treasures*. These both are interwoven together.

Many of life's failures are people who did not know how close they were to success when they gave up.

If we did all of the things we are capable of, we would literally astound ourselves.
-Thomas A. Edison

If You Get Into A Ditch, Don't Keep Digging

How do we identify if we are using our gifts and talents fully in our lives? How do we know what they are? What should I do if I discover I am completely off track?

Several years ago I recall as I was just beginning my life as an "adult" fresh out of high school. I really admired many of my friends who simply knew early on what they wanted to "become" as an adult. During my senior year in high school everyone was announcing their decision of which college and major they had already chosen. One of my friends declared that she planned to be a child psychologist. She attended the same college as I, and eventually after getting a little sidetracked with a couple of unsuccessful marriages, raising two children mostly as a single parent she eventually earned her Bachelor's in Psychology. She began working with adolescents and children, later earning her Master's and has since become a highly successful mental health therapist. I could elaborate on many of my friends who seemed to jump right out of the starting block after high school knowing their direction, and years later were spot on with their chosen career.

I, on the other hand right after graduation felt lost. I was completely undecided upon any direction for my major, and didn't decide upon which college I would attend until just the month before classes started. I told my parents that I wanted to sit out for a year, and go work out in the "real world," hopefully figuring out a career choice in this way. My parents were firm in telling me," I was going to go to college *now*, no matter what."

I found myself unloading and getting settled into my new dorm room, along with at least several thousand other freshman students. It was August, and I had celebrated my eighteenth birthday just the week before.

That week I registered for my first classes. During the pre-computer era this process was about as stressful as one could imagine. I unfolded my course booklet, and wrote down six classes in pencil on my registration form at one of the designated tables. Then I picked the shortest of half a dozen different lines leading up to the registration counter, and there were at least 50 students ahead of me. It took me at least an hour to reach the counter. The lady took my paper and thumbed through her master class listings, and drew a line through five of my six classes. Then she wrote down my information for one class, and gave me back my paper.

She stated pointing at my crossed out classes," These five classes are full and are closed."

I was incredulous," All five!"

"Hmm, hm. You need to go back to the table and find new classes, then get back into line."

I walked away, at first astounded. Then I followed suit with all of the other students, and started running back to the table to see how quickly I could scribble down five new classes and jump back into line. It was a frenzied race for us all, in a blind attempt to sign up for the last morsels of classes available that none of the Sophomores, Juniors, or Seniors wanted when they pre-registered the previous semester. At the end, I had spent nearly six hours standing in line and had managed to get only five classes, three of which were completely different from the ones I had originally planned.

I finally started my first semester of classes. Even though I had no earthly idea what to list for my major, I thought that listing *math* looked much better than *undecided*. Although I had made straight A's and taken every possible math course I could squeeze into four years of high school, I found my 5 credit college algebra class no longer fun. I discovered that I didn't seem to connect to my teacher, and my first exam in that class was marginal. I continued through the class and finished, but with my first-ever C in math. I struggled in my required *western civilization after 1648* class enough, that had I not withdrawn half way through I would have failed.

During my second semester I decided to change my major to political science and took a couple of political science classes. I was gun-ho with this choice until towards the end of the semester, I managed to get a meeting with my advisor.

I thought I was so fortunate that my appointed advisor was the head professor of the political science department. He asked me what I planned to do with my degree.

My answer was, "My goal is at age 25 to be in the House of Representatives. At the age of 30 in the Senate.

Then at the age of 35 to be the first woman president of the United States."

He was silent for a moment and then very matter of factly declared, "Well, as a woman with a degree in political science, the best you can hope for is to get a job working as a secretary in a government agency."

I sat silent for a moment, and my eighteen year young be*lie*f system decided at the time, that he must really know. Since he was the *head* of the political science department, I gave him the respect of being an authority.

My mother spent many years working as a secretary during a time when women simply weren't given promotions to any higher positions. I remembered her sharing with me about training all of her male bosses, each one of whom she had a similar college degree, and they were hired with no experience. Similar to most of the other girls in high school, my mom made me sign up for a typing class. On a good day I could type about 20 words per minute, and I knew I had no desire or ability in this area.

Shortly after, during this semester I started getting frequent sore throats. It seemed that every few weeks I was sick, and this affected my attendance in classes by being down for a few days at a time.

I finished my second semester of classes with less wind in my sails. I had taken another class of *western civilization before 1648* with a different instructor, and still struggled and dropped the class. My grades after one full year of classes were marginal, at best. One might never have guessed from my recent grade cards, that during high school I had taken all college prep courses and had graduated with a 3.4 average.

After finishing my first year, I went home and was fortunate to get a summer job working in my dad's aluminum factory. During this time they hired their employee's kids who were attending college. It was a great way for us to earn a good wage for a couple of months to help out with school costs. Also, they were happy to give the college kids the hottest jobs during the summer that nobody else wanted to do. I was assigned to work in the section that took apart the large cast iron crucibles and spouts, cleaning them after they were used to pour the molten aluminum. I learned what it was like to work in a hot factory, and to be on a rotating shift. We worked seven days on day shift and got two off. Then we worked seven days on second shift, and got another two off. Then seven more days on midnight shift with three off, and then it started over again.

I returned to school, and this time decided to list my major in Agriculture. I had worked every summer from age 13 to 17 either detasselling corn, picking corn, weeding beans, or as a pest management field scout. So this seemed like it would be a good fit. I picked up a couple of agriculture classes including the required chemistry class.

One of my friends lured me reluctantly into joining a sorority. She convinced me that since it was a service sorority, it would be a lot of fun and much different from a social sorority. I found that it took up, I am sure, every bit as much time to pledge a service sorority as any other. Also there were many parties, events, and functions we were required to attend. I found myself caught up more into the partying aspects in which this university had a strong reputation. I admit that we did have a lot of fun, but it was quite a distraction from studying.

That semester my sore throats started recurring again, each time with more severity. I became so sick, that I missed a couple of weeks of school. I remember that there were days that went by that I could barely remember. My roommate became really concerned once I had a 104 degree fever, and became more and more non-responsive. Because neither one of us had cars on campus, she called the campus police and the two of them nearly carried me out to his car, and drove me to the emergency room. I remember vaguely being given a shot, and getting held up at a counter, and someone putting a pen into my hand for me to sign papers. Lying across the back seat of the police vehicle, I recall my roommate arguing with the campus police officer that he had to take her to a pharmacy to get my scripts filled. Afterwards, I was poured back into my bed where I stayed for a few more days. I recovered, but only somewhat. On my days that I was somewhat normal I had a continuous fever which fluctuated from 100-101.

I finally went to a new Doctor telling him this had been going on now over a year. He told me my tonsils needed to come out. I finished out the semester with mediocre grades, and even an F due to not being able to get caught up in all of my classes.

I went in for my tonsillectomy about ten days before Christmas during my holiday break. My surgery was at 9 am and I didn't wake up until into the evening. There was a roomful of well-wishing visiting family members and friends. When I first awakened I felt overwhelmingly queasy, and managed to grab a bed pan just in time to grossly spit-up a stomach-full of blood. After finishing, my first words I attempted to form were an apology. I found that my words were slurred and I could barely get my tongue to move. A few minutes later, I couldn't keep my eyes open and was asleep again.

The next time I awakened was the following morning, when the nurse was bringing me my breakfast tray. She made sure I was awake and told me I had to eat. Sitting before me was a tray having bacon, eggs, toast and orange juice.

Now my second attempt to speak was just as difficult as the previous night. I still couldn't move my tongue as it was a major effort. My words were still slurred and slow.

I said slowly and with struggle, "I thought I would get ice cream."

She was firm," No, the Doctor wants you on solid food *immediately*."

" I can't hardly move my tongue...."

"Your throat will be sore for awhile, that's to be expected," she barked at me as she cut me off and whisked out of the room.

I examined everything on my plate in complete disbelief. During this time I didn't like eggs, and looking at them made my stomach turn, and that was the only soft thing on my tray. I turned my attention to the toast, and decided to give it a try. I slowly chewed. I never realized how much one needed the tongue for eating. I could definitely tell that this all seemed really strange. I worked and worked at it, and about 45 minutes later when she came back in to take my tray, all I managed to choke down was one wedge of half a piece of dry toast and one bite of bacon. She didn't say a word and hurried my tray away.

About an hour later another nurse came into my room and told me I would be released soon. She had me get up to take a shower and put on clothes. I found that I was so weak I could barely walk. She went and got another assistant to help steady me to take a brief shower. A little later my Mom came and took me home.

She helped me into my bed, and I slept a few hours until she brought in dinner and woke me up. I was happy to see that it was hamburger helper, at least something softer on my throat. It was still the same, chewing and swallowing my food was a major effort. It took me nearly two hours to eat one small serving, half of what I might have eaten before my surgery.

My next week at home I stayed in bed, and was awakened about three times a day to spend about two hours "working on eating" about half a meal. I managed to get myself into the shower once. I decided to step on the bathroom scales to discover I was down to 116 pounds. I was 119 pounds just before I went in for surgery. My last "normal" weight I could recall was at the end of high school when I weighed 136 pounds and was five foot six and a half inches tall. Being the late bloomer, I was just finishing my last growth spurt and was nearly five foot ten inches. As I looked at myself in the mirror, I looked gaunt and like a ghost. My size ten clothing simply hung off of me like a gunny sack. One might never have guessed that two years ago I was running on the Cross Country team and Track, and was strong and in vibrant health.

Christmas came, and this year I was disappointed that I was unable to do any of my usual shopping for my family. After Christmas I finally moved from my bed to the couch, and slowly began keeping awake a couple of more hours during the day.

Nearly four weeks after my tonsillectomy it was time for me to return to school. My body was still very weakened, and I yet had a tongue that seemed to be traumatized and lethargic. My bodyweight was up to 118 pounds and only slowly gaining.(As a Doctor today, I can look back at my experience and determine that none of this was at all usual. An educated guess tells me that during my surgery it is highly probable that the hypoglossal nerve most likely was nicked, injured, or possibly even slightly cut. The hypoglossal nerve is responsible for much of the major aspects of voluntary motor control of the tongue and for speech. Nerve tissue is normally very slow to heal. It only heals on average 1 mm per day. The four month healing time which it took in my case to be able to speak and eat normally again is in alignment with this possibility.)

This semester I changed my major to pre-forestry since I love camping, hiking, and the outdoors, thinking being a park ranger might be a lot of fun. During the first month it was quite an effort for me to even get to my classes. Often each of my classes would be immediately after another. I discovered I couldn't walk to the other side of campus in less than the appointed 15 minute time frame, and was late much of the time.

I still attended many of my sorority activities, now as an "active" member. My grades still were only about average, and this time my nemesis was a required organic chemistry class. Halfway through the term I dropped the class, as I was failing.

About three months into the semester, I seemed to be gaining some more weight back and finally started speaking normal, eating again without effort and seemed to be getting stronger. I felt well enough to take a part-time job bussing tables at a restaurant.

During the previous few months I managed to also fall head over heels in love, and found myself in my first major relationship. As my Sophomore year in college was coming to an end, I was able to find an inexpensive one bedroom apartment within walking distance to campus. I signed the lease and before the end of the semester we both moved in together. Both of us had part-time jobs and planned to work through the summer, and live in our newly found love nest. Neither of us had mentioned any of this to our parents, as we knew they would never have approved.

At the beginning of the summer I found out that I was offered a position again working at my dad's factory. This time I didn't get selected to work inside the plant, but on a four member crew keeping the companies' hundred acres of land all mowed throughout the summer. The pay wasn't as high as working inside the plant, but it was still nearly double what I was getting paid at the restaurant.

I quit my job at the restaurant, and took the job at home planning to come back on the weekends to visit during the summer. Everything seemed to work out really well during the first few weeks. My parents thought I was coming up to spend time with my "friends" on the weekends from my sorority.

A few weeks into the summer when I returned for one of my weekend visits, I noticed a couple of personal items in the bathroom. Once there was a different brand of deodorant from either of ours in the medicine cabinet, and a new red toothbrush. When I mentioned them, I got a vague answer which satisfied me at the time.

About a month before classes were about to begin, I arrived at my apartment. As I approached the door, I saw several boxes and my suitcase piled up on the front porch next to the door. I was greeted by the person who apparently used the red toothbrush. I was told "we need the key, *now!*" The one I thought was the love of my life stood sheepishly in the background.

I answered, "What's going on?"

"You need to give me your key and get your things and go. You are not welcome here, either!"

Bewildered and heartbroken, I surrendered my key with little fight, and gathered the boxes one by one into my car. As I bawled the three hour drive back home, my sorrow turned into anger at myself. I knew I couldn't tell anyone when I came home what *really* happened.

It sunk in on the way home that not only was I inadequate to be with the person I loved, but that I now didn't have anywhere to live. Classes would start in a month and all of the dormitories would already be full, and finding another apartment to rent would be a slim chance this late. I had spent two years in college, and felt no closer to figuring out any kind of career path. The classes I had registered for in the upcoming semester included music and piano classes. The more I thought about everything in my life, the more I just felt I was done. Everything I had attempted to do in the previous two years had been a failure. I had failed in school, my health only recently was getting better, and I couldn't even maintain any kind of a relationship.

Once I returned home, I avoided everyone for at least a day. My Mom knew something was wrong because I was home early, but gave me my needed space. Finally, the next day I announced that I wasn't going back to school and I quit. I contacted the school and withdrew from registration. This caused quite an uproar. But I was serious, and declared to my parents," I'm going to go work, and figure it all out this way."

I started keeping an eye in the newspaper. Then I saw a job listed for a part-time disc jockey at one of the local night clubs. I went and applied, and immediately got the job. It was like a dream job for a nineteen year old, since I loved music and dancing. I had worked there a couple of weeks and it seemed to be a really good fit.

It was about a couple of weeks before all of the colleges started back to school. My Mom showed me where one of the other local colleges was having a career day. She noticed that this school had a program in communications, and thought I should at least go and talk with them. I dropped my stubbornness for a moment, and went to speak with them. I returned home proclaiming, "Okay, I will return and take *one semester* of communications classes. But I'm going to quit if it doesn't work out."

A couple of weeks later I was in school again. I absolutely loved all of the classes and my instructors. I made A's in all of my communications classes, and A's or B's in everything else. I re-discovered that I had a love for writing, and wrote feature articles for our college newspaper and became the photo editor. Only a few weeks into my new disc jockey job I was promoted to the lead, because the other disc jockey was fired.

Everything in my life seemed to completely turn around. I eventually graduated from college with honors, and was awarded several inter-collegiate press association awards for my writing and photography. I even braved another relationship, which was at least somewhat more successful than the first. My health rebounded and became even stronger, as I found time to immerse myself in athletics such as softball, running, and weight training.

If we take the time to examine this couple of year period in my life right after high school, there is much to recognize in the signs and symptoms. It all demonstrated that I was completely off purpose. I simply wasn't accessing or fostering anything in my life which was connected to my greatest *talents* or purpose.

At the very beginning, I had voiced my opinion that I should sit out of college for a year. My parents were afraid that if I didn't go right to college, that I would get distracted with marriage or kids and decide not to go. So right away I was attempting to do something in my life to please others, and not myself. As long as I had didn't have any direction, my grades suffered right away. Even when I became excited about majoring in political science, I simply allowed the department head to throw my dream out of the window. After this, I floundered in and out of at least two more majors in which the classes were less than inspiring to me.

My second year of school I allowed a well-meaning friend to convince me to join a sorority. I once again did not use my voice, and chose to simply go along and become involved with an organization which added more to my troubles than eased them.

Interestingly, I started having challenges with my health, specifically throat issues right after beginning school. Each time that I didn't speak up for myself and use the power of my own voice, I progressively became more and more sick. Then even once I was given the potential help of receiving a tonsillectomy, there were more complications. After the surgery due to an accidental surgical trauma, I could barely speak and eat food for about four months. Not only does this exhibit the *effects* of my failure to fully use my voice and *talent,* but also the law of *karma,* or cause and effect. Whether I misused my voice, or didn't use it at all, the results were the same. As we know, there are never any accidents, and everything in our life which seems good, bad, or in between all occur due to us attracting it into our life. Unfortunately, during this time of my life I had not learned any of these concepts, and my lessons were difficult.

Lastly, as I moved forward into my first relationship, I yet again did not use my voice to acknowledge it to anyone in my family. I was secretive, and even telling them outward lies about my true activities. It makes perfect sense that since this relationship was founded in secrecy and mistruths to our families, it couldn't possibly survive for very long.

Herein lies a great example of floundering away from one's special *talents*. If we look back at the parable, it is plain to see that my life was described in it as well. I was similar to the man who was given one *talent* and hid it away in the ground in fear. This is similar to my allowing all of the other people in my life, whether being authority figures, or friends to push me here and yonder until I was really lost. Since I was unwilling to step out and insist on finding my own way, it was similar to allowing my *talent* to be buried and in disuse. My own lackluster way of allowing others to control my decisions, directed my destiny into a black hole of nothingness. Soon the Master, or universe responded to my actions and took everything away. My body suffered and was nearly totally lost, and I agonized emotionally just as the parable describes is inevitable.

Of course, it is difficult to recognize all that we need to realize while we are in the middle of moving away from our talents and gifts. I think that most of us can see periods in our lives such as this, when we are off of the wagon. The key is to use our *discernment* to figure it out as soon as possible, so we can turn things around.

How exactly do we recognize when we are drifting away? One key is to ask ourselves how we feel. Ask yourself how most of your days feel. Do most of your days feel like there is struggle? Do most of your days feel more peaceful? Are you always upfront with your family about your life? Are there things you withhold from your family? Does your health look vibrant? Or are you grappling with various health conditions? If you do have health issues, which area of the body are they located? Are your relationships with others mostly peaceful and loving? Or is there more often stress in your relationships with others? Are you actively serving others in a way which you feel happy and joyful most of the time? Or does it feel like a great effort and you do not always enjoy how you are serving in your work or community? Do you feel like you are growing in your life? Or do you most often feel like you are stuck in the same place? Do you perform activities for yourself which you love and enjoy? Or do you find you have no time for anything for yourself? Does your life mostly seem to flow with financial abundance? Or do you often notice that you experience financial strain? Your answers to these questions can give you quick guidance as to where your life may be at any given moment.

Turning Points Are Always Pivotal

So if we can determine that we are not fully using our *talents* in our lives, then what can we do to change? It is not necessary to wait until we hit rock bottom in our life to decide to change.(Although there are some of us who do seem to need to get our lessons the harder way.)

Towards the end of my two year saga, there came a particular place where I finally reached my *turning point*. It happened for me shortly after my three hour drive back home, following the last straw of my relationship ending. I *for the first time* took an inventory of every aspect of my life. Next, I admitted to myself for the first time that nothing was working successfully in my life. I became frustrated and angry with myself, and allowed myself to stew in my own emotional juices fully for about a day. Then I *surrendered,* and simply gave up. I acknowledged that I didn't have the answers, and let go of "trying" to figure it out on my own.

Next, I simply announced I would quit school to take a break and then work it all out later. Even though my parents were opposed, this time I stood my ground, and used my own voice for the first time by truly taking my own stance. I recall I had no idea what was in store for my future, but I felt that I simply had to let go, and trust in taking a different approach.

As I look back, it is amazing to me that literally in a matter of one month after taking these steps, my whole life pivoted into a new and improved direction. The right and perfect situations for me seemed to appear. The job I landed as a disc jockey, was a dream come true. Then shortly after I discovered a degree program, I might never have found before, and was back in a different college having a completely different uplifting experience. My level of growth soared during this time, and was the stepping stones for even more progress and opportunities after graduating from college. I was really on track because I was actively developing my true *talents* and gifts.

This is a great example of the transformations which are possible after we take action towards creating our own *turning point* in life. Once we are actively moving and using our own best *talents*, there are no limitations to all of the opportunities which may unfold for us.

What would our world look like if every human-being fully used our *talents* to the same extent as Thomas Edison? What if like Edison, when adversity came we simply closed our eyes and went inward, allowing the next divine idea or solution to simply present itself to us? What if every human-being *continuously* strived to develop all of our *talents* to become greater and *never* stopped? What if we take action on our inspirations, and continue to create and contribute throughout all of our life? What if every day we felt absolute passion in everything we do? What kind of wonderful world this would be?

When I look at the four T's of giving, I often feel that *treasures* and *tithes* really seem to overlap and are fairly similar. Both *treasures* and *tithes* are usually represented by money, but could also be other gifts which we may give of ourself which have either a financial, or non-financial value. The difference of these two are simply determined by *which* organization, or person it is who are receiving our gifts. If the organization, or person *is not* one in which spiritually feeds us personally, then the gifts we give to these are our *treasures*. If the gifts we give to an organization *is* one in which spiritually feeds us personally, then the gifts we give to these are called *tithes*.

Both of these are essential components to giving. Complete books have been dedicated to explaining the importance of these two in our lives. There are many varying thoughts surrounding that a certain percentage of our income should be dedicated towards this giving. It is beyond the scope of this book to fully examine every aspect of these two. However, ensuring that we regularly give of ourselves in these two areas of our life, are yet another key aspect towards moving into a full expression of *divine love*.

Some examples of giving our *treasures* might include: donating canned goods to the local food pantry, giving money to a charity that supports Native American children, giving our old computer to the local school, having money removed from each paycheck to go to a couple of United Way charities, taking a Thanksgiving meal to a family in need on the holiday, and giving short-term financial support to a family member who is struggling.

Some examples of giving our *tithes* might include: giving a regular financial donation to the spiritual center or church in which you attend, donating two truck-loads of dirt to help repave the parking lot at your spiritual center or church, donating several items for your spiritual center's annual yard sale, and donating financially to a non-profit organization which provides you and others spiritual books and information.

When we look at these two areas, it is these which have a key connection to the level of financial abundance in our life. Not only do these two impact our ability to fully give of ourself to others, but they influence us directly on what is available for us to receive. Many have called this concept *the law of circulation,* and we have called it the law of *karma,* or law of *cause and effect.* This area is no different than any other in our life. Everything which we send out in our life, including our gifts of *treasures* and *tithes* carry a creative energy, and it will come back to us.

Do I readily give my *treasures* to others? In what ways? Are there other ways I may do more? Do I readily give my *tithes* to others? In what ways? Are there ways I may do more?

7

To Thine Own Self-Love

What Goes Around...

There are many people grounded in all various religious and spiritual groups who have been taught the importance of *giving*. However, seemingly there are very few who have been taught that *receiving* is equally as important as giving. Yet *receiving* is one of the six important components of *divine love.*

In fact, this is one of the most often overlooked components. When this is completely absent in a person's life, it is very easy for the person to eventually become greatly unbalanced. This can often lead to eventual significant health problems.

Many of us are taught in the West that we are to think of others first and not of ourselves. Also many of us are raised to be*lie*ve that it is always better to *give* rather than to *receive*. The intention behind this is overall noble, to hopefully teach our children as they grow into adults to not be selfish and uncaring towards others. However, what this seems to develop in most people, is a sense that all *giving* is good and all *receiving* is bad. The truth of the matter is that while *giving* is a good thing, *receiving* is also just as good, and best when there is an equal balance of these two in our lives.

One typical example of this which we witness very often is when one person gives another a compliment. At work your boss may come up and say," You really did a great job helping to organize the company picnic this year. Everyone really had a great time."

Years ago before I fully understood this concept I was one of those people who would deflect any compliments I received. I might answer," Aw, I really didn't do very much, and I nearly messed up as I didn't have enough chairs or spoons for the ice cream."

When we deflect a compliment such as this, we deny ourselves the opportunity to *receive* a gift of higher energy *given* by the other person. We also deny the other person to *give* of themselves this gift of higher energy. So it is the same as deliberately placing a block between ourselves and another not allowing this loving exchange. Ultimately, this is a disservice to ourselves and others. The person who responds to others in this way may think she is being modest and unselfish, but actually she is obstructing herself and the other person from having a higher level connection which serves both of them.

A better response to your boss might be, "Thanks so much. I am so glad everyone had a great time. I really enjoyed helping out." As you can see this dialogue instead allows a free circulation of flow of higher energy.

This is what is meant by "Whatever we *give* we *receive*. And whatever we *receive* we also *give.*" I was able to fully grasp this concept several years ago after first becoming a certified *Reconnective Healing* practitioner by Dr. Eric Pearl. As a Doctor utilizing this healing method for my patients, I loved learning how to use these energies. After I *received* the training I was so intrigued that I could feel these energies not only in my hands, but moving and fluttering in different areas of my body as I facilitated sessions for patients.

While I would stand in the room to *give* these sessions to my patients, I can normally feel the energies moving in my body. After the sessions, my patients most often relate feeling the energies and describe the changes they notice. Most often they notice improvements either in particular aspects of their health, relationships, or spiritual awareness. During the first couple of years performing sessions for my patients, I noticed most of my own health conditions began to clear up gradually over time. While performing sessions for my patients, I occasionally would feel the energies pooling into specific areas of my body. Later I would notice that old health conditions of mine were simply going away. This is when I truly experienced how it is, when we *give* to others fully and freely, that we also *receive* and the two are truly circular and connected to each other.

Other ways we might *receive* from others might include gifts which may be tangible or intangible. Examples of this might be a neighbor stopping by your house to give you a bag full of fresh vegetables from his garden. Maybe your friends come over one Saturday to help you paint your house. Or it might be as simple as someone allowing you to go ahead of them in line at the grocery store, because they see you have only two items.

The other method of *receiving* which is available to each of us and equally important is that which occurs during our *meditation,* or stillness. It is during this state that we are able to tap into all that is. This is where we open ourselves fully to *receive.* This is the place where *grace* exists. It is here that Edison *received* his next inspiration for an invention. It is here that we may *receive* peace, clarity, solutions to our problems, and increased awareness. It is here that we may *receive* everything possible that we might imagine, and everything possible that we can't imagine. It is here that we can *receive* all that we have forgotten.

What is the best way to ensure that we are balanced and are *receiving* in our lives?

The Greatest Secret Revealed

Meditation has been practiced since the beginning of time in all of the most advanced civilizations. Most every sacred historical text either indirectly or directly refers to meditation. *The Bible* references it in at least 31 different verses, *The Quran* in 27, *The Orthodox Jewish Bible* in 23, and it is found in *The Book of Mormon* in 28 verses as well.

Recently, there have been numerous scientific studies which verify the many benefits *received* through the practice of regular meditation. Most of the studies consistently show that regular meditation practice increases relaxation in the body, and tends to normalize the blood pressure. One shows that meditators typically need less sleep at night than non-meditators. More research has revealed many physical changes created in the brain.

A study by researchers from Yale, Harvard, Massachusetts General Hospital, and the Massachusetts Institute of Technology verified meditation is associated with increased cortical thickness of the brain. The structural changes were found in areas of the brain that are important for *sensory*, *cognitive,* and *emotional* processing. They were most fascinated to find that meditation practice could change anyone's grey matter of the brain. The study participants were typical people with jobs and families, who meditated on average 40 minutes daily. Magnetic resonance imaging (MRI) showed that regular practice of meditation is associated with increased thickness in a portion of the cortical regions related to *sensory*, *auditory*, *visual* and *internal* perception, such as *heart rate* or *breathing*. The researchers also found that regular meditation practice may slow age-related thinning of the frontal cortex.

Present day science is verifying that which has been known since the beginning of time. The practice of meditation is the greatest vehicle for humanity to *receive* all that we are aware of that is possible, and all of which we are unaware is possible. Meditation is the gateway which every person no matter where one lives, age, social status, religion, financial position, regardless of *anything*, all have equal access.

The regular practice of meditation is the key which allows us to not only develop a physiologically balanced and healthy body, but to access everything. Meditation allows us to find the solution to any issue. It allows us to experience first-hand that we are truly connected to everything. During meditation we witness through our own awareness that which cannot be described in words, and simply know. This is the means to our growth in awareness in every aspect of our being and life. It is here that we encounter the essence of our own reality. We do so by entering into the place of stillness, where there is nothing and everything all in one.

Meditation is the one vital practice that every Great Master who has come to our planet first practiced, and mastered themselves and then continued to teach others. Since we know that it was a major practice and teaching of the famous Masters such as Jesus, The Christ, and Gautama, The Buddha, then it only makes sense that we should make this our practice too. This makes sense if we wish to *awaken* to our own true nature and increase in our own awareness, that we must practice the same as the Masters.

Do You Go To The Bathroom?

I know that there are those of you who may find the concept of practicing meditation a little foreign, or even kind of scary. You may be saying, I don't know anything about that. I don't know where to begin. What if I don't have the time? What if I discover something about myself that I don't want to know? Or worse, why should I even bother as I could *never* be like any of them?

When I first met Sai Maa over thirteen years ago, the notion of practicing meditation was *extremely* unfamiliar to me. Same as with all of the other Masters, this was the primary teaching that Sai Maa taught us.

I recall sitting in the group just as confused about this concept as ever. As she was leading us throughout the meditation practice, I kept thinking how I didn't know what I was doing. I wondered if I was doing any of it right, and was just sure that I wasn't. My mind was going a hundred miles an hour, into all sorts of doubt in my own ability to meditate. I saw the others who all appeared to know exactly what to do, following her in the practice. I look back and now realize how crazy it was that I was sitting before a Master who was teaching me directly, yet thought there must be some special "technique" that I didn't know. My first full weekend retreat I spent with her distracted by all of my own doubts of my own inadequacy.

Sai Maa told us the importance of practicing meditation each day. She explained that we should create our own special space in our home just for meditation. We should have our own chair or seat on the floor exclusively for this purpose. A few years later I understood the importance. It is because as your individual energies become accumulated over time in your special chair or seat, it makes it easier to move to a higher meditative state. When you return and sit in the same chair over and over, eventually you will notice that it takes much less time than before to reach a deeper state. Some of this comes naturally due to more practice, and some is because the energy in your sacred space has become ramped up and residually stays in that area. We also could place a small table, called a *puja table* in our space. We may include on it photos of the Masters, ourselves, special crystals, candles or other items to create our own sacred space which also assists to increase the vibrational energies of the whole space. It is important that we place a picture of ourself along with the Masters, as we too have the same Divinity and shall remember fully soon too.

My second-three day retreat with Sai Maa became the turning point for me. During these years Sai Maa would have about a two hour introduction on Friday evenings giving new guests a chance to meet her. She would usually speak to everyone giving a discourse of some fundamental teachings, then facilitate a guided meditation, and finish with chanting(singing) songs. Same as usual that evening, I started into the meditation taking a breath, and still questioning if I was doing any of it "right."

This time it was different. About halfway into the meditation I noticed that my mind finally seemed to stop thinking all of the thoughts. I felt myself drifting and into a place where I lost all of the sense of my outer surroundings, and I was in a place of silence and peace. Then I saw Sai Maa walk into this *silent room,* and instruct me as she motioned to the surrounding space that this was where I wanted to be when I meditate. This was the place that I should come, and I *was* doing it correctly.

Later that night after the program, I shared this experience with a couple of friends. I am not sure whether they thought I was simply being delusional, but I knew absolutely I was blessed to be in the midst of a Master. It was at that moment I realized with Mastery, everything is possible.

The weekend program continued all day Saturday and Sunday morning. At this retreat we were sitting on metal folding chairs. It was difficult for me on Saturday to stay focused, as after the first three hours of sitting my back side became really sore. Also, I was distracted because during the meditation Sai Maa was getting onto a man who kept leaving his body. Apparently, he was doing it for fun and seemingly to aggravate Sai Maa. I wondered how in the world someone could *deliberately* do that? I figured that I simply must have been the most ignorant beginner in the whole room.

Sunday arrived, and this time I followed in suit with the others by bringing the fluffiest pillow from my motel room. This seemed to help immensely. One of Sai Maa's assistants reminded us just prior to her arrival, that these would be the last few hours we would get to be with Sai Maa for at least a few months. She suggested that we should open ourselves up as completely as possible, to fully experience this last portion of our time with her.

During meditation I decided to simply open myself completely. I remembered the place of stillness I experienced on Friday night, and thought maybe I might be able to go there again. I seemed to move to that place of peace easier this time. Then I just completely opened myself up, and allowed whatever might be there to come. Then it happened. Every aspect of my being simply became beyond any words. I could see myself. I was the most brilliant white effervescent light. At the same time, I could feel the light coursing throughout every aspect of my body. The intensity was so strong, I thought maybe this was what happened to people I had heard rumors of having spontaneously combusted into a grease spot. As a Chiropractor, I equated it to feeling every single nerve fiber throughout my body engorged with light, and electricity like it was on fire. Yet it was more than that. I started feeling every kind of emotion possible to experience, especially all of the lower ones, as if they were being wrung out of my system like a sponge. The tears were flowing uncontrollably, and the intensity was such that I thought I might start sobbing hysterical from the emotional release. I opened my eyes just long enough to grab a tissue for my nose. I thought opening my eyes might have stopped it. I closed my eyes, and immediately continued the experience. I witnessed myself as a large, formless being of light. Then I saw two other light beings same as I approaching me. One came very close and the other stayed a little further away. I knew the one closest to me was Sai Maa. We each were the same size, and had all of the same radiance. I was overwhelmed with the combination of the brilliance, the emotional release and ecstasy all at once.

During this time, Sai Maa had noticed me in the back of the room and had motioned for someone seated in front of me to check on me. I felt someone's hand lovingly positioned on my thigh checking in on me. Shortly after, Sai Maa ended the meditation and told everyone to take a break.

I opened my eyes. All of the sensations finally stopped, leaving me only in a pool of my own emotional bewilderment. I was still tearful as I heard Sai Maa call upon me saying, *come hear my beautiful child.* She called me to the front of the room to speak with her. The only thing I could think immediately after, was that maybe I finally figured out how to meditate. And that it was a heck of a lot more intense than I ever imagined.

I approached her, and she asked me how I was doing. I choked up and told her I had thought my body was going to explode. She shook her head as I continued to tell her that I saw myself. She said *yes* in agreement with me, getting more excited. I told her that I saw her too and someone else, and that we are all the same. She kept saying yes, that I was absolutely correct. Then she was just about to explain something to me. I am sure it would have cleared up all of my confusion, and I interrupted her to ask a completely unrelated question. Today I know that it is important to *never* interrupt a Master, when they are about to give you an important message.

It took me at least two or three years afterwards to fully understand what had happened to me. Had I been patient and allowed her to explain, I am sure it would have saved me a lot of time. At that time I had absolutely no frame of reference for this experience. It didn't fit much of anything I had ever been taught in all of the traditional religious teachings from my childhood.

Throughout the years as I have continued to actively practice meditation daily, and have never had this same type of experience again. I learned through this gateway, called *meditation* that we are truly all Divine in nature and the same. We each are a brilliant light-being beyond any description available here, and there is no separation. Each and every one of us *are* the Divine Source. I was so blessed to *receive* this understanding and knowledge first hand. And it is *only* through *personal experience* that we can fully learn that which is true and eternal. This is why it is so important that we each find the time to practice meditation.

It is the Divine doorway which allows us each to experience everything. A Master will never simply give you the esoteric teachings, and tell you that you must accept all which she teaches through blind faith. She will say, allow me to *show* you how to discover the truth to everything. It is through your *own personal experiences* that you will ascertain your own wisdom and truth. Everything which is eternal is simply waiting for us. It is always there. Whether we decide to start seeking now, or wait another thousand years it will be still there waiting and available.

Sai Maa would tell us over and over the importance of practicing meditation. Once she was telling us, yet again, that we needed to have a daily practice. One woman argued that she simply didn't have enough time. Sai Maa asked her, do you go to the bathroom during the day? She answered, of course. Sai Maa said, then you practice meditation while you are sitting in the bathroom. The rest of us found this pretty comical. But she was trying to get across that it was important to simply get started *somewhere*.

During my first year with Sai Maa I was like the typical Westerner, who really didn't get the importance of daily meditation. So I practiced once in awhile when I thought about it. That was about once to twice a month. Then during my second year as I began to understand better, I created a small space as she suggested and was able to practice once to twice a week.

One day I was reading a book written by Paramahansa Yogananda, the first Spiritual Master to come to the United States from India during the 1920's. He also taught all of his students meditation and recommended daily practice. However, the light bulb went off for me when he likened meditation to that of learning to play the piano.(It happens I was learning to play the piano at the time.) A person wouldn't expect to be able to learn to play the piano very well if they only practiced once in awhile. One could only expect to learn to play well, if it is practiced every day. The more time we spend practicing, the better we might become. This is the same as in the practice of meditation. One becomes better at meditation with more practice. I will add on to his analogy that we have the opportunity to remember our own Divinity, and *receive* more when we practice daily, and are able to increase our time.

Immediately after reading this, I was able to truly get it. I decided to meditate every morning, and became very disciplined. I found that soon there was a palpable shift in my life. I started to experience everything in my life differently.The obvious occurred, as well as the not so obvious. I became better balanced and peaceful. I noticed that many things which would have disturbed me before no longer did. Or, if there was an upset in my life, I seemed to get through it much easier and faster. Then the important aspect that I noticed, was a gradual and continuous increase in *awareness*. Many aspects of my perception of living here started to change.

I found that within only a few months of practicing in the mornings, that I wanted to practice again during my lunch break. It simply became a habit for me, that I would never wish to stop. Once in a great while if I am somewhere that it isn't possible for me to meditate first in the morning, I feel mostly off balance until I eventually can find some time in my day to reconnect. Today I feel my best explanation is that it is similar to having a battery, which can go for a little while and then needs to be *plugged in* to recharge. When we deliberately plug ourselves in, we are able to revitalize every aspect of our life.

There are lots of books and teachers of meditation. What I have learned is that there is no *right* or *wrong* way to meditate. There are countless different methods, and one works just as well as the other. The important thing is to simply get started.

Often someone new to meditation may get started, and feel disappointed thinking that nothing is happening. Each person will have a unique experience in meditation. It is just like learning a new instrument, in the beginning it may be helpful to get some lessons to start. Just because you don't notice anything doesn't mean that nothing is happening.

About three years ago I bought my first bamboo plant. It was pretty small and I didn't really know much about them at all. I bought it during the first day of a weekend I was at a Chiropractic conference. I left the plant in my car during the day while I was in class. It was during the middle of the summer and at least 110 degrees in my car. That night I took it to my room. Then the next day it was in my hot car again. I finally got home with the plant, and within a day it was limp and nearly dead. No matter what I tried, it was simply too far gone. A few weeks later someone gave me a new bamboo plant, and explained to me that bamboo needed to *continuously* have a water source, stay mostly at room temperature and needed some light. Now a couple of years later, I have made sure my plant always has plenty of pure water and is near a window sill. I have watched it in turn spiral and grow up into a strong and vibrant plant at least a foot more taller.

My bamboo plant reminds me of what happens to us when we regularly connect to our own source during meditation. Similar to the plant, we slowly and gradually start to spiral upward becoming more strong and radiant. If we are taken away from that source for very long, or are not connected very often, we start to wilt and eventually die similar to the plant.

Also, if we look at the bamboo plant everyday it is hard to notice that there is much growth at all. But if I had taken a photo of it three years ago and compared it to today, I would notice the plant has actually grown at least a foot during this time. Likewise, the growth in ourselves from day to day after practicing meditation may seem subtle, but after a period of time the changes will be noticeable.

Actually, it is impossible for us to ever be completely disconnected from our own divine source. However, when we consistently make the concerted effort to *plug in,* we will grow and experience transformation in our lives.

Use Your Imagination

Although there are probably countless methods for practicing meditation, the easiest approach to get started is practicing with the *breath.* One of my favorites which I switch around and use frequently include the use of *affirmations,* or what are also called *mantras.* The other completely non-structured end result of practice, is simply slipping into the *silence* and getting lost. The latter seems to simply come over time naturally. This most often occurs towards the end of a session. This silence is the place where the thoughts finally cease, and we *experience* our connection. At the very beginning one may not find the silence. This is fine. It is the same as learning anything new, each person progresses at one's own individual rate. Then eventually after some practice, one may notice for just a few seconds that all of the thoughts are gone and there is no notice of the body. It might even feel like you have found a blissfully peaceful new space where there seems to be nothing, yet everything. This experience may be different for each person. As you continue your regular practice, eventually a few seconds of silence will grow to a minute, and a minute to a few minutes or more.

When we begin it is important to be somewhere quiet, and as mentioned before, to use the same chair or cushion on the floor each time. It is important to sit comfortably with the spine erect. Initially, we want to focus our attention on our breath. During most breathing meditations, we should use the breath through our nostrils only and not through the mouth. Close your outer eyes, and take a deep breath in and *imagine* that above our head there is a large light in which we are connected. Then we *imagine* seeing a tube of light running into the top of our head, and coursing throughout our whole spinal cord through our feet and into the earth. As we take an *in* breath, we imagine that we are drawing that light above us through the tube into our body and down into the ground. Then as we begin to exhale slowly, we imagine each of our breaths are pushing and pulling this light in a circular motion, throughout the body into the ground and above the head. We *imagine* this cord of light which we are attached, as a bright dazzling golden color. Continue to slowly and rhythmically draw a breath *in* seeing the light from the breath coursing onto the cord of light and increasing its intensity. Then slowly release the breath *out* continuing to watch the pattern of light moving throughout the body. Slowly continue this same pattern of breathwork. If you are a beginner, start out for about five minutes. As you become more comfortable with this practice, you will gradually wish to increase the amount of time. At anytime you may feel you wish to stop the rhythmic breathing, it is okay to do so and sit in silence. This most likely will occur naturally with greater practice. At first many people find it difficult to sit in silence for longer than a couple of minutes. This is all completely okay, as with practice it will become easier, and you will notice that you can seem to stay there even longer.

At the beginning, it is not unusual to experience difficulties in keeping the mind from drifting in its thoughts. You will have times that you can't stop thinking about the shopping list in your head, or the next thing you are supposed to be doing that morning. This is all normal, and it is best to simply allow the thoughts to come, and not to attempt to hold them off. As you continue to practice, this will occur less. However, it is important not to worry about this, as even those who have more experience in meditation still occasionally encounter this too. Oftentimes a new meditator will claim that they aren't seeing any of this *supposed* light anywhere. This is when it is important to simply continue to keep open, and simply use your *imagination*. Imagine seeing the light dancing above your head, and streaming through your body. Soon enough you will begin to notice the vast benefits, and subtle energies you may have never noticed before.

"Logic will get you from A to B. Imagination will take you everywhere." - Albert Einstein

The next common practice of meditation is through the use of *affirmations* or *mantras*. These are specific, usually short phrases or words which may be spoken, chanted or even simply thought. These may be used in your own native language, or possibly in Sanskrit.

Sanskrit is the oldest language both written and spoken. It is the language in which one of the oldest sacred documents was written, *The Vedas,* in India around 1700 BCE. Many various mantras have been developed and used in this language in Eastern religions including Buddhism, Hinduism, and Jainism. We now better understand the principles of how each spoken word carries a certain level of energy. We can surmise that such a language which has been in existence for over 3500 years, has had countless people during the longest period of time speaking, chanting, and thinking these words. This allows us to understand that there is a very great level of energy embedded into the words of this language. It is much like each word spoken by the countless numbers of people throughout the years, has carved a path into the woods. After more than 3500 years the path has become so deep and well-worn that anyone using this same trail is not only sure to stay on course, but easily move towards the chosen destination. This is the reason so many spiritual teachers may teach affirmations in Sanskrit.

There are many great affirmations to choose. I find it is most helpful in the beginning to simply pick one or two that really resonate with you. Then practice using those affirmations consistently at first. Later, if there is a certain situation in your life, or something you specifically wish to move more into your life, then it is okay to change. It is important to not change your chosen mantra too often. Remember that you are creating your own pathway every time that you practice. Every time you practice you are strengthening that even more into your life. Meditating with a *mantra* is very similar to practicing a new chord on guitar. At first it may seem a little awkward, and all of the tones seem a little strained. But eventually you will hear all of the notes come through with greater practice. Then as you continue practicing, you may notice other qualities in the sound you never heard previously. Eventually you will have that one mastered, and be ready to start on the next, or may go back and play that one again effortlessly.

Most spiritual teachers instruct students to use the mantra along with the breathing. So this teaching is to take in a deep in breath through the nostrils, and slowly exhale simultaneously chanting, or speaking the affirmation slowly during the out breath. The full affirmation should be completed by the end of the outbreath. Next, take a deep breath in again through the nostrils, and slowly exhale again repeating the mantra.

Many teachers recommend the use of a *mala,* or what Westerners might call prayer beads. These have been used throughout the years to assist in keeping count during this practice. A *mala* typically has 108 beads. Certain numbers have been considered divine throughout time. Some are 108, 16, 3, 1 and there are many others. Each time we speak our mantra, we are sending out a specific energetic imprint which is allowing that energetic vibration to cause an activation in our life, and the life of others. Repeating this specific vibration into the universe a certain number of times, allows it to be more aligned and to give a greater level of power in the universe. It is similar as if we buy a new reading lamp in our house. The instructions state that it is most optimal to use 40 and 60 watt light bulbs. But instead, we decide to plug in a 20 watt bulb. The lamp will have to work harder to use this frequency bulb, and the resulting power output of the lamp will be most likely more diminished, and much less vibrant than had we used the proper wattage bulb.

When first learning this practice it might be beneficial to start by repeating your mantras three times. When you feel comfortable and are increasing your meditation time, you may increase to 16 and eventually 108. This is also in accordance to the length of your meditation. A mala, or prayer beads can be easily purchased on the internet, or in many international/spiritual retail stores.

Sanskrit Mantras

Om –*The primordial sound of the universe.*

Om Namah Shivaya –*I honor the divine consciousness of Shiva*

Om Shanti Shanti Shanti – *Invocation of peace*

Om Mani Padme Hum -*invokes the powerful benevolent attention and blessings of Chenrezig, the embodiment of compassion.*

The Gayatri Mantra:

Om Bhur Buvaha Suvaha
Thath Savithur Varenyam
Bhargo Devasya Dheemahi
Dhiyo Yonaha Prachodayath.

- *We contemplate the glory of Light illuminating the three worlds: gross, subtle, and causal. I am that vivifying power, love, radiant illumination, and divine grace of universal intelligence. We pray for the divine light to illumine our minds.*

English Mantras/Affirmations

I am Love –*Invocation of love.*

I am Peace –*Invocation of peace.*

I am Joy –*Invocation of joy.*

I am that I am –*I am divinity(God) presence that I am within.*

I am the Resurrection and the Life – *Invocation used to resurrect our own eternal, divine and everlasting nature.*

I am grateful –*Invocation of gratitude.*

These are some basic *mantras* which are excellent to get started. Eventually, you may create your own as you continue to advance in your practice for your own situation. There are two major points to remember in creating your own mantra. Keep it as simple as possible, and always keep it in the present tense by using the words *I am*.

Here's some great examples to use and some you want to avoid:

Avoid: I am wanting to live a life of great health.(This is too passive and wordy.)

Instead: I am living a life of great health.(This is short, more powerful and fully in the present.)

Avoid: I am expecting that I am living a life of financial abundance.(Too long and confusing words, and not in the present.)

Instead: I am experiencing financial abundance.(This is more powerful, and fully in the present)

Avoid: I am able to serve others in many different ways.(This is ambiguous and too long)

Instead: I am serving many people to heal.(This is short, specific and in the present)

The most important thing to realize in your practice of meditation, is to pick and choose what *you* feel drawn to use. No matter what, there are no hard, absolute rules. Remember to use your *imagination* and allow yourself to be divinely guided in what seems right for you. There are many different teachings in meditation, and it is not at all a requirement to have decades of practice, and know all of the advanced methods. It is crucial to simply get started. Then practice, practice, practice, and have fun with it.

"Whatever forms of meditation you practice, the most important point is to apply mindfulness continuously, and make a sustained effort. It is unrealistic to expect results from meditation within a short period of time. What is required is continuous sustained effort."

-The Dalai Lama

Remembering Ourself and Others

The next major component of Divine Love is *Divinity*. This realization may be experienced through the practice of meditation. Divinity is: the state of realizing one's self is directly from God.

This is the key component of *Divine love* which so many people have faltered away, or have yet to know. It is the recognition that *every* single person on this planet is of a pure, *Divine* essence. Each are connected to one another, and equally connected to the *One Divine Source* most call *God*. Also, it is the concept that we are not only connected with this Divine essence, but are also one and the same.

Most Westerners have been taught that there is some large, usually male God somewhere "out there" in the cosmos who watches everything. If one doesn't live "right" and follow all of "his rules" just the way "he dictates," then when we leave this planet he will judge us. Then, of course he may either throw us into some sort of hell-like fiery place if we were bad, and into a heaven-like place if we were good.

I recall being taught this concept very early as a child, and felt this made no sense to me. I questioned this idea immediately, and fortunately it propelled me onto my own search at a tender age to discover what was really true.

We don't know a millionth of one percent about anything.

-Thomas A. Edison

It is very easy for anyone to explain this concept, and state that the truth is that we each are all *Divine* and are one. This not only includes our sisters and brothers, but also that we are one with the *Divine* and loving essence of all of creation we call *God*. However, there are those not yet ready to comprehend this, and others who find this to be quite a stretch outside of one's comfort zone.

This is important to realize that *no* person can simply tell another this concept, or teach it in any theory in a way one can fully understand. This is the time that the *only* way to really learn and comprehend this, is through actual *personal experience*. The *only* gateway which leads to this experience is through meditation.

Once we are able to have this experience, there is no unsurety afterwards. This is how we are then able to know with absolute certainty that everyone no matter what position, status, or demeanor has the *Divine* presence which courses throughout all of us connecting one and all together. It is from this place that we are able to have the highest level of respect, and experience the greatest level of *divine love* for ourself and others.

"In that day you will know that I am in my Father, and you in me, and I in you."

-John 14:20 Bible English Standard Version

What Is So Great?

The final component of *divine love* is *gratitude*. Gratitude is: the state of feeling or showing thanks or appreciation for the benefits received in life.

Gratitude is very similar to looking at the age-old question, *which came first, the chicken or the egg?* When we look at *divine love* and *gratitude*, it is the same conundrum. We know that these two energies are intertwined intimately together. It is simply not possible for one of these to completely stand-alone without the other.

Often times, it is easy to see the relationship of these together. Remember the last time that you first laid your eyes upon, and welcomed a newborn baby into your family. First there is that highest feeling of love for this new little being. You think of this one who has chosen to be a part of your family, and at the same time we get washed over with the greatest feeling of *gratitude*. We are simply grateful for this tiny being, and are in awe of this seeming miracle just received into our world.

Other times it is more difficult to see the connection between *gratitude* and *divine love.* However, we know that each of the numerous research studies have proven that the regular practice of *gratitude* in ones' life helps to create many benefits. It includes a significant increase in the various aspects of health and overall happiness in our life. One such example is a study performed in the Eastern Washington University psychology department. It determined that the more grateful a person is, the less that individual suffers from depression. This study found that clinically depressed individuals practiced significantly less gratitude (nearly 50% less) than the non-depressed people in the control group.

This is yet another indication of how directing the attention of our thoughts onto that which is of a higher vibrational energy, such as gratitude, attracts more of those higher benefits into our life.

Stop Focusing On The Ditch

I remember my driver's ed class when I was 16, and so diligently working to learn all of the rules of driving. I remember the most difficult task for me was learning how to keep my car on my side of the road and in my lane when I was driving. Not drifting onto the middle yellow lines or off the road onto the white lines, and not freaking out when an oncoming car approached from the opposite direction was all a challenge for me. Finally, I got into driver's education, and my instructor helped me to learn the little secret which worked for me. He told me to "stop looking over into the ditch." He said, "If you keep looking over at the ditch, that's where you are going to drive your car. Keep your eyes on the *center of your lane* and that's where you'll go." So as long as I kept focusing upon the ditch, my car would keep drifting over that way. Likewise, if I focused upon the double-yellow lines in the middle of the road, I would gradually drive my car over those too. So he advised me to keep my gaze focused on the middle of the road. Amazingly, I discovered when I kept my focus on the middle of the road, my car no longer drifted off where I didn't wish to go. This was the key I learned to staying in the center of my lane.

Similarly, wherever we place our attention in our lives is the direction we will drift. Are we focusing on all that is good and great in our life? Or are we concentrating more on our struggles? Do we focus on the fullness of the water we just poured into our glass, thinking how much we enjoy drinking clean water and so appreciate that we have plenty? Or are we concentrating on the empty space in the glass, questioning already whether there is enough water to quench our thirst, or if it would be better had there been a few ice cubes?

One evening, the famous violinist Itzhak Perlman was in New York to give a concert. As a child he had developed polio. Getting onto stage is a little more challenging for him since he wears braces on both legs, and walks using two crutches. Perlman moved across the stage slowly, until he reached the chair in which he seated himself to play. He took his seat, signaled to the conductor to begin, and began to play. No sooner had he finished the first few bars, then one of the strings on his violin snapped with a report like a gunshot. At this point he was close enough to the beginning of the piece, that it would have been reasonable to have brought the concert to a halt while he replaced the string, then begin again. But that's not what he did. He waited a moment, and then signaled for the conductor to pick up right where they had left off.

Perlman now had only three strings with which to play his soloist part. He was able to find some of the missing notes on adjoining strings, but where this wasn't possible, he had to rearrange the music on the spot in his head so that it all still came together. He played with passion and artistry, spontaneously rearranging the complete symphony right through to the end. When he finally rested his bow, the audience sat for a moment in stunned silence. And then they rose to their feet and cheered wildly for him. They knew they had just witnessed an extraordinary display of human skill, ingenuity, and tenacity.

Perlman raised his bow to signal for quiet. "You know," he said, "it is the artist's task to make beautiful music with what you have left."

How often are we faced with events in our life which are both major and minor challenges? As part of our natural human experience, each of us have these appear from time to time. It is these situations which give us the greatest opportunity for growth.

Most people usually have that one person at work who after entering a room causes everyone else to scatter like ants. She is the one who seems to nearly enjoy lamenting on and on about all of her troubles. She still talks about her ex-boyfriend running off with someone else, emptying out her bank account even though it happened nearly two years ago. She complains about the high cost of gas and groceries, blaming it all on the government. Next, she engages anyone who will listen on her latest gripe that the recent 1% raise by the company was an embarrassment, and she feels reluctant to tell any of her friends as they all got 3-4% raises in their workplace. She goes on and on to anyone who she might be able to pull in to her story.

Hopefully, we also know someone who walks into the room, and within a few minutes there are several people seemingly being drawn to her. She speaks to others how incredibly mild the Summer has been, and that she has gotten the most beautiful green peppers and squash out of her garden this year. She speaks with others about the same company raise and is excited. She mentions that she hears there are other corporations in the same industry that couldn't give employee raises, and shares how she feels their company must be doing really well. Her personality exudes *appreciation* for most everything. Even on a day when she gets a flat tire on her way to work, she comments that she is so glad it happened in a really safe place just off the busy highway. And then how two people stopped to help, and were so nice as one of them offered to drop her off at work.

This is similar to our previous analogy of our two plants of *fear* and *love.* However, each of these are *components* of these two, which are *gratitude* and *complaints*. Obviously, we want to look at our life and ask if we are spending most of our time moving over to water our *tree of gratitude,* or more time growing our *tree of complaints?*

It is pretty amazing how so many parents work to teach their children at an early age the importance of using the words *please* and *thank-you*. This has been woven into the fabric of our society to teach our young people to be polite, so hopefully the child will eventually blossom into a courteous adult. It seems that as children, we learn to give a well-practiced, rote *thank-you* when another person gives us something. It might be when you are three as you are given your favorite blue popsicle, we know how to recite *please* just before and *thank-you* immediately after being handed the treat.

As we get older, we eventually start to learn to also thank others for more intangible things. If someone gives us a ride home from track practice, or we were given extra tutoring in english at school. All that we are mostly taught as we grow up is to *affirm thanks* for the *tangible,* and *intangible* benefits we may receive from other people.

However, there is another whole realm of practicing *gratitude* which often is overlooked in our lives. There is also all of which occurs to us throughout our life, which are the *tangible* and *intangible* benefits we may receive from the *events* and *circumstances* in our life. This concept moves us more into the esoteric domain of the practice of gratitude. This is the area many have difficulty understanding and fully embracing. Yet it is a crucial area, which if we fully grasp the dynamics will enhance our greatest growth.

Each day in our lives we experience a chain of these events and circumstances. There are those that we mostly welcome and enjoy, as well as others that may be unpleasant to a greater or lesser degree. It is our perception and reactions to these, which determines whether we are living a life filled with plenty of gratitude, or are not.

Green Eggs and Ham

There are times in life where one can become very grateful when we have endured a difficult condition. We may find that when it has improved even just slightly, we feel great appreciation. I am sure everyone who has been in the military any length of time, has quite a string of such stories.

Roughly 30 years ago I was diligently working to survive my Army basic training. It is amazing how when we are placed into a stressful situation, we often are forced to deal with older unrealized traumas which often come to the surface.

When I was a child, both of my parents worked and I stayed with quite a few different babysitters. I recall being dropped off early in the morning, and wasn't quite school age yet. This particular babysitter was a mother of three boys. One was a year younger than I and not in school yet, and the other two were older and in school. Everyone else would normally eat earlier and be gone, at the time her youngest son and I would sit at the table for breakfast.

I remember my first morning a small bowl of runny, well butchered, and chopped up eggs were slid in front of me. She had barely cooked the eggs over-easy, then slipped them into a brown melamine bowl, rhythmically chopping them up until there was a gooey yellow and white mess in a pool at the bottom of the bowl. She slapped a spoon down in front of me, as it was the only possible utensil to use. I simply watched her in disbelief. At first I wasn't quite sure what she had fixed for me, as my parents cooked eggs and left them still intact. After receiving an explanation that they were *really* eggs, she hovered nearby waiting for me to dig in. I blinked my eyes reluctantly stating," But I *don't like* eggs."

Unfortunately, this was the era where adults *made* children eat foods they didn't like, regardless. *And* it was the age that all babysitters were simply to be minded. If you didn't, there was a full report to your parents, and later you were in the *worst* kind of trouble possible.

She finally scolded," This is *all* you are getting and you had *better* eat."

I stared down into the slimy mess and finally shoved a spoonful into my mouth. As soon as I attempted to swallow I began to gag. She didn't seem to have much compassion, as it also was the days of the *two bite rule.* It was never enough for a child to just take one bite, but you had to take a second bite before you might possibly get released from the food that you disliked. I choked one more down, doing everything possible to restrain myself from heaving it all back up again. After this I was reprimanded some more and told, "I was *bad* because I didn't eat my eggs like her son."

This same exact scenario of scolding and belittlement occurred at least 2-3 times each week, (whenever eggs were served) for the duration of the couple of years that this sitter watched me. Each and every time I forcefully had to swallow them down, and the taste never did improve. This was the beginning of my root aversion to eggs. As the years progressed, I avoided eating them no matter the method of cooking or coaxing.

It was now at least fifteen years after all of that, and I was in my Army basic training at Fort Jackson, South Carolina. I generally decided that the Army seemed to like making every aspect of the training difficult. Even going through the chow-hall to eat was made stressful for us. It was all about strict order and discipline. We filed into the hall in a perfect line. Each time the line moved you were to snap to attention, take a few steps forward and snap back to parade rest. Once in front of the food line, you held your plate out and food was slapped onto your plate. The server stated," Broccoli?"

Your answer was either, "Yes Sir/Maam," or "No Sir/Maam." Then the food was either slapped onto your plate or not. Unlike stories I heard from those who went through Army basic training years earlier, we were given a choice. Every time I went through the chow line for breakfast, eggs were served and that was I think the only item in any of the meals I said, "No Maam/Sir, to have smacked onto my plate.

During our regular training we were up and going at 4:30 in the morning, and lights went off at 9:00 at night. The days were so packed with road marches, weapons training, and more that I recall feeling starving when it was finally chow-time and exhausted when lights went out. Most of us wrote our families to send us care packages of food. The drill sergeants would make us do pushups at mail call. Each letter required a payment of 10 pushups, and each care package was 50 pushups. We simply *existed* for our letters and care packages, but hoped to not get them all in one day. Three letters and a care package all in one day, meant dropping and giving them 80 good pushups until they were fully satisfied.

Then our meals were timed. The rule was that we had 10 minutes to eat after the last woman in our platoon received her plate. There was no talking allowed, but it didn't matter as we were too busy shoveling our food down for that. One evening at dinner everyone in our platoon had just gotten our plate and had sat down for a minute. Our drill sergeant came in and barked at us to get up and go get in formation, *right now*. We each inhaled whatever food we could, and had to throw away the majority of the rest. We went out and stood in formation waiting for well over an hour, and she never came to get us. Another Drill Sergeant in our company finally asked us why we were waiting. We explained what had happened, and he said since we did get our plate for dinner we couldn't go through the line again. He sent us back to our barracks, and those who had care packages of food opened them up and we shared with each other.

Then the Army finally gave me my moment, one of the turning points in life that makes such of an impression you just never forget. We were in the seventh week of our training, and finally out on the long-awaited field training exercise called *bivouac*. The Drill Sergeants touted that this would be the ultimate test of all of our skills, and we would get a small taste of what it is like to be in the field and in war-like circumstances.

It was the first week of December, and although we were in South Carolina it was still cold. We had been issued cold weather gear, but were not allowed to wear it. Instead, we carried all of it, and everything else we needed in our rucksack. As a squad leader I carried two canteens of water, extra magazines, a first aid kit, and protective gas mask all strapped onto my body. Then my rucksack had about 35 additional pounds stuffed into it, and we carried our M-16 rifle and wore the pre-Kevlar *steel pot* helmet. Most of the time we were probably carrying at least 60 pounds of weight.

After at least a couple-hour road march we set up our tents as a *base camp*. We were all happy to realize that we lost the weight of the *shelter half,* or half of a tent and sleeping bag from our rucksack after setting up our tents. Then at least a portion of the time, they allowed us to leave them behind in our tent.

The days we were on our bivouac, the Army was in the middle of moving from using the old C-rations to the new MRE's or Meals, Ready to Eat. We were finally marched to the Camp chow tent, where we each were given our first C-Rations meal. We stood in line to fish out one can of a main entrée out of a warm trough of water, and were given three more cans of food which were a vegetable, and fruit or dessert. Each ration also included a package of salt, sugar, plastic spoon, toilet paper and two pieces of beechnut gum. We each sat on the ground wondering how we would get into all of these cans to eat. Our Drill Sergeant told us that there was one can opener, called a P-38 in every sixth box of C-Rations. During that first field meal, even though a couple of people were able to share, out of 40 in my platoon about 7-8 people managed to open about one can of their food to eat. The rest of us found the gum. I took two of my four unopened cans and slipped one into my left and right cargo pockets in my uniform pants.

That afternoon we were running across fields slamming our bodies into the ground, low crawling, and jumping into foxholes as tracer bullets were being fired over our head. By the time I reached the second foxhole, I realized my two cans of C-rations were banging against and painfully bruising both of my outer thighs. I hastily pulled them out of my pockets, and left them behind in one of those foxholes.

Dinner-time finally rolled around. We were given C-rations again. This time there were about 13 of us who had procured can openers. I still didn't manage one yet. Even though this time some of them became slightly faster at using the one inch folded can opener, tempers really flared as yet half of our platoon did not get into even one can of her food. Half of us had now fully missed two meals, and the rest had eaten minimally. This time I simply tossed all of my unopened cans back into one of the tubs.

Once it was dark we were taken to a night fire course. We were told that live tracer bullets would be shot over our heads by a few feet. We ran down hiding behind various obstacles, until we kept reaching barbed wire. Some were high enough that we could low-crawl the length of it, and the rest we needed to lay on our back with our M-16 clenched as close to the body as possible and slide under the length of the wire in this way. The weapons firing overhead were loud, created a haze, and smelled strong of gunpowder. We could see the M-60 machine gun muzzle flashes in the distance lighting up the black sky, and bright red tracer bullets streamlining just above us. The adrenaline heightened every sense as each of us knew live rounds were being shot at us.

Finally, we were marched back to our base camp. Once returned, we divided up our schedule for guard duty. We were informed that unlike in the barracks where we were authorized 7 ½ hours of sleep each night, in the field it was only 4 ½. I finally hunkered into my down sleeping bag exhausted, cold, and as all of the excitement was seemingly finished, I realized that I was really hungry. It seemed like only a few minutes later I was awakened for my two hour guard duty.

It was so cold that night, as much as possible I kept my back up against a tree to attempt to keep warmer. I kept repositioning my hands on my M-16, trying to find the best place to keep my fingers from freezing while they were touching the metal. My best efforts were useless, as the next day I noticed places on my fingers which were white and numb with frostbite.

I finally was relieved off my post, and was dead to the world sleeping with my cold M-16 in my sleeping bag. At about 3:30 am a couple of the Drill Sergeants came and raided our camp dressed in black clothing as the *enemy*. We awakened to gunfire, yelling and we were mostly confused and running to take positions into the woods. After about an hour we were finally ordered back to our camp. One explained that they had managed to take at least two of our soldiers as hostages. They yelled at us because they were able to easily go past our guards on two of the four sides of camp. Not surprising, we made quite a few mistakes, and they went through item by item the list of what we did wrong, and the couple of things we did correct.

Along with dawn arriving it began raining. We were marched over to the mess tent for breakfast. It started pouring down like a monsoon. Each of us stood in line with cold, wet feet, and ponchos glistening as our Drill Sergeant barked seemingly with delight," Normally when you are in the field, the Army authorizes you one hot meal each day. This is your one hot meal today, you *best* enjoy it."

The mess tent was drab Army green, and had just enough room to cover the cooks and the food from the rain. The food had been transported from the regular mess hall, and sat open in large rectangular metal trays. One by one, we each walked down the line getting the food slapped onto a large stainless steel sectioned tray. The cooks didn't bother asking this time, just knowingly slapped generous portions of everything onto the plates for each of us.

One of the first two soldiers who received their food attempted to hunker just under the tent at the end of the line out of the rain. Our Drill Sergeant shouted," Get your (blank – blank) out from under *my* tent. As lousy as you did this morning, only about *half* of you should even *still* be alive!"

I stepped under the tent and they served me a couple of slices of bacon, fried potatoes, two biscuits with a heap of sausage gravy, and a great big serving of scrambled *eggs*! It initially looked like the best breakfast ever in my life. Then I had to step out from under the tent. There wasn't anyplace to go stand to get out of the pouring rain. I stood and looked at my bacon, potatoes, and eggs now each floating in water, and raindrops hitting so hard they seemed to splash out of the pool of water. The gravy also was quickly becoming thinner and diluted. I paused for a moment and just gave thanks. I could hardly believe that I was finally going to get to eat a full meal. I ate everything on my plate and absolutely relished and enjoyed it all. For the first time since I was a young child, I ate *eggs*. I could feel my body slowly shifting from the shivering, beyond hunger feeling, to that of satisfaction and warmth.

Even this day, I remember how there was such of a deep level of gratitude that washed over me. I savored every single bite, and I ate *all* of my scrambled eggs. I discovered that it certainly is possible for us to overcome the old unpleasant things, which may try to haunt us from the past. I still think this cold, wet and soggy breakfast, may have been the best meal I ever had in my life. Today I have learned to eat eggs and I still enjoy them.

We spent two more days in the field. At my next meal of C-rations, I was so delighted that I finally got my own can opener. My heart jumped for joy and I not only felt a huge relief, but great gratitude. Each of the remainder of my meals in the field, I managed to open and eat at least 3 of my 4 cans of food. Today I still carry my original P-38 can opener on my key ring. Not only has it been a handy tool throughout the years, but also when I look at it I am reminded of everything which brings me such gratitude.

Today I can look back at my earlier situation as a child, and my experience during my basic training and be very grateful for both. If I had never undergone this challenge as a child, I would have completely missed the opportunity as an adult, to receive such of a high intensity level of growth from this chain of events during my Army training. Oftentimes, it is possible to see that even the most unpleasant situations in our life can bring about the greatest prospects for transformation. This is the reason that it is important to have gratitude for *everything* which shows up in our life. As soon as we recognize that even the most disagreeable events we may experience are teaching us important lessons, it becomes much easier to give more appreciation for these as well.

When I was about at the same age as I faced this challenge with my babysitter, our family would go every Sunday to visit my grandmother. She bought me a set of Dr. Seuss books. I would sit and read with her every Sunday, *Green Eggs and Ham.* It actually was my favorite book of the series. I recall that she was insistent that I read *that* book to her every Sunday. Even when I was reading way beyond that skill level, she would still have me sit with her and read that story. The essential story for those unfamiliar is about Sam, who *did not* like green eggs and ham. At the beginning of the story, he would not eat them anywhere. Then towards the end of the story he eventually shifted, and discovered that he *did* like green eggs and ham and he could and would eat them everywhere. Does anyone else think *hmmm?*

We each have events in our lives which impact us so strongly, that we remember them throughout the rest of our life. Often these are *turning points*, which allow us to reflect more clearly the empowerment of being grateful for so much in our life.

It is often just such times as this that something we usually take for granted is either lost, or becomes more scarce, and this gives us the opportunity to learn more about gratitude. A better approach would be to simply be grateful now for *everything* in our life. This includes *all* of our circumstances, each event, person, simply everything.

Cultivate the habit of being grateful for every good thing that comes to you, and to give thanks continuously. And because all things have contributed to your advancement, you should include all things in your gratitude.

— Ralph Waldo Emerson

We know that when we use our *thoughts, words, feelings,* and *actions* to express all in our life for which we are grateful, it tends to attract more of that into our life. Are we thinking, feeling, and expressing gratitude each day in our lives? What are the *tangible* things, people, relationships, situations, and circumstances in our life which we are grateful? What are the *intangible* situations, events, and circumstances in our life which we are grateful? The daily practice of gratitude is important for us in our life.

Divine love simply would not exist without *gratitude.* We also know that as we bring more of this into our lives, we also are inviting a greater experience of health and happiness as well. Make sure every day that we are making regular trips to water our *tree of gratitude.* As we make this a regular practice, we begin to witness every aspect of our life blossom.

8

Wind Beneath My Wings

Once again, we must examine the four major essentials key to actively pursue our *awakening* journey. We have fully explored all of the major aspects of *divine love*. Now we must remember there are yet three other important legs, which are needed to create a strong "chair" to support us as we continue to move forward in *awakening*. The second leg of our chair is *power*. Power is defined as: the ability to act or produce an effect.

Many people often have many negative connotations in relationship to the word *power*. Often this word is thought of as being synonymous with control. Which then leads many to think that those people who are in a position of power are *also* controlling of others. Some of the people who first come to mind are dictators, such as Adolf Hitler and other well-known political or business figures, who managed to negatively influence large numbers of people.

However, *power* is similar to any energy on our planet which may be used for the highest and greatest purposes, or for the lower and manipulative purposes. There are actually many people who have learned to tap into this limitless field, and have accomplished many *great* things. *Power* in its purest sense is another important energy which when we fully understand it, we can learn to harness and reap all of its countless rewards.

Mastering others is strength. Mastering yourself is true power.
– Lao Tzu

Living On The Edge

During my undergraduate school I had an unforgettable teacher for my Literature class. He must have told us dozens of times, " If you only remember only one thing from my class, remember that *life is literature* and *literature is life*." This has stuck with me throughout the years. I have seen that this has always been absolutely correct.

If we borrow this same type of phrasing, we can apply this same concept to *power*. It is important for us to always remember that *power is passion;* and *passion is power*. When we recognize that these two are intimately connected, it is much easier to understand how to incorporate this vital element into our life.

Passion is defined as: a strong feeling of enthusiasm or excitement for something or about doing something. So if we look at power and passion, we can easily see how these are both linked.

We have learned the importance of our thoughts, words, and actions and that these create the reality and conditions in which we live. We must understand that each of these are simply empty shells merely having inert potential, until they become activated. They only become creative in our lives once the emotional component of *feeling* charges them. One of the higher levels of *feeling* we can express which moves these from working *passively*, or not at all, to working as a palpable, *active energy* in our life is *passion.*

When we remain focused, excited, and filled with *passion* about any task and continue this feeling *consistently* over time it, will always lead to the expression of greater *power* in life. If are able to fully display in our life passion in all that we do, it will create a major effect(*power*) in every area of our life.

It is possible that everyday we could live a life in which we get up in the morning and go to a job that is, "okay," for eight hours. Then we come home, eat dinner, and watch television for three or four hours, go to sleep, and repeat the same thing the next day. This is a lifestyle which is essentially lackluster, and most likely contains little *passion.*

Throughout my years in private practice, I always enjoy learning more about my patient's home life. It not only helps me to understand their background and needs better, but to know more about them. I am amazed at the times that I discover those who seem to have very little of anything in their life that excites them, or gives them any joy. I have engaged several people in conversations similar to this.

"So tell me what are some of the things you like to do for fun?"

Often there is a long period of silence as they are trying to think of something. " Umm, I don't know."

"Oh, there *must* be something that you enjoy doing."

Usually more silence, "Uhh, I guess I just have a regular life."

"You don't have any hobbies that you enjoy? *Any* certain activities that you like? Any kinds of movies or books you read? Outdoors or gardening?"

"Nope, I guess not so much. I just mostly work and maybe watch a little TV."

"Then tell me about your job. How do you like it?"

" Well…. it's just a job. It's a paycheck and pays the bills."

Seemingly all of the coaxing in the world brings out nothing. The first few times I heard this years ago, I was simply astonished. As a person who has a long list of hobbies and fun things she *wishes* she had more time to do, it was really difficult for me to understand.

Today, I understand that this is an example of one who is simply *going through the motions* of life. If one examines such a person's life closer, we would find that we would be fairly hard pressed to find much, if any passion in any portion of his life. Therefore, we would also notice no real power, and little overall growth. Often those who spend much of their life staying in such of a zone of comfort, at some point usually have some incident or even a string of events which cause a disruption. Hopefully this will often shake these people up towards shifting from living a passive and safe life, to becoming more fully engaged and active.

> *There is no passion to be found playing small- in settling for a life that is less than the one you are capable of living.*
> *– Nelson Mandela*

Passion Meets The Pavement

It is easy to think of all of the different famous people throughout history who lived their lives filled with passion, those are the ones we hear about most of the time. However, there are plenty of people not so famous, who we can look to their stories and find great examples to inspire us. Often times we don't have to look any further than within our own family. I am so fortunate to have had multiple family members, who have greatly inspired me with the passion and power each lived throughout their lifetime.

My only major regret in my life, has been that I wish I had asked my grandparents to share even more with me about their lives when I was a child. The examples they demonstrated throughout their lives always motivated me to strive to live my life more like them.

My Grandmother was born in Iowa in 1888. She was a middle child of nine and grew up on a farm in Iowa.

When I was a child, she lived about a two hour drive from our home. Every Sunday after church my older brother and I were loaded into the car to go for a visit the rest of the day at her house. My earliest memory, as I mentioned, is at the age of four sitting next to her reading my new Dr. Seuss books.

She was very warm and loving, yet as needed firm as well. Dressed most always in a cotton pastel colored dress, her hair was neatly parted at the side with waves of gray swirling and glistening of timeless wisdom. During this time she lived with two of my great-aunts, each of them having moved in together after the transitions of their husbands.

I fondly recall all of the times after we ate lunch that we would play different games together. If we sat at the table we would either play an older game called *carrom,* and an even older game which was in German, we simply called *the german game,* or *scrabble.*

 Often just before we sat at the table to play these games, she would get down on the floor with my brother and I and play a game we called *pick up sticks.* They were about eight inch long colorfully painted wooden sticks which we dropped onto a heap on the floor. The object was to carefully pick each of the sticks up without causing any movement in any of the others. Whoever could pick up the most would win. My grandmother was a strong competitor, and never simply allowed us to win. Kneeling on her hands and knees(yes, gracefully in a dress), she would get her head low to the floor and carefully eyeball exactly how to maneuver her chosen stick away from the others. She would roll with laughter just as much as either of us, if any of us made a funny mistake. She usually would beat both of us managing to pick up more sticks than either myself or older brother.

As I got a little older my favorite board game became *scrabble.* She played this game so often with us, her friends, and sisters, that she would wear out a board every year. We would buy her a new one for Christmas. Needless to say, she was really good. The whole family played together, and I can't recall anytime anyone ever beat her. We always needed to keep the dictionary nearby. She mostly used words, even my parents had never heard. We would look them up in the dictionary, and they were amazingly always there. Every different game we played not only was she an excellent player, but she did everything with just as much excitement, joy, and fun as I did as a child. It wasn't until years later that I discovered that not every grandparent was just normally like this.

One summer I was the age of eight, my parents took my brother on a vacation and left me at her house for a week. I quickly discovered that my grandmother had a usual daily routine.

The first morning I awakened fairly early, being sandwiched in the comfort of a heavy hand quilted blanket. She ensured I had made my bed, and then I was herded into the bathroom to quickly wash up and brush my teeth. I came out into the hallway and was surprised to see her waiting on me. She said," Every morning right after I get up, I first exercise and do some calisthenics before I start my day." She stood before me in white cotton pajamas, which the pants were loosely draped off of her slender hips down to just above her calves. Her top was also white, and loose fitting, with sleeves just below her elbows. She stood erect and raised her arms in a strong V position above her head. She began. "I begin by doing at least ten toe touches," she bent over and alternated, touching each toe in perfect form. I was delighted, and quickly joined in with her.

"This is like what we do in gym class," I rejoiced. We finished those pretty quickly. At this time it never even entered my mind, that my grandmother was age 81.

"Next, I get on the rowing machine and use this for 5 minutes." This machine looked similar to a bicycle except that you pulled the handlebars up towards yourself, and simultaneously pushed a solid straight bar down with both of your feet. The motion this simulated was that of a rowing motion. As she pumped her arms and legs vigorously, I laid down on the floor nearby and performed a couple of sit-ups.

"Grandma, can we do some sit-ups too?" I was simply enthralled to discover that she seemed to love to exercise as much as I.

A couple of minutes later she laid down onto the wooden floor next to me. "You'll have to show me what to do," she encouraged me.

"Just put your hands behind your head like this, and then sit-up until you touch your elbows to your knees," I demonstrated. "See, it's easy!" We do 20 in our gym class. She pulled up and did a near perfect sit-up. I started counting," One, two, three, four, five….." She kept up with me until I got up to about eight or nine and then started laughing. We both continued laughing and giggling, until I got to 20 and stopped. Next, we both got up and she helped me get onto the rowing bicycle. It was hard for me to get the rhythm with my feet, but I kept working at it.

She got onto the other exercise bike and announced, "Lastly, I ride the bicycle at the very end for ten minutes." We both finished, and she didn't seem nearly out of breath as I.

Next we got dressed and ate a good breakfast. She had me come sit next to her. I had brought three or four library books for the week. I read at least a few pages of one of my books to her. She commented on how she thought I was becoming a really good reader. I stopped reading and asked," Grandma, what was it like when you were growing up?"

She paused a moment and answered,"Well, you know we didn't have a television or even a radio when I was your age. We lived on a farm and had cows and chickens."

"Wow, so you grew up a lot like my dad did on a farm?"

"Yes, I suppose so. I remember one time my older brothers dared me that I wouldn't jump off of the roof of the barn into a snowdrift," she smiled, and started to chuckle," I was a little bit younger than you. I jumped into the snowdrift and it was way over my head and I got stuck. They had to go get our parents to help dig me out. Then *they* got in all kinds of trouble for that."

We both laughed together. A loud squealing noise began piercing through our merriment. She noticed me flinching a little at the noise. She reached into the front of her dress and tugged out the large silver, disc-like speaker on the cord she wore around her neck.

" Is my hearing aid squeaking?"

"Yes, it is." I grimaced until she reached behind one of her ears and turned a tiny knob until it finally stopped.

"Is that better?"

"Yes, it is fine now."

I thought for a bit, then gathered my courage," Do you mind telling me what happened when you first lost your hearing?" My Mom had explained to me somewhat, but I was curious and wanted to know more.

She paused for a moment studying my serious look.

"Well, I was six years old and became real sick with a sore throat. Eventually I had a red rash all over. You know that there weren't the kind of treatments then like there are now?" I nodded. She continued," They finally said it was scarlet fever. Because it was so severe, I lost most of my hearing afterwards."

"Did they let you go to school after that?"

"I was so fortunate that I was old enough that I had a good vocabulary already. Someone from the hard of hearing society was sent, and I was taught how to read lips. Then I was able to go back to my regular school with the other kids. It wasn't easy at first, but I got much better over time. And today I am *so* thankful that there are hearing aids."

I was glad too. Now I better understood why I was always told to look at her, whenever I was speaking. That was when I first started to realize what a truly remarkable life my Grandmother had been living throughout the years. I wondered what it would be like to grow up without very much hearing.

Next, we went outside and she let me water all of the flowers alongside the house. She taught me the names of each different variety and we both had a lot of fun.

That afternoon while she worked the newspaper crossword puzzle, I read a little more. Then at 2:30 the television was turned on. First, we watched the game show called *Password.* She explained the rules to me, and soon I was playing along and both of us were shouting out words at the TV. She was faster than I, and was getting the answers to most of them before the people on TV. I was pretty impressed. Next, *Jeopardy* came on, and that was well over my head, but she was getting quite a few of those correct too. Every weekday afternoon the television went on for precisely one hour, and we played along with the game shows.

On Sunday morning we watched the evangelical program with Rev. Billy Graham. I also noticed that Sunday morning and every evening, my grandmother read from her bible and devotionals. She showed me her *Guideposts* magazine, and several pamphlets and book by Dr. Norman Vincent Peale. It was a well-worn copy of *The Power of Positive Thinking* written by him.

A couple of times during the week she came outside and played a ring toss game with me. I was allowed to choose whichever board games we played each day. I chose *scrabble*, of course, nearly every time. When my parents arrived to pick me up at the end of the week, I felt such of a greater love and understanding for her.

It wasn't until years later that I was given a better glimpse of the level of passion, faith, and gratitude my grandmother had lived through all of her years. I knew that she had worked as an accountant over forty years during her life, well before I first knew her. She had worked first at a bank, and later at a large school supply company. We found a carbon copy of a letter in her belongings, that she had sent to the president of a local bank in which she was inquiring to obtain employment. It was amazing to me to see her level of passion and tenacity. What makes this exceptional is that this all occurred during the early 1900's, she was considered handicapped, and a woman seeking non-traditional employment. Unfortunately, we were unable to locate her original letter in time for this writing, but here is my best recall at its essence:

Date: 1907

Dear Mr. Bank President,

It has come to my attention that your bank has an opening available in the bookkeeping department. I wish to inform you that I have excelled in, and completed several accounting courses.

I am tenacious, hard-working, and well-detailed working with numbers. I am a very fast-learner, and would become a great asset to your bank. I know that I have all of the qualities that you are seeking in a person for this position.

The best possible decision to benefit your bank, and you, is to hire me for this position. I know that if you make any other choice than this, it would be a great mistake.

I am looking forward to meeting with you soon.
Sincerely,

I am pleased to say that after reading her letter, the bank president interviewed and hired her. This was her first job at age 18. She continued to work in a full-time career as an accountant, during an era when this was unusual for most women.

She married later than most women during this era. She met her husband from *The Hard of Hearing Society,* in which she was one of the original organizers and founder. She was in her 40's when the two became married.

A couple of years after her marriage, her youngest brother's wife passed suddenly leaving him with eight children on his own. My mother was the youngest of them at the age of four. She was sent to live with her for awhile. This went so well, after four years my mom chose to be adopted by them. Four years later, my mom's new father and her husband passed unexpectedly as well.

My grandmother was simply the most passionate, faithful, disciplined, and grateful person, I have ever had the opportunity to know first-hand. No matter what obstacle showed up in her life, she was always steadfast in her faith(inner-knowing that everything was in divine order). Everything she did in her life exuded passion, joy, and love for others.

She lived such a full life and greatly impacted all of those around her. Her *thoughts, feelings, words,* and *actions* always seemed to match the highest levels of love. My grandmother enjoyed excellent health throughout her years, and survived all of her brothers and sisters. She lived independently in her own home until the age of 97. It was only when she started having difficulty with her vision and couldn't read lips as well, that she needed to go into the nursing home. Four months later she made her peaceful transition.

This is the last letter I received from her three weeks before I left home, and entered active duty in the Army. It inspired me at the time, and throughout the years whenever I read it again.

Sunday, September 18, 1983

As the time of your departure draws near, you are very much on my mind. I think of you in strange places alone, and then I realize that you will not be alone – ever. God, who has been with me will be with you, and He loves you even more than we do.

God has been good to me. He gave me a wonderful mother, and we had many happy years together. When she died and I wanted a husband, He gave me a wonderful one, Charles. Then, when I wanted a daughter, He gave me a lovely one, Helen. Then came lovely grandchildren and Joshua(first great-grandchild).

You will be seeing many new places, and I expect to see them too, through your letters. Be happy.

I found a new Bible verse lately that appeals to me. "Commit thy way unto the Lord and trust also in Him and He will bring it to pass." I can turn my eyes over to God and then TRUST Him.

My nightly prayer is that God will so ENFOLD me in His loving care that my life may be the UNFOLDING of His purpose concerning me. In other words – that God's Will be done. Then I say the same prayer naming my relatives and friends.

God bless you always.

I am so blessed to have had such a person touch and inspire my life. It is those who have passion in every area of their life, who are truly powerful. This is an example of one of the way-showers, who came before us that are our teachers. We owe it to each of them, that we are lifted by the foundation they so diligently built for us.

It is just as when we witness the magnificence of the eagle soaring higher and higher. With wings spread, they know just how to maneuver perfectly into the unseen current of wind. You will notice only occasionally do they need to make an effort to flap the wings. It is the current that lifts them to greater heights. It is the same invisible current of passion, which empowers us and raises us as well. If there isn't passion in our life, there is *no* power.

Passion is energy. Feel the power that comes from focusing on what excites you.

-Oprah Winfrey

The other most passionate person I presently know is my spiritual teacher, Sai Maa. This is just one aspect most everyone notices after first meeting her. Every facet of her personality radiates passion. It is such of an important quality, that she has taught several retreats during the last few years just on the topic of *passion*.

Now it is time to ask ourselves. How much passion do I have in my life? What areas of my life do I have passion? Which areas do I not? Am I using the passion and power in my life for the greatest good and service for myself and others? If we really examine these answers, most of us will find one or more areas in our lives which we might improve. How can we move more passion and power into our lives?

The 20 Percent Principle

There is a principle which was first noticed and named the *Pareto Principle* after its proposer Vilfredo Federico Damaso Pareto (1848-1923), a French-born Italian engineer. He observed that where a large number of factors contribute to a result, the majority (about 80 percent) of the result is due to the contributions of a minority (about 20 percent) of the factors. Investigations suggest, as a business example, that some 80 percent of the sales of a company are generated by 20 percent of its customers. 80 percent of the inventory value is tied up in 20 percent of the items. 80 percent of problems, are caused by 20 percent of the reasons. Although it has not been proven as a scientific law, it does seem to appear consistently in many different areas. It is also called the 80/20 principle, Pareto's Law, or principle of imbalance.

Similarly, if we look at any organization whether it is a social, spiritual, or business organization, typically the same 20 percent of the people do 80 percent of the work in running the organization. Now you are probably wondering how this might possibly relate somehow to passion and power?

It is simple, if we use this same principle to look at our life. When we know that by definition *the majority(about 80 percent) of a result is due to the contributions of a minority(about 20 percent) of the factors.* We can us this same rationalization when we look at our life.

We might look at every aspect of our life as a big organization. We can break our life into various categories. These might include career, relationships, family life, spiritual life, education, and hobbies. We should separate each of these, and move through each one individually. Ask, how much passion do I bring into my career? Relationships? Family life? Etc.

Here's an example: I typically work eight hours in a day at my career. After examining all of the activities of my day, how many of them am I doing with fully engaged passion? We calculate the approximate total time feeling passion. Is it at least 20 percent of the time? If so, that is great. Think of this as the threshold we wish to cross. Once we are able to reach this level of passion, this will provide for 80 percent of our career feeling very productive and meaningful to us. Next, go through each of the other areas of your life and perform the same procedure. Did every area make it at least to the 20 percent level? Were there certain areas of your life that missed the mark? If you made the mark in every area, congratulate yourself. As we know from this principle, if there is at least a 20 percent level of passion in your life all across the board, this is the driving force for about 80 percent of all aspects of your life.

Finally, take a close look at every activity that you were able to identify that you presently engage in passionately. These are usually the activities that while you do them, you completely lose all track of time. Think of ways to expand upon these, and bring more of this into your life. Often, if we look back at our childhood, some of the first activities which we loved to do and were drawn towards can be a great clue to help us. Do you remember loving to draw or paint? Did you enjoy music? Did you love to spend time digging in the garden? Did you enjoy taking apart your bicycle or other mechanical things?

Ultimately, these lives of ours were never meant to be lived by simply "going through the motions" of our daily activities. It is important to take a close look at each area of our life, and determine whether we have passion. It is *passion* which leads us to being powerful in our life. It is *power* which decides whether we are really living our life fully and completely, or not. Am I soaring as high as possible, with *all* of the available wind beneath my wings?

9

Wisdom Of The Ages

By three methods we may learn wisdom: First, by reflection, which is noblest; second, by imitation, which is easiest; and third by experience, which is the bitterest.

— Confucius

As we continue on our journey, there is yet another essential leg needed on our chair, so we may be fully supported. It is so important that we garner as much *wisdom* as possible into our lives. Today we live in such of a fast-paced era of higher technology and seeming knowledge, that this valuable aspect of our life gets forgotten by many. Also, there are those who feel that increased knowledge is most valuable to pursue, and may be mistaken that greater knowledge always means greater wisdom. This is simply not the case.

There are a varied array of definitions and understandings of the meaning of *wisdom*. These are the most important meanings for our needs. *Wisdom* is: a wise attitude, belief, or course of action. *Wise* is: the ability of an individual to have a deep understanding, keen discernment, and a capacity for sound judgment.

Unfortunately, in more recent years, people here in the West are not taught from an early age to revere and respect those who have greater years of age. Although there are a few exceptions in the West, typically those living in the Eastern countries tend to look to the elder generation as a valuable part of society who possess much relished wisdom. Particularly the Japanese people display a high example of this in their society. It is interesting that not only is there an elevated reverence for the elders in this society, recognizing they possess the greatest level of wisdom, but the people who live here also have the highest average lifespan of all countries. Might this possibly be one of the contributing factors? Absolutely! Wouldn't it be wise(no pun intended) for us to learn this from others?

Of course, simply having a greater number of years of life, does not automatically endow the person with a greater level of wisdom than one who has fewer. What it does imply, though is that this person has had *more opportunities* to gather wisdom than the younger one.

So if we establish that simply having lived a longer life than others, and gathering more knowledge than others does not automatically give us wisdom, then what exactly does? If we examine some of the key words in our original definition, these may point us in the correct direction. At the core, we must examine our *capacity* to have deep understanding, discernment, and sound judgment. These are what in turn determines our attitude, and steers us in the eventual course of action in our life. Overall, wisdom is really an important factor we really need to nurture and grow in our life. Why is it so important?

Learning To Swim With The River

When I was 15 my parents took my brother and I out on the Ohio River often in our motorboat. Frequently, we would find a little sandy patch along the shoreline to stop and dock the boat. This time we stopped along a small peninsula, which split up the middle of the river. I was an avid swimmer, and loved to go out into the water and swim. As soon as we beached the boat I was in the water immediately.

My mom hollered out," Why don't you come put on a life jacket?"

"Aww, I don't need it. Those just get in the way of *really* swimming. Besides, I *just* passed my senior lifesaving," I reasoned. After all, I *was* on the swim team and typically swam at least 15- 20 laps of the pool at each workout. *And* only two weeks ago I pulled my 200-plus pound flailing and fighting lifesaving instructor out of the pool during my final exam. I felt pretty invincible in my aquatic capabilities. I continued swimming about 10-15 feet past the back of the boat until mom called me back in to eat lunch.

As we ate our sandwiches, my parents were talking to another couple who had docked their boat near ours. They seemed to hit it off well with them. My dad and her husband were completely engaged in discussing the differences in mercury and evinrude boat motors, horsepower, and other technical boat lingo. Our boat had a mercury engine, and theirs had an evinrude. A few minutes later, my parents were offered if they wanted to go out in their boat and he would let my Dad "take his for a spin."

My brother and I were left with our boat and told they wouldn't be gone for long. My brother didn't seem to mind, as he was still finishing eating. At age 19 and likely going through his last growth spurt, he was eating nearly twice as much as the rest of us. I was happy, as this meant I had more time to go swim.

After watching my parents speed off with the other couple in the boat, I waded back into the water. I could feel the smoothness of mud squishing between my toes as I walked further out. The water was the warmest closer to the shore and was cooler as I moved out more. As I continued further out, I noticed larger pockets of cool water with small punctuations of warm here and there.

Once I was at what seemed to be the final place I could still touch the bottom, I lunged off into the deeper water like pushing off of a starting block. I first swam regular freestyle, wondering what it might be like to swim all the way across the river. I thought how this felt like swimming laps in the pool, only better. I moved next into the breaststroke, and then it eventually dawned on me that maybe I should start back. I noticed that suddenly the water seemed more rough than it had been closer to shore. I turned and noticed, I was at least 150-200 feet past the back of our boat. This is when the reality first struck me that I really wasn't in a swimming pool, as I could feel the current pushing against my body. I saw that as I stopped and simply treaded water for a minute, that I was drifting along downstream.

I knew I needed to start back towards the shore *now*. I looked into the distance and attempted to align myself with our now distant green boat, and started swimming back. With every stroke I took, I felt the current pushing against me. I looked up towards the boat, and saw that I was no longer in line with it, and I was being swept down river. I steadily pushed on taking the longest, strongest and most deliberate strokes I could muster. I now grasped that I simply couldn't beat the current. I remembered how we had been trained to swim diagonally of the current in a situation such as this. I started to allow it to take me and swam along with the waves diagonally.

As I continued down river, I could feel the undercurrent becoming stronger and colder. Another minute or so and I would completely pass the length of the peninsula in which our boat was beached. I knew if I allowed that to happen, I would be completely in the middle of the river. At least fifteen minutes had passed since I had first attempted to swim back to shore. I knew that I was getting tired, and the current seemed to be a constant tug. I kept swimming and was coughing and choking, as I kept getting gulps of water instead of air.

Although the body was getting weary, my mind was still very active. I knew to just keep focused, and swim diagonally with the current. I made one more big push using all of my strength to try to get to shore, hoping I might make it before the current took me into the middle of the river. I splashed, heaved my arms as hard and fast as I could muster, and sputtered out more water all to no avail. It seemed like the river was going to win. I was completely exhausted. I knew I had to rest. I finally laid back into the water, and simply allowed myself to float face-up. I thought if I could just rest a minute…

As I was still for a moment, I thought I heard the panicked voice of my brother screaming my name in the distance. At this time in his life, my brother didn't know how to swim.

I alternated floating on my back a minute to rest, and then treading water. No matter which I did, I was still fighting the powerful undercurrent. I had no idea that this was what was meant by an "undertow" I had heard in the past.

Next, I heard the distant sound of a boat engine starting. A couple of minutes later, I saw my brother whisk around to me driving our boat. Words couldn't describe how happy I was to see him. I was jostled around by the new waves he had created, and spat out water still gasping for air.

"Are you alright!?"

I barely sputtered out a quick, "unhuh." I saw his look of grave concern, which is unusual to see coming from any teenaged sibling.

He placed the white plastic ladder over the edge of the boat for me to climb up. Normally, I'd climb right up that and over into the boat easily after 30-40 minutes of waterskiing. But not so today. It took every bit of my remaining energy to heave one foot onto the bottom step of the ladder. Then he grabbed both of my arms and pulled me up over the edge into the boat. I fell onto the floorboard like a big slippery fish who just put up a great fight, and finally had to surrender. I coughed and hacked more water up for another two or three minutes, then weakly pulled myself up into the seat. He started driving us back to shore.

" Do you know how much you scared me?"

I still couldn't really answer him just yet.

He nervously continued," I didn't know *what* to do, and I knew you were in trouble. I know you are a really good swimmer, but the river today is pretty rough. Do you know that you could have *drowned* out there?"

I nodded and managed an, "Unhuh, thank-you."

He docked the boat back up onto the shore. I continued to occasionally cough up more river water for awhile, and rested. My parents came back, and by then I was able to tell them the whole story myself.

This day I learned quite a multitude of lessons the hard way. A few included the dangers of ego, perseverance, overcoming fear, and gratitude.

I am so grateful that my brother saved my life. At this time he couldn't swim, and didn't like water. Although he had been taught to drive the boat somewhat, he wasn't supposed to drive it without my parents present. He knew I was in trouble, and had no other choice than to come get me with the boat. He overcame a lot of fear on that day. Just a couple of weeks after this incident, my brother began to teach himself how to swim. During this time, my parents had an above ground swimming pool, and by the end of that summer he had taught himself how to swim.

During the time that I have lived near the Ohio River, nearly every year I typically hear in the news that one or two teenagers have drowned. Everytime I hear this, it takes me back to think about this event, and how I am ever so grateful.

This illustrates a prime example of how a lot of *knowledge* on a particular subject does not automatically equilibrate into a great level of *wisdom*. There is no question that during this time I was a really good swimmer. I had taken every possible swimming class at the YMCA, including senior lifesaving. I was good at waterskiing, and had been canoeing for several years. I had lettered on my high school swim team as well.

The first thing that jumped into the way of wisdom was my strong *ego*. Often when we feel we have a lot of knowledge, or excel in a certain area we may think we are above others in this area. We think that we can throw by the wayside anything reasonable, that most people need to stay safe. We think it just doesn't apply to us, and we are infallible because of our superior abilities. I thought that life jackets were only needed for weaker swimmers.

The next thing that interfered with my use of any wisdom, was my own *ignorance*. Although I knew all about many watersports, I didn't really know much of anything about river currents or their potential influences on swimming. When I carelessly swam too far into the river oblivious to the current, this was another component which put me into danger.

Finally, I didn't use any *discernment*. This is when we look at the big picture, examining each of the different factors to help us determine the wisest course of action. I was anxious to simply be in the water as much as possible, and didn't consider anything else. The water was a little rough that day with a stronger wind. I was pretty careless, that I went out farther away from the shore than usual. It was my inability to discern any potential hazards, and use any type of good judgment, which kept me from possessing any level of wisdom.

This above example depicts precisely what happens in our life if we lack wisdom. When we lack wisdom it is easy to get caught into the current, being pulled in a direction away from the way you intend to go. It didn't matter how much *love* I had for swimming. It didn't matter how much *power* and *passion* I put into my swimming. When I used *no wisdom,* I was simply caught in the current and taken to the opposite place of where I wanted to go and nearly drowned. This is what happens to us everyday, if we aren't working to cultivate greater *wisdom* in our life.

What does it look like to use wisdom? What are the ways we can bring more of it into our life?

The saddest aspect of life right now is that science gathers knowledge faster than society gathers wisdom.

— Isaac Asimov

Learning To Avoid Distraction

About ten years ago, during the first few years that Sai Maa was coming to the United States, she told us about some of her travels in India. She came to a town and met a well-known Guru(spiritual teacher). He invited her to stay at his ashram(spiritual community) for a couple of days.

She had been there only a short time, and he told her he had been waiting for her. He said he had been waiting a long time, and he *knew* that she was the one. He offered to Sai Maa to take over his ashram. He emphatically encouraged her to take it, and it would all be completely hers.

Sai Maa said that his ashram was beautiful and huge, he had continuously thousands of spiritual devotees who came regularly to see him. She told him she couldn't take his ashram. He was insistent that he was so sure she was the one, whom he had been waiting for so long to come.

During this time, Sai Maa had only recently started coming to the United States regularly. When she was in country she would travel from California to New York, stopping off at four or five different locations between the two to give weekend retreats. During these earlier years, the retreats I attended mostly were in either Bloomington, Indianapolis, or Chicago having between 40-70 people on average. I would guess if I included all of the locations and couple of foreign countries where Sai Maa was giving her programs, during this time there might have been about a total of 500 of us who were her students. One would have thought that an offer such as this to take over a large ashram in India, instantly having thousands of students would have sounded very appealing to her.

Sai Maa told him no. She thanked him for his extremely generous offer. Yet she knew that if she took his ashram, she would not be able to continue to come to the United States and serve the people here, nor those people from the other countries.

She continued to explain to us how there are times that something that really looks like it would be a good thing to do, might really be a *distraction*. She was able to *discern* that if she accepted his offer to take over his ashram, this would have taken her away from her primary mission to serve as many people as possible in the West.

If we fast forward now at least 10 years later, Sai Maa has continuously given programs throughout the United States, Canada, France, Belgium, Australia, Germany, Japan, and probably others I have forgotten. Although I am sure there is no way to accurately count her current number of active students, I would guess at this moment there are between 4000-5000 of us worldwide. I know that Sai Maa has met and touched the lives throughout these years of at least tens' of thousands of additional people. Last month I went to see Sai Maa in Denver, and there were over 1000 people there to be with her at that one event. All of this could never have happened if Sai Maa hadn't used her *wisdom* to make the best decision ten years earlier. There are countless numbers or people in the West who might never have received the great benefits of learning from a Master.

If we look closely at this example, we can see each of the key elements being used properly. First, if we look at *ego,* there was nothing of the sort in Sai Maa's mind. She relayed to us that she felt honored, and displayed great humility to him. Some others might have been attracted to this offer and accepted it easily, happy to have an instant spiritual community with little effort.

The next factor often seen wherever there is a lack of wisdom is *ignorance.* We think of this whenever one does not have adequate or complete information about the situation. This occurs also when we do have the needed information, but we choose to *ignore* the importance of it. Sai Maa was well informed in this example, and understood the magnitude of the decision she was making.

The other factor we see in wisdom is the full use of *discernment.* We know that discernment allows us to see all of the different nuances, which are needed to use our judgment to make the best decision. She looked at each aspect of this offer that this Guru was giving her. She had a clear picture of everything, which assisted her in making this decision. She also was able to determine that even though this seemed like a wonderful opportunity, it really would be a *distraction,* which would ultimately lead her astray from what she knew was her major purpose.

The Art of *Being* Wisdom

So the key elements we need to work on to develop *wisdom* in our life are: *eliminating ego* through *increasing humility, eliminating ignorance, using discernment,* and learning to *identify* and *eliminate distraction.*

There are countless different ways in which various experts and lay people alike attempt to define and explain the *ego.* I have heard every kind of argument surrounding what it is, or isn't. There are some who feel it is necessary to have *some* ego, and others do not. It is similar as if we were to send ten different people into a dark room, which has been closed up for a long time. Each person after some time would come out having ten completely different descriptions, attempting to quantify the experience. Rather than attempting to wade through such a murky, controversial area, it is much easier to simply focus upon its polar opposite.

When we shine a bright light into an old, closed up room, instantly much of the darkness disappears. The light allows us to see what is *really* in the room. This is much the same as when we focus upon bringing a greater amount of *humility* to our life. Bringing humility is just like pointing a brilliant light into the shadow, and the shadow simply vanishes.

Humility is: the quality or state of being humble. *Humble* is: not thinking or feeling of oneself as being greater or better than another. It is important to note that this *does not* mean that we think of ourselves as *less than* another. It is vital for us to understand this as well. How do we become more humble? How can we practice humility?

There are a wide variety of different qualities we typically find in one who is humble. When we practice humility, we listen more to others and typically speak less. When we are practicing *active listening* such as this, we also are practicing humility. It is allowing others to voice *their* needs, or concerns in a situation without discounting or eliminating their importance. It is recognizing when the time is right to stand back, and allow others an opportunity to step up into a position which will allow them to grow. This is especially true if it is something which you have already experienced, and have obtained some mastery. Finally, *humility* is acquired in our life as a natural by-product, when we truly begin to understand our own *divinity* of ourself *and* others. Once again, the only way to truly bring this understanding into our life is through personal experience. The way to encounter our own *divinity* is through the practice of meditation. This will lead us to *respect* the divinity of ourselves, others, and every living thing. When we come to know first-hand that we each are connected, and One of the same Source, it is no longer possible to think that any one of us might be greater or less than another.

If we understand that *ignorance* means: the state of being ignorant. *Ignorant* is defined as being uninformed or unaware. It is also when we choose to *ignore* information in which we *have* been previously given.

Once again, rather than attempting to quantify, somehow contain, and eliminate an undesirable quality from our experience; it is better to simply focus upon, and increase its opposite. We must always focus our energies upon that which we choose to bring *into* our life, and *not* upon that which want to eliminate. When we take this approach, that which we wish to eliminate simply falls to the wayside. We know that *bringing the light* to this includes increasing our *awareness*, becoming better *informed*, and *paying attention* to the information which we already know or have been shown. Once we have *decided* to move forward in our spiritual journey of *awakening,* the right and perfect teachers, and books will begin to appear in our lives. It is simple; start reading the books and practicing what they teach, and listen to the teachers and practice all that they teach you. This is the way to become *informed* and to increase your *awareness.* Finally, *pay attention* to *everything,* and take the necessary steps to incorporate it into your life.

It's not what you look at that matters, it is what you see.

-Henry David Thoreau

That which is the natural next step after *paying attention* in our life is *discernment.* This is the ability to see and understand people, things, or situations clearly and intelligently. This is the component of wisdom which requires more practice and diligence to develop in our life. The first step, as mentioned previously, we must be *paying attention* to what is occurring in our life in every aspect. We must ask ourselves *and notice,* "What is happening in each of my relationships, career, family, and spiritual practice?" We must *really* be willing to look at all of the details. We must determine which of these are going really well, and which of these are not. Then we must ask ourselves, "What is not working, and why?" Then the most difficult task is we must completely remove ourself from the middle of our life. We must use our *imagination*, pretending that we are sitting up in the bleachers at a distance. At this vantage-point we can see every aspect of the game we are playing. Then ask yourself, "What can I see clearly here, while I am fully removed and simply a spectator?" It is important to be completely honest with yourself, acting like your own best friend who is telling you what you *really need* to hear. Finally, take whatever it is you have discovered into your meditation with you, and listen. You will be able to see the situation much more clearly. Guidance may come immediately, or within a couple of days. At the end of taking these steps, you will most likely have a greater ability for *discernment*. This is by far the most difficult aspect of *wisdom* for us to attain in our life. *Discernment* is not so easily taught to others, and is truly an art which takes some practice to master.

A close cousin to discernment, and an absolute requirement for complete *wisdom*, is to be able to *identify* and *eliminate distraction. Distraction* is: the state or act of being distracted. *Distracted* is: being unable to think about or pay attention to something. Needless to say, during this age of high technology, we experience a myriad of distractions all around us. Of course, there are the obvious ones such as television, computers,and cell phones. But there are many others which are not as obvious, which have a tendency to show up in our lives. It is through the use of our *discernment* that we are able to *identify* that which is a *distraction* to us. If we look at our life and are able to see that there is an activity, situation, or relationship which interferes, or takes our attention away from our purpose here, this is a *distraction*. We may take the same steps as those we use for *discernment.* We must move ourself away from the middle of our life, and examine everything from the sidelines again. The important thing to understand, that a *distraction* may *seem* like it is a good thing, but it ultimately will take you off-track from your purpose. It is just like intending to drive your car to Florida, and instead you make several detours and end up eventually in Minnesota. Each of the detours is a *distraction*, and you never get to your planned destination. *Distractions* come in all shapes and sizes. They may be obvious and simple, such as spending too much time watching television, or not-so-obvious and complex. Agreeing to take a promotion in your career which requires longer working hours, and a position which you are not well-suited to perform, is a distraction which takes a greater skill for us to see.

Obtaining *wisdom* in our life requires that we deliberately must continue to practice each of these. Remember that *wisdom* is truly an *art*, which cannot simply be taught. However, if we can recognize that everything occurring in our life is *not* random, or accidental, but has a specific, and divine purpose to teach us; this is where we start. Over time, and after repeated efforts, we eventually will gain greater *wisdom.*

10

Master's In Discipline

Our fourth leg and, just as essential as the others to support us on our chair, and in our spiritual journey is *discipline*. *Discipline* is: training that *corrects*, *molds*, or *perfects* the mental faculties or moral character. And orderly conduct or pattern of behavior. *Discipline* may often be related to *structure*. Typically, when our life has a greater overall structure in our day to day activities, it is much more likely to have discipline than if our life is mostly unstructured.

This is an important characteristic within humanity, which I have noticed during my lifetime has become more and more diluted with each new generation. I know there are many reasons why discipline has diminished in the West, however, our task is to simply understand its importance, and learn how to bring it back into our lives again.

If we examine our definition again, there are the key phrases, *orderly conduct, pattern of behavior,* and *training that corrects, molds, or perfects the faculties or character.* If we distill this yet a little bit further, we may reduce it even more simply, *discipline* is: *an orderly pattern of behavior and training that improves the faculties or character.* This is the simplest definition we will use to help us understand.

Why is discipline so important? As I hinted before, this is an area that particularly in the West has continued to dwindle with each passing year. It seems as everyone's lives' become busier due to the newer technologies, we have such an information overload that most have allowed the technology to control us, rather than us controlling it. This has lead us each passing year with less *structure* in our lives, and greater chaos.

A few days ago, my partner and I were on the walking trail near the river. A woman with her apparent grandson were walking past the opposite direction. Her grandson looked about age twelve, and was reluctantly shuffling about ten feet behind her taking short, lackluster steps. In an exasperated tone she asked us," We started on this trail up by the fire station, are there any mile markers along this route?"

"No, there are not." I answered.

"I need to know when we have walked a mile, so we can turn around." Nearly apologetically, she explained," He's in the Boy Scouts and is doing this for one of his merit badges." The boy now caught up with her, and with angst written across his face was listening to us.

We thought for a moment," A mile from the fire station should be about up there by the flag poles." my partner pointed into the distance.

"Thank you so much." she continued walking and the boy grimaced.

"Oh *man!* Can't we go back *now?*" He pleaded some more with her. She didn't answer him. He rolled his eyes and shuffled his feet, continuing reluctantly up the paved path behind her again.

I thought to myself, "Wow, modern day boy scouting has *really* changed!" Although I am sure that this is probably not the typical boy scout, it definitely is quite a symptom of what is happening right now.

This example fully illustrates what life looks like for a person who has no discipline. Although this is a younger person, it makes no difference, as it would look the same for an adult.

If we break this down, we see a person who has chosen to be part of an organization. This boy belongs to the boy scouts. Then, he has most likely set a goal for himself to obtain the next rank. All of the different scouting organizations require a certain number, and type of merit badges, which must be earned to obtain promotion to the next rank. Each of the merit badges have a list of tasks which must be learned, and performed to earn the specific badge. This boy either chose, or was required to obtain this particular merit badge. I am sure it likely was the one for *hiking*. It is apparent, one of the tasks he needed to perform was to take a two-mile hike or walk. So we could probably deduce a couple of things from this scene with this boy. He really *wanted* to obtain this merit badge in hiking, but he *didn't want* to have to hike the whole two miles.

How often do we have a goal we wish to attain, *knowing* that there are certain requirements, and yet we see if there is a shortcut, or an easier method to obtain it? This is what we do when we are lacking the *discipline* it really takes to reach our goals.

In this example, because this boy lacked the ability to keep focused on his goal, *and* to push himself until he reached it, his grandmother was the one who had to nearly drag him along. The only difference between this incident in a child and in an adult, the adult will most likely not have someone there who will *make* you continue until you reach your goal.

So this scenario shows us that if we lack discipline in our life, it is unlikely that we are going to make progress towards any of our goals. This would likely create a pretty frustrating life for us. Once again, it would be similar to having our goal and purpose to drive to Florida, and this time the engine of our car simply sputters along. We not only don't have the momentum to ever make it to Florida, but we will end up stranded, out in the middle of nowhere.

Some people regard discipline as a chore. For me, it is a kind of order that sets me free to fly.

-Julie Andrews

Dedication is another quality we will notice in a person who has a high level of *discipline*. Our dedication to a particular activity means we devote our time, and energy regularly towards that activity. Typically, if an activity, cause, or goal is important to us, this will lead us to devote and dedicate our energies regularly. Having a regular pattern, and training which molds our faculties or character, practiced over time, will result in our having discipline.

You Are Your Possibilities

Oprah Winfrey is a well-known celebrity who has demonstrated throughout the years, how *discipline* in her life has allowed her to reach great success in most every area of her life. During this writing, she reportedly has a current net financial worth of 2.9 billion dollars, and is the first African American woman to become a billionaire. She typically is wildly successful in most anything she attempts to do. What is her secret to this kind of success? Not only does Oprah embody each of the other three major factors, *Love*, *Power*, and *Wisdom* as we have previously discussed, but also she has a great level of *discipline*.

Oprah Winfrey was born in 1954 in Mississippi. Her parents were unmarried and broke up soon after her conception. Oprah had a difficult childhood, and grew up poor, in a small farming community. She was also sexually abused for several years, leading to going through pregnancy and losing a baby at the age of 14. Shortly after, she was sent to live with her father in Nashville, who was a barber. Her father was strict with his discipline, and felt that education was important.

During high school, she became an honor's student and joined the speech team. She won several speech team awards, and obtained a scholarship for college. At age 17 she won the *miss black tennessee beauty pageant*, which lead her to receive an offer to work part-time at a local radio station broadcasting the news.

After graduation from college, she worked at her local television station becoming the youngest, and first black female news anchor at the station. She moved to Baltimore in 1976 to be a co-anchor for the news. By 1978 she switched from news reporting, and became the co-host and host of two different local talk shows.

Finally, in 1983 she moved to Chicago, taking over a low-rated morning talk show, which within a few short months became number one in Chicago. Afterwards, her show became syndicated and was broadcast nationally starting in 1986, being renamed *The Oprah Winfrey Show.* Since this time, her show has set every kind of record throughout talk show history. Starting in the 1990's and thereafter, Oprah focused her show primarily on self-improvement, literature, and spirituality. She made a conscious decision to provide viewers with uplifting, and positive informative programs. At this writing, she currently has her own cable network station, called *OWN(Oprah Winfrey Network),* and produces her own programs having spiritual foundations such as *Super Soul Sunday.*

If having a top-rated international talk show, touching millions of people's lives each day weren't enough,

Oprah also starred in at least two movies including *The Color Purple*. She has co-authored at least five different books, and published the *O Magazine*. She is personally active in several philanthropic causes. She has been ranked for many years as one of the top 50 most generous Americans. She has donated, and started numerous charitable projects throughout the years. One of her projects includes building, and funding a school for disadvantaged girls in South Africa.

I am sure this only *somewhat* covers all of the facets of her life. *What I know for sure,* Oprah has positively touched over, and over, millions of people's lives. I first saw her program in 1986, and have witnessed throughout the years the way she has blossomed and transformed. She has assisted to shift the lives of multitudes of people. What a difference *one* person can make in this world! But it all never would have happened without *discipline.*

Here's her own description of a typical day:

6:00 a.m. Woke up. " I was going to get up at 5:30, but at 1 a.m. I sent an e-mail to security saying, 'Give me an extra half hour.' I got to the office about 6:30 and got on the treadmill downstairs in the gym. [While on the treadmill] I play Scrabble on my iPad, against the computer."

7:30 a.m. "I got in the makeup chair, then did two shows."

11:30 a.m. "I drank a green drink—spinach, parsley, a little bit of apple juice, celery, and cucumbers in a blender—and made some phone calls. I had to call Africa, and you have to do that before everybody goes to bed over there."

12:35 p.m. "I got back in the makeup chair—I was running late—and then did a show with Barbara Streisand."

2:00 p.m. "I came back upstairs, called the bank with any transfers that needed to be made, money issues. Then we had meetings about the next week's shows, what we have coming up."

7:50 p.m. "This was an early day since I was on the treadmill [again] by 10 of 8. I'd already done 45 minutes in the morning, so I did 30 minutes. Actually, it took 34 minutes to finish my Scrabble game, and I stayed on to 35 to round it off. The guy next to me was at a level-50 incline, and I was at 10. I was embarrassed to stay at 10, so I moved to 20. I was like [*panting*]—but I was going to keep it there."

8:50 p.m. "This almost never happens, but I came home at the same time as Stedman [Graham, Oprah's longtime love]. I made him something for dinner—leftover shrimp and rice, a little salad with lettuce, olive oil. I shaved some truffles, chopped up rosemary. I made it for him; I had a rice cake with almond butter. I'm trying not to eat past 7:30. I sat at the kitchen table and we talked for maybe 30 minutes, then I went to bed.

10:00 p.m. "I took my little stack of books to bed. I was trying to figure out what the next book club [selection] was going to be." [She chose *Great Expectations* and *A Tale of Two Cities*.]

11:10 p.m. "Lights out."

When we look at her typical day above, which she mentions is shorter than usual, we first see a certain level of *structure*. It appears that she spends about 12-13 hours performing career-related tasks. Then she spends about an hour and 20 minutes exercising. She mentions her food for lunch is a green drink, and for dinner, a rice cake with almond butter. It has been well-publicized through the years, that she has a tendency to struggle with her weight. It is apparent she is always looking for ways to become more healthy. This exemplifies her level of *dedication* to taking care of her own health needs through a daily dietary and exercise regimen.

Additionally, during one of the scenes of her program, *Behind The Scenes 25,* she showed the viewer's her meditation space in her home. She shared that each morning before she starts her day, she takes time for meditation, prayer, and reading the *Daily Word*. This is her time to be with something greater, to stay connected and better focused through her day. This displays yet another daily practice which demonstrates spiritual *discipline*.

One of the characteristics about Oprah Winfrey which isn't reflected above, is that it is well-known that she strives for excellence in everything that she does. Not only does she expect this in herself, but also in all of those who surround her. Some people have even described her as a perfectionist. I watched the camera follow her behind the scenes at her *Legends Ball*. In 2006 she planned this three day celebration at her home to honor 25 of the most legendary African American Women in entertainment, art, and civil rights. She was absolutely meticulous, personally overseeing every single detail. The celebration took months of planning, and truly honored these women for the years of *dedication* and *discipline* displayed throughout their lives, which paved the trail for many others. The weekend turned out highly successful, not only honoring women such as Rosa Parks, Coretta Scott King, Tina Turner, Diana Ross, and Alice Walker, but inspiring everyone who witnessed the event. During the weekend, Oprah Winfrey stepped back, and simply allowed it to unfold slowly like a blossoming flower. There were many memories shared of personal hardships, and gains, many tears, and laughter. Through her *love, power, wisdom* and *discipline,* she created an unforgettable weekend for all of the honoree's. And it was a highly inspirational one for all of the rest.

Oprah Winfrey's life demonstrates to us that it doesn't matter whether an individual is born into the most dire circumstances such as being in a minority race, and sex, living in poverty, or suffering from abuse. Each of us have the opportunity to rise to greater heights, and the ability to *serve* multitudes of humanity.

I can readily identify with her challenge of choosing a non-traditional career path as a minority woman in the South. Only a few years after she was first breaking her trail, I too, was attempting to obtain a job in radio or newspaper after graduating college. As a *Caucasian* female, after nearly every interview, I was told directly, or indirectly that I wasn't hired due to being a woman. It was always followed up with an unreasonable explanation, which if it happened today would definitely be a lawsuit. This occurred multiple times in Kentucky and Indiana in 1983. After so many roadblocks such as this, I finally enlisted in the Army so I could have a career in my chosen field. During 1986 when *The Oprah Winfrey Show* debuted on national television, I was stationed at The Pentagon serving as the official Army photographer there. One of the civilian photographers had a small, 9" black and white television at his desk. It was never turned on until 4:00. If he, or any of the other four of us were not out on assignment, he would gather us up to come watch "Oprah." I felt so inspired to see her, and to know how she came up from a humble background. We all really loved her, and her show.

She shows us that even when life seems like it is soaring out of control, it *is* possible to bring it back around and move back on course again. Often there is a *turning point,* when our life is able to make that shift from spiraling downward, to spiraling upwards again. This seemed to happen for her when she was sent to live with her father. It is here that she received the *structure* that she needed, and learned how to develop *discipline.* She was able to fully develop her talents to move forward, and become successful in her life. This formula she learned, and simply continued to apply to each of her aspirations and goals throughout her life.

What I learned at a very early age was that I was responsible for my life. And as I became more spiritually conscious, I learned that we are all responsible for yourselves, that you create your own reality by the way you think and therefore act. You cannot blame apartheid, your parents, your circumstances, because you are not your circumstances. You are your possibilities. If you know that, you can do anything.

- Oprah Winfrey

Now that we have seen examples which allow us to comprehend *why* discipline is so important in our lives, it is time to learn *how* to bring it into our life. First of all, we need to take a hike back over to our bleachers so we can get a good view of our life-game, once again. We must separate ourself and take a good look.

Does our life appear to have any *structure*? Do we go to sleep and wake up at about the same time every day? Do we arrive at our work or other activities at least 5-10 minutes early? Do we have any regular exercise routine? Do we eat our meals at the same time each day, choosing healthy foods? Do we have a *regular* spiritual practice of meditation or prayer? Do we practice it at the same time daily? Do we attend our chosen special activities *regularly* in which we are committed? (These are activities such as attending a spiritual center, meditation group, book-study, exercise class, sports group, hobbies, etc.) Do we have a routine in which we spend time with those who we are in a relationship, such as family? If you said *yes* to all seven of these, congratulate yourself that you have *structure* in your life. If there are *any* no's, it is important to look closely, and take steps to create a regular schedule for yourself. It is important to *decide* what are our goals, and most significant in our life. Then begin to start action steps to move ourselves into a life having better *structure*.

Am I *dedicated* to every area of my life? Look at spiritual growth, career, relationships, health, hobbies, and family. Do I actively pursue activities in each area which allows a greater level of growth? If any areas are weak, ask yourself why? What is my level of *dedication* in any weaker areas? What are my priorities, and what goals do I choose to set for myself?

Is there any specific *training* that I need to assist me to reach my goals in each of the areas? What is my plan to obtain the *training* I need in each area? Examples might include, reading a particular book, going on a spiritual retreat, going back to college, taking a nutrition class, signing up for a tai chi class, enrolling in business coaching, or taking a music class.

Am I giving my complete energy to each activity in my life? Do I put 100% of myself into every task I perform? If not, ask why? Look at your level of *dedication* again in the weaker areas.

The other day, one of my patients told me she was walking in the parking lot on her way into a grocery store with her grandson. They saw a large item of trash on the ground and witnessed a store employee walk right past it, ignoring it as he went to round up the grocery carts. She stopped her grandson, and they watched as he pushed a couple of the carts past the same article on the ground, leaving it as he continued with the carts into the store. She looked at her nine-year old grandson," When the day comes that you go to work at a place, and they are *paying* you, if see trash on the ground, that is *your job* to pick it up." This is one example of how it may appear when we really lack *dedication.* If we look at our life and find an area which is weak such as this, we must determine if this is due to laziness, or a signal that it may be time to look for something else.

Finally, to really have true *discipline* in our lives, we must honor *all* of our commitments we have made to ourselves and others. Our *commitments* are all of the activities which we have determined are a *priority,* and in which we have *dedicated* ourselves. This means that when we have a commitment, we follow through no matter what. It means going to work, even on the days you don't feel like it. It means arriving on time to help your friends move, even though you would rather be *anywhere* else. It may be turning down taking a day-trip with your family, because you promised yourself to finish an important project. You might have decided to return to college to obtain another degree; so you attend all of your classes, putting your *full* effort into all of your coursework. If you have made spiritual growth your high priority, you may spend 30 minutes practicing meditation when you first awaken in the morning, and 30 more minutes at the middle of your day.

When we weave each of these together, the end result is a life which has the fourth essential component of *discipline*. We may say that without exception, each of the most successful people throughout time, in all fields learned how to be *disciplined*. Therefore, as we continue our spiritual journey, that which will move us the fastest toward our goal is acquiring as much *discipline* in our day to day life as possible.

11

Powertools For The Path

There is available certain specialized knowledge every Master who has walked on this planet, has known and actively practiced until they gained mastery. Hence, this is the reason they are each called a *Master*. At least a portion of this has seemingly been hidden, and unavailable to the majority of people for many years. Previously, these teachings have been passed along orally throughout the ages, from the Master to the student. And only as soon as it was determined that the student was ready. During this new era, more esoteric teachings have become available, in writing, and accessible to everyone.

There are many advanced tools that are available for us to use in our daily lives, in which whole books are dedicated to explaining all of them. If we attempted to study, and practice all of these at once, this would be like a 16 year old first learning to drive, and being given a car, motorcycle, tractor, school bus, semi-truck, 32 foot recreational vehicle, and an airplane. If the prospective driver started learning all of these at the same time, it might take quite some time before we would expect *any* of these to be minimally mastered by a new driver. On the other hand, if one vehicle were selected, and after adequate practice, we would expect that eventually the driver would reasonably master that vehicle. So in this case, we would want to choose the most easy to understand, and easily accessible vehicle. The logical choice is to start out learning to drive a car. A car is very versatile, and will supply most of a person's transportational needs.

Similarly, we have access to several different advanced tools. Each of these can assist us in our daily life. Just like when we first learned to drive, we must first understand the concepts and begin regular practice.

Once again, if we attempted to learn everything and practice with every one of the different tools available, it might seem a little overwhelming to many of us. Therefore, it is better for us to choose one, which is the most versatile, for us to learn which can supply many of our needs. The reality is that there are actually twelve different advanced tools, and seven which have been fully made available for us during this time.

The Seven Sacred Flames

Now that you have come to understand the fundamental concept that every aspect of our life is surrounded and permeated with *energy. And* that we are continuously creating our own reality with the *level of energy* we infuse into our *words, thoughts, feelings,* and *actions.* It is time to take it to the next step.

I recall how relieved I felt when I first found out there were seven sacred flames available for us. It was similar to being bounced around in a sea, then discovering there are invisible lifelines which will show up and rescue you when you call to them. However, you must first know that they are there, and how to make the call.

We know that our *words, thoughts,* and *feelings* are creative in ways which we can witness in our lives, such as affecting the people around us, our health, careers, or other events. So we know that these impact all that we can see. Does it make sense, that since our *words, thoughts,* and *feelings* are all *energies* that we can't see, then these would *also* influence *other energies* that we *don't* see? Our answer is, of course!

Now, what if we have available *certain* energies that are here all of the time, that we don't see? We know that gravity is one unseen energy which is here at all times. It makes perfect sense that there are others. It is also reasonable to know *that our words, thoughts, and feelings,* with knowledge and practice can affect these unseen energies. There have been certain documented accounts of Yogis from India during meditation levitating off of the ground a few feet. This is a visible example of how *our* unseen creative energies are able to influence other invisible energies. In this case, the Yogi's deliberately emitted energies are influencing the field of gravity, which allows the body to raise up off of the ground. It is not necessary that we each learn levitation, but it shows us that if we are open, practice, and allow, that we really have *no limitations*.

What are the *seven sacred flames,* and why are these important to us? These are energies which typically are unable to be seen, or perceived in the outer world. But they can be seen, perceived, and utilized in the inner world, after some practice. But first we must arm ourselves with the understanding that they exist, then we may learn how to use them.

There are seven of them which are continuously available for our use. Explaining each one in depth, and attempting to understand and learn them all at once, is a great way to become very frustrated quickly. Instead, we are going to focus on just one. If we only learned and mastered just this one, and never learned *any* of the rest, we could still become an adept, similar to all of the great Masters who have walked on this planet.

The Violet Transmuting Flame

This great flame, perfect for our use right now is *The Seventh Ray*. It is called *The Violet Flame of Transmutation*. The Ascended Master Saint Germain is the Master who is in charge of this ray, and is greatly responsible for it becoming available for our use on this planet.

An *Ascended Master* previously was a human being, same as us, who lived upon this planet through multiple cycles of lifetimes until reaching a higher state of awareness. Once a certain level is attained, the person *ascends* to a greater level in which no more cycles of birth are required on this planet. Then these higher beings assist, and serve humanity to learn to do the same. Jesus, The Christ, and Gautama, The Buddha are two well-known examples of Ascended Masters.

Some of the known previous lifetimes of the Ascended Master Saint Germain include, the prophet Samuel in the 11th century BC, Joseph- the husband of Mary and father of Jesus, Saint Alban- the first martyr of Britain in the 3rd century, Merlin- the great alchemist, and prophet in the 5th century at the court of King Arthur, Roger Bacon- philosopher, Franciscan Monk, teacher, and scientist(1220-1292), Christopher Columbus- discoverer of America(1451-1506), and Francis Bacon-philosopher, statesman, literary master- authoring *The Shakespearian Plays*, and other works under pen names(1561-1626). He made his ascension after this lifetime. Having a strong desire to continue to serve the people on this planet, he was given special permission to return in a physical body again. He appeared as "Le Comte De Saint Germain," a "miraculous person" who astonished the courts during the

18th and 19th century in Europe. Here he was known as "The Wonderman of Europe." During this time, he lived as an immortal being for over 300 years throughout Europe. He spoke all languages, played any musical instrument, demonstrated alchemy activities in front of friends, and maintained the appearance of a 40-year-old man. He also could materialize in one place, dematerialize a few moments later, and re-appear several hundred miles away. Today, Saint Germain is in charge of *The Violet Transmuting Flame,* having served, and continuing his service to humanity in ways beyond our greatest comprehension.

Benefits and Actions of the Flame

Each of the seven flames have unique specific qualities and actions. Some of the main qualities and actions of the *violet flame* include: freedom, transmutation, transformation, diplomacy, and application of the science of alchemy. The color which is associated with it is violet.

The *violet flame* is considered one of the most important flames for redemption, transmutation and freedom. One source states that the flame's violet color is actually a combination of the blue and pink rays. The blue ray's action is *power*, and the pink ray's action is *love*. These two combined energies create a balance between the divine feminine and divine masculine to become an incredible ray for our use. There are countless benefits, which could take up volumes to explain thoroughly. We are going to focus upon the actions which are the most important for us to understand, so we may readily apply this in our lives now. It stands ready for us to use anytime. However, we must know *what* we may use it for, and *how* to bring this into our lives as a divine tool.

The main role of the *violet flame* is that of *transmutation. Transmutation* is the act of changing, or converting a lower energy vibration, or substance into a higher energy vibration, or substance. One application is to call, or invoke the violet flame to *transmute*, or cleanse any misqualified karma which we have created from our current lifetime, or any of our previous lifetimes. Learning to use it in this way, allows the flame to clear many possible obstacles from our life caused by our lower energetic karma. We still will learn the necessary lessons needed, but most likely in an easier, and gentler way.

We literally may decree or invoke the *violet flame* into any situation or aspect of our life, and it will *transmute* any discordant energies allowing divine transformations to occur. We can use this in any of our relationships, our family, career, spiritual growth, and health. Literally, if you have *any* difficult situation in your life, and you invoke the *violet flame* to work in that area, it will go to work clearing, and moving everything involved into the direction of divine order. There are simply countless applications for its use in this way.

When I first met Sai Maa over thirteen years ago, she immediately taught us about the *violet flame*. She told us to use it for anything, and everything. She has facilitated meditations with us countless times showing us how to use this flame. She taught us it was important before each of our meals, as we bless our food to put the violet flame into it before we eat it. I have practiced this with every meal since she first taught us. Today I understand the benefit much greater than I did before. A friend of mine lived several years in a monastery. He explained that it was typical that the most highly revered, and loving monks were the only ones allowed to cook the food. They understood that the love and joy these higher evolved beings radiated would go into the food which they cooked, and benefit everyone.

I remember all of the times I ate my grandmother's food growing up. She made everything from scratch, my favorites included her yeast rolls, milk gravy, strawberry shortcake, and ice cream. She simply loved to cook, and put the most joy and passion into her cooking. We always marveled at the great taste of her food, and showered her with compliments. She always said to us," You are just tasting the *love* in it." She was absolutely correct. Likewise, when we put the *violet flame* into our food deliberately before we eat, this ensures that all of the food we put into our body energizes us.

We may invoke the *violet flame* into every cell and tissue of our physical, mental, emotional, and all of our subtle bodies. It can *transmute* anything which is dissonant in these bodies into energies which can serve us. Anything which is adversely affecting our health, or spiritual well-being can be transformed. Once again, it requires consistency and practice.

Any difficulties in a relationship can be divinely shifted as well. It is important when we use this tool, that we simply allow whatever is our most beneficial outcome to manifest. If we attempt to control our relationship, or any situation into the way we think it *should* be, we may be settling for something less than what we otherwise would receive.

An example of this often occurs when we are in a relationship with another. Perhaps the first few years seem great, and then over time both people start to have difficulties. There may be a great lack of communication, or both people have seemingly moved into different levels of growth in their lives. If one begins to bring the *violet flame* into the relationship, and notices that it seems to accelerate the differences, it is best to simply allow it to do its work. Many of us become attached to *making* a relationship last, when maybe it is really time to release it. If we hang on, this not only contributes to our own suffering, and lack of growth, but causes the same for our partner. If we simply allow, and the relationship is finished, *and* we release it, this makes us available for another greater, and new experience that may be just around the corner.

On the other hand, there may be times that we move the *violet flame* into a distressed relationship, and it may take an action which allows the solutions to come to the surface. This is the time that we must be able to use our *discernment* to enable us to decide the next best course for us to take. It may be that there is a way for resolution we hadn't seen previously, which will become more apparent to us.

There are other actions of the *violet flame*. It is also known as the comfort flame, the flame of diplomacy and ceremony, and the freedom love flame. The creation of comfort, no matter the form is considered another action. The *violet flame* is also a tool, which will assist you to attain spiritual freedom. When this occurs, you may become limitless and be able to realize, and direct every aspect of your own divinity. This, is the greatest and true realization of freedom.

There is absolutely no relationship, situation, event, person, substance, or *anything* in which we cannot invoke the *violet flame* in which it will not create a transformation. Throughout the years, I have used the *violet flame* in so many ways. After 13 years of regular practicing, I am sure there are numerous other applications for its use, and I have merely skimmed the surface.

I have used it in my personal relationships. I have used it in my professional relationships. I use it throughout every portion of my physical body and subtle bodies. If I see a person, animal, or anything alive which is struggling physically or any other way, I send it to them. One may put it into the weather. It may be used to clear homes, or any building of lower energies. It may be invoked to surround you during any dangerous moment to help protect you. It may be sent to others who you simply think may need it to help them with *anything*. It can energize any food before it is eaten. It can be placed into plants and flowers to help them grow healthy. These are many of the ways I have used it in my life.

Clouds and Angels

Roughly three years ago, my Chiropractic clinic was located in a rural town of about 2800 people. Every year in August they celebrate the corn harvest with a *sweet corn festival*. It is a week-long event with the festival in the city park, and on one evening there is the annual parade. The parade route is at least two miles long, and runs down the length of mainstreet through the center. It winds around the major highway that runs through the edge of town. Typically most every business in the town and its surrounding areas has a float in the parade, and all of the people come out to watch. Aside from all of the businesses, the girl scouts, the boy scouts, the kiwanis, the little Miss and Mr. sweet corn festival candidates ride in convertibles, fire trucks, and politicians all are decked out alike. This was the first time that I wasn't in the parade. The previous time, there had been at least 90 vehicles or floats total in the line. On this day there were about the same.

Usually *everyone* in town and from the surrounding areas would come for the parade. Most would line up their folding chairs all along the streets starting at least an hour before. There were probably at least 2000 people in their chairs lining the streets this day.

I closed up my clinic a little earlier than usual, remembering the parade started at 5:30. My Chiropractic clinic was sandwiched in the middle of a small strip mall. I came outside to an empty parking lot finding my sole Hyundai Elantra parked across the lot. I looked up the street and saw a mass of people all crowded into the grocery store parking lot. I walked to my car and tossed my briefcase inside on the seat. I knew that even if I wanted to leave town, there would be no way until the parade was finished. The main parade route was the only way out of town, and was blocked by the police car in front of my office.

I sauntered across the empty parking lot, crossing the railroad tracks and sifted in with the waiting crowd. We were standing at the corner at the end of main street, where the parade would reach its midpoint, and elbow onto the highway towards the park near the end of town. I saw a man who I knew. While we waited for the parade to arrive, he gave me more details than I cared to know about the local town news and gossip. I finally attempted to change the subject.

"Looks like we have great weather for a parade."

"Yeah, I think they called and checked for today. There's supposed to be some chance of a little rain, but not *anywhere* close to here." He puffed up officially.

"Well, that sounds great. This is the first year I didn't get registered in the parade, just too busy to get anything together in time." I smiled," I guess I'll just get to watch, for once."

It seemed like we were waiting forever for the first of the parade to arrive. I saw *Little Miss Kernel, Little Mister Kernel, Little Miss Sweet Corn Festival, Miss Sweet Corn Festival* in their shiny red convertibles, a couple of fire trucks blasting sirens, and one of a dozen members on the state representative's re-election team handed me a brochure and a popsicle-stick fan. Then I noticed that some darker clouds seemed to be rolling in from nowhere, and it became cooler. It started sprinkling, and within another minute it was raining just enough for me to be wanting an umbrella. I decided to start walking back over towards my car. I thought," What a bummer for everyone to be getting wet in the parade." It was literally at the peak moment of the parade, and *everyone* was outside. I got into my car, and within a minute I saw the owner of the auto parts store driving his train into the parking lot and behind the building. Every year only for the parade, he drives a black antique train, with seats for at least six, complete with the old steam whistle which he toots for everyone throughout the town. This time his train was empty, and I saw him with a grave look bouncing, and driving his train as fast as possible behind our building.

Suddenly, the rain started coming in sheets, the once bright and sunny day was now gone, as I barely could see out of the windshield of my car. The reality was finally occurring to me that this was becoming a major storm. I looked out of my windshield now, and could no longer see the police vehicle parked in the street, and everything simply looked black. I briefly contemplated making a run for my office. But I could feel the wind and rain pelting my car, and knew it was at least 500 feet *and* I would still have to unlock the door. I decided to stay put.

Next, I thought to myself, *I know that there simply are no accidents, and I was right where I was supposed to be.* As the rain became stronger, and the outside looked blacker, I heard the pounding of hail pummeling my car. It was ear piercing, sounding like machine gun fire ricocheting off of my car. At that moment, I was surprised my windows were not breaking. Many thoughts flew through my mind in a fraction of a second.

I immediately closed my eyes, and called to the *violet flame.* I invoked it first to surround my car. It was difficult to keep myself calm. Now, I not only felt my car heaving back and forth from the force of the hailstones, but the wind now was lifting my car up off of the pavement and bouncing it back down. With each gust, it picked me up off of the ground, tilting the car sideways slightly and dropping me back onto the concrete. I opened my eyes just long enough to decide to push my jostling briefcase from the passenger seat to the floorboard, and put on my seatbelt. Then I closed my eyes again, and attempted to center myself and keep calling in the *violet flame.* I simply kept as focused as possible, surrounding myself, then the whole town, and as far outside of town as was needed with the flame. I again reminded myself that I was here in this moment for a reason, and it was *not accidental.* I kept working to stay focused amongst the chaos.

At the moment I really understood the full danger, I quickly prayed to Sai Maa and all of the other Masters for help. I thought about the thousands of people that were outside for the parade. What was happening to them? Then I refocused myself back on the *violet flame,* once again.

Then just as quickly as everything started, the winds started to slow down. I could hear the missiles of hail now receding to about a strike every several seconds. My car was no longer getting picked up off of the ground, and I could now see out of my windshield. I couldn't believe that there weren't *any* cracks on my windshield at all. Another minute and the hail and rain stopped, the gray clouds were gone, replaced by large fluffy white clouds, and a clearing sky.

I got out of my car, and walked around it, still feeling dazed and the surge of adrenaline from all that had happened. My car had three-inch circular dents covering all over the hood, trunk, and right side of the vehicle. The left side looked completely untouched. I noticed the same side headlight and tail-light were both smashed out. All of the windows didn't have even a small crack. I crossed the parking lot, amazed at the remnant hailstones gathered in a clusters here and there, and at the front door of my clinic. I gathered a few up into my hand, with our 90 degree heat, they were reduced to the size of large marbles. Now the driver of the train, and owner of the building joined me as we walked around the perimeter of the building checking for broken windows and damage. We found no damage to windows, and exchanged our excited stories of the storm. I heard a siren in the distance, as the all of the town must have been surveying the damage.

I waited for the police to clear the street, and then decided to start my 50 minute drive home. Tonight it took me nearly two hours, as I left a town that now looked like it had been war-torn. There were tree branches everywhere, vinyl siding slung throughout the streets, and splintered, uprooted trees. During my drive home, I sent out prayers of gratitude, and that as much as possible everyone would be safe. The small town made the 10 o'clock news that night, and the next two days. I found it interesting that the meteorologists couldn't really agree about what happened, whether there was a tornado, or a severe storm. They did agree that there were over 100 mile-per-hour winds and baseball-sized hail. They estimated the property damage to the community at over a million dollars.

I went to my clinic the next day, and it was nearly like the National Guard had been called to duty in our town. There were utility trucks all over with people repairing powerlines, and phone service, dump trucks with workers picking up debris, and the sound of chain saws cutting up trees. My clinic was one of the fortunate few in town to have electric restored that day.

I started seeing patients, as usual, with everyone having their own harrowing story to share with me. I heard stories of how people all up and down the parade path opened their homes up to everyone who didn't have anyplace to go for shelter. A local café herded a whole float full of girl scouts inside to keep them safe. All of the rest of the people on open floats abandoned them in the streets, and either were taken into a house or business during the storm. By the end of the day, I had much of the story of the storm pieced together. I was so happy to discover there were no deaths, and only a couple of minor injuries.

The major thing I felt, and noticed others mentioned, was an overwhelming sense of gratitude. So many told me that they just *knew* that we somehow had been protected, and just thanked God for this blessing.

One of my last patients told me her story. She related that she and her husband had parked their van in a parking space behind an old medical building, and left with their daughter to watch the parade. Just as the parade was starting, she had just decided to move the van to a different place closer to the parade route. Once the storm started, her family ran and took shelter in their van. Afterwards, she saw that in the same place where she had previously moved the van, there was now a large uprooted tree which smashed into the medical building. And it would have crushed their van had it still been there. She told me she looked to the sky and gave thanks for her family being safe. She noticed a funny cloud formation, and snapped a couple of pictures on her cell phone camera. She showed me them. There were a pair of cloud formations that looked amazingly, just like a pair of angels moving through the sky. Both were a profile view, having fluffy curly hair, a soft face, and a sweeping long gown. Both had a serious look as though they were busy and quickly moving towards their next task. She was so convinced these were angels, she told me she had posted them on her Facebook page for everyone to see. I smiled, and agreed that we must have had *a lot* of help on that day.

It took about three months for the town to recover, and repair from all of the damages. I am sure not any of us who were there will soon forget our experiences from that day.

Making the Call

Now that we better understand the *violet flame*, how exactly do we invoke, or call upon it to assist us? This is very similar to meditation, that there is no right or wrong way. There may be some certain words we may use that are more powerful. Otherwise, it is most important to remember that this is continuously available to us, simply waiting for us to call.

Hopefully, by now you are regularly practicing the meditation methods that were described earlier. In the beginning, it is best to start learning to use the *violet flame* during your meditation practice. As you continue to practice, you may use it whenever you wish during your day for anything in which you may notice a need. Most of the time, it is best to practice during your meditation period.

One of the keys to practicing, is to always put your *full feeling* into working with this energy. This is the time to allow your *power* and *passion* to come through by using your voice and thoughts in a mighty way. It is important during this activity to keep focused, and not allow your mind to wander to other things. When we begin to use the *violet flame*, it is similar to using a mantra during meditation. The following are some great examples to help you get started. Some of these are original ones Sai Maa taught me, and others I have modified and used at different times for various purposes.

Decrees and Invocations

- I am the *Violet Transmuting Flame* in manifestation and action.
- I invoke the *Violet Transmuting Ray* into every cell, tissue, organ system, atom, and subatomic particle of my physical body, every aspect of my emotional body, mental body, and all of the spiritual bodies. I invoke the *Violet Flame* to transmute *everything* which does not serve into pure light and love, and that which does serve. I invoke that this flame *shall be* continuously *activated* and *energized*, continuously *established*, and continuously *anchored* throughout all of these systems and bodies. By the grace of my beloved Saint Germain, and so it is!
- I invoke the *Violet Transmuting Flame* to transmute everything which does not serve in this food into pure light and love, and that which does serve. By the grace of Saint Germain, so it is!
- I invoke the *Violet Transmuting Flame* into every aspect of my relationship with _____. I invoke the *Violet Flame* to transmute everything within this

relationship that does not serve into pure light and love, and that which does serve. I invoke that this flame *shall be* continuously *activated* and *energized*, continuously *established*, and continuously *anchored* throughout every aspect of this relationship. By the grace of my beloved Saint Germain, and so it is!

- I invoke the *Violet Transmuting Flame* to penetrate every aspect of this home, throughout every room inside of the house and surrounding this home. I invoke the flame to completely transmute anything which does not serve into pure light and love, and that which does serve. I invoke that this flame *shall be* continuously *activated* and *energized*, continuously *established*, and continuously *anchored* throughout every aspect of this home and its surroundings. By the grace of my beloved Saint Germain, and so it is!

- I invoke the *Violet Transmuting Flame* to move into every aspect of this storm, penetrate every portion surrounding me and as far reaching as is needed. I invoke the *Violet Flame* to transmute everything which does not serve into pure light and love, and that which does serve. I invoke that this flame *shall be* continuously *activated* and *energized*, continuously *established*, and continuously *anchored* throughout every aspect of this storm and all of its surroundings. By the grace of my beloved Saint Germain, and so it is!

- I invoke the *Violet Transmuting Flame* to move into every aspect of this (name the situation). I invoke the *Violet Flame* to transmute everything within this (name the situation) that does not serve into pure light and love, and that which does serve. I invoke that this flame *shall be* continuously *activated* and *energized*, continuously *established*, and continuously *anchored* throughout every aspect of this (name the situation). By the grace of my beloved Saint Germain, and so it is!

It is important to remember to be so grateful for having this wonderful gift which is available to us. At the end of my meditations, I try to always offer my deepest gratitude. Every time we activate this energy, not only is the *Violet Flame* moving into action on our behalf, but a myriad of lightbeings and Masters, such as Saint Germain go to work in our lives assisting with whatever we are calling to clear. How incredible it is to know all of this help is available, simply waiting for us to make the call. It is appropriate to repeat the invocation, for most of these three times during your meditation. Most often, it is not enough to invoke the *violet flame* once into a significant situation, and expect to see something change. If there are difficult circumstances, it is more beneficial to invoke the *violet flame* into them everyday. Do this consistently for at least a week or more, until you can see that there is a shift starting to occur. Just like anything else, more practice brings greater mastery.

The above invocations simply give you an excellent format, and place to start. As you continue to practice, you may wish to create your own invocations. It is most important that you create these from your own feelings and heart. The list above gives you a starting place, and simply know that there are countless ways to use the *violet flame.* It is also important to start your invocation with the words *I Am,* or *I,* for the same reasons as in a mantra. When we are using any of these energies, there is only the present. The power of this energy is the greatest when we use our full, genuine feelings, and in the present tense, or our current situation. Also, using the words *I am* also calls, and activates our own *divine source* or *presence.* It doesn't matter if you use it for general, or very specific applications.

The most important thing is to remember that it is that invisible lifeline available to *each* of us whenever there is *any* need. Simply make the call, and use this incredible spiritual powertool.

12

The Spiral Ladder We Climb

All of nature on this planet contains certain shapes which are found throughout everything. Whether it may be a leaf of grass, rabbit, or a human being, all have certain shapes which are in common. All living things have DNA in each cell. DNA is *d*eoxyribo*n*ucleic *a*cid, which is simply a substance that carries genetic information in the cells of plants and animals. It is contained in each cell, and has the shape of a double-helix. Today scientists are intrigued with unlocking the mysteries of the DNA, and are beginning to realize that this structure holds the key to understanding everything within a living organism. What is intriguing is that these double-helix strands form a spiral shape and contain codes. Some of these which scientists have explained, and many more which they have not.

Why is the structure of DNA important to us? If we look at the double-helix shape, we can see that it seems to continuously spiral. Since we know that DNA is a major building block in every one of our cells, it makes sense that this same pattern may also be a foundation in our life. Below shows a depiction of DNA's typical spiral pattern:

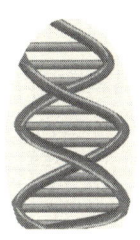

This same pattern occurs in our life as well. As with everything, it takes understanding, and then some practice to be able to see this pattern working in our life.

One of the major things that tends to occur to anyone who has decided to put feet to the pavement and actively pursue the spiritual road, is accelerated activity. I have witnessed many people just getting into a practice, and working to weave some spiritual-like aspects into life, and *Pow!* Suddenly there is one event, then another event, then something *else* unexpected. Then soon after there is frustration, this person thinks, "I just finally start getting it together, am *taking* the steps I am supposed to take to become more awakened, and now all of *this?!*"

Absolutely!! When everything surrounding you seems like it is in constant flux, and just one thing gets settled, then another starts- *congratulations,* because now you are *really* on your way!

So how in the world do we handle, and even comprehend all of these things coming in so fast at us? Why is all of this happening to me, when I am working on my spirituality? What can I do?

It is *because* you are working on your spirituality. When a person opens up and says, "I'm ready," to the universe, and the doors are even cracked just a little, the proverbial flood gates are opened up wide. Then every *next* thing that you need to work on in your life will come to you, *guaranteed*!

Progress has not followed a straight ascending line, but a spiral with rhythms of progress and retrogression, of evolution and dissolution.

-Johann Wolfgang Von Goethe

Many sources say that during one lifetime, a person who is mostly unaware, and has an absence of the pursuit of spiritual activities will have the opportunity to clear *some* of their previous *karma* from previous lifetimes. However, a person who is actively pursuing spiritual advancement, will be given the opportunity to clear *much more* of their previous *karma* from other lifetimes. As every kind of challenge seems to come into all areas of our life, at times it is difficult to realize that this is a blessing, but it really is. It does make sense if we think of it as having opened ourselves to learn more lessons, so they are brought to us to benefit and grow from them. It is simply because we are sending out our thoughts, intentions, words, and actions to advance our spiritual awareness, that we are attracting back the situations we need to be able to grow. So how can we learn to deal with all of this coming in at us all at once?

First, we must understand one of the little secrets to our universe which is imprinted throughout nature, and reflected in our DNA. There is a distinct pattern in life. If we look at its double-helix structure, we see that it moves as a spiral. It is critical for us to understand that not only does this key structure *inside of us* move in a spiral pattern, but all of the events on the *outside of us* move in a spiral pattern as well. Think of it as simply a *divine pattern* which every situation and event in our life uses. We see these in *every* aspect of our life; relationships, career, family, spirituality, and health.

The Perfect Spiral

One of the most common areas we find this is in our personal relationships. A typical scenario may be that you move into your first serious relationship at the age of 17. The two of you are together nearly two years, and the last couple of months you both start to have frequent fights. Both of you are attending college, and you each are about ready to declare a major. Your partner plans to choose a major in theatre arts after taking a course in it, and loving it. You both have disagreements over the importance of a well-paying major. You voice to your partner that you feel it is more important to choose a major which will provide a greater income in that field after college. You are unable to allow your partner to decide without intervening with an argument. Your partner feels so much pressure and discord, that the relationship is ended.

A year or so passes, and you start dating someone that you meet in one of your engineering classes. You feel happy, and think this is great as you both will get jobs in a well-paying field after graduation. Your new partner graduates, and you graduate the following year. Both of you find good jobs starting out in a couple of engineering firms. Both of you decide to get married. About six months later, your partner suddenly gets fired at work. Every other engineering firm in the area has said no to hiring your partner. Soon you both have arguments over paying bills. It was important to you that you *both* should drive expensive cars. After many months of searching for viable employment, your partner finally gets hired as a server at a large-chain restaurant. You both struggle financially since your partner's income is half of what it was previously. You decide to sell one of the cars, and your partner feels you should trade the other in for a less expensive one. You refuse, and this ensues many more arguments over money. A few months later, your partner gets selected for assistant manager training, and really loves working at the restaurant. The increase in pay still wouldn't come close to your partner's previous income, and this is disturbing to you. More financial arguments continue, and this time after four years into the relationship, you get divorced.

It takes you a couple of years to grieve this loss in your life. During this time, you have recovered your finances and managed to keep your car. You just were promoted to the next level in your company, and now are looking to buy a condo in a nice neighborhood. A friend invites you to a pool party, and you meet someone. This time you decide that you are going to be careful, and *really* get to know this person. Both of you have instant chemistry with each other, and this relationship develops very quickly. This person seems perfect as you both are professionals, and you both enjoy having nice cars, and seem to have most everything in common. After dating each other for over a year, you get married again. You sell your condo, and move into your partner's larger house. After moving in, you find that your partner seems a little bit controlling, and somewhat private over the finances. This doesn't disturb you, as you relish how the two of you are so much alike in tastes. You both enjoy buying, and having great clothes, eating out at nice restaurants, and driving classy cars. You have a baby together, and you have never remembered a happier time during your life. One day your partner is out of town for a few days at a business convention, and you bring in the mail. This is the first time you have brought in the mail in months, as your partner is always seems to be first at the mailbox. After shuffling through the mail, you notice a credit card bill addressed to both of you. It wasn't a credit card that you recognized at all. Upon opening it, you discover that you are a joint cardholder, and the card has a $40,000 limit, which has over $36,000 in total charges on the card. After your partner returns, you demand to know immediately *everything* about the finances. You find out that after your marriage, your partner added you as a joint account holder to multiple credit cards without your knowledge. The two of you now owe over $95,000 in credit card debt within the first eighteen months of your marriage. Worse yet, you discover that at least two of the cards are behind in the payments. A surge of arguments, fighting, financial counseling, marriage counseling, bankruptcy, and eventual divorce comes again within the next two years.

So now you decide that you are better off to stay single, abandoning the idea of getting into another relationship. You now have joint custody of your child and are raising her as a single parent. Three years into making payments on your 5 year bankruptcy, your company downsizes and you get permanently laid off. You are unable to find another job in another engineering firm, and eventually your unemployment runs out. In desperation to keep up with your customary lifestyle, you accept a full-time position working in sales for a furniture company. And you are hired in a part-time position working at a retail store. A few months later, you get cut from your part-time job, and are struggling enough financially that you are considering moving back in with your parents.

If we look at the first three situations in this person's life, it might be easy to think that these issues are simply due to some difficulties in communication in each relationship about money. However, if we look closer, we can see that it is more than this. The last situation shows us clearly that once more, even in the absence of being in a relationship, the same type of problem emerges again. So we know that this is *not* simply caused by the choice of partner in the relationship, but it goes deeper than this. By now, it is easy to see that this similar pattern simply keeps repeating itself over and over. It is much easier to see this pattern looking from the outside of this situation, than it is to see it from looking at it from the inside.

Relationship studies agree that the most common argument that couples have in their relationship is about finances. One study states that, "money is...fraught with layers and layers of meaning." Similarly, in this example we can see that there are likely *layers of meaning* behind these financial issues. These show up not only during relationships with others, but the same issues come up again outside of being in a relationship.

How can we better understand how this works?

The Relationship Diagram

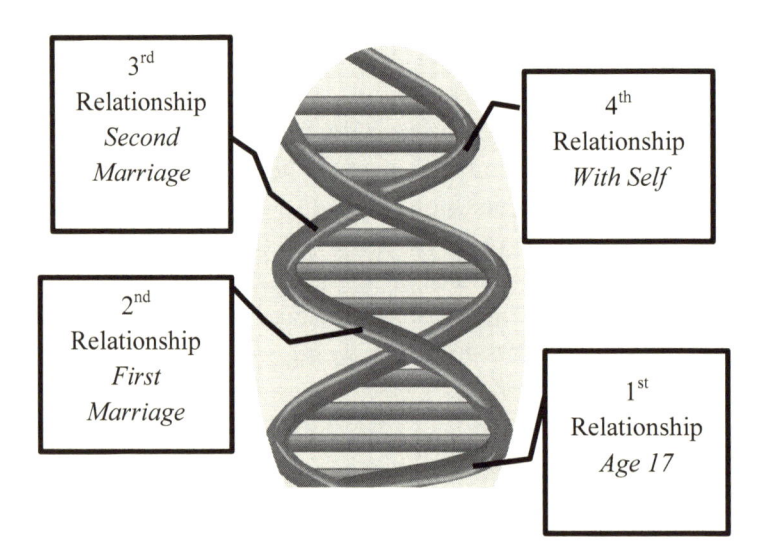

```
┌──────────────┐                    ┌──────────────┐
│     3rd      │                    │     4th      │
│ Relationship │                    │ Relationship │
│   Second     │                    │  With Self   │
│   Marriage   │                    │              │
└──────────────┘                    └──────────────┘

┌──────────────┐                    ┌──────────────┐
│     2nd      │                    │     1st      │
│ Relationship │                    │ Relationship │
│    First     │                    │   Age 17     │
│   Marriage   │                    │              │
└──────────────┘                    └──────────────┘
```

This is where we must be able to put all that we have learned together to really *discern* what is happening in our life. Once again, we need to take a short hike over to our side-line bleachers, so we can get a better view of what is occurring in our life. We must ensure that we distance ourself, to be able to see our life just like someone who is looking on from the outside.

Analyzing Our Spirals

As you see, our first relationship at age 17 belongs at the bottom of our spiral. Often even during our teenage years the very first occurrence of a very definite pattern will begin. In this case, this is the first romantic relationship of your life. Everything may seem to be going fairly well until it is time for each of you to declare your own major, or career-path you each intend for your life. It is most likely that you were taught at an earlier age, having a well-paying career is one of the most important elements to having a successful and happy life. This is what your family had taught you throughout the years, and you simply embraced this without question. It is likely that you were taught that it is important to have nice clothing, live in a better neighborhood, and drive a fine car. This was your first experience away from home, and being exposed to a different way of thinking. Your partner surprises you in finding a passion for performing in theatre arts, and completely changes direction. Your partner most likely was doing the same as you, pursuing a major which ensured a well-paying career. Suddenly, your partner decided to take a different course which ultimately would allow your mate to have greater enjoyment in life. Herein was a great first opportunity to witness, and consider a different approach toward careers and life than was taught to you from your family. Instead of seeing that there might be another way to live life, learning and opening up to other possibilities from this example, you chose to close down and resist. You resisted this concept so strongly, that you eventually pushed your first love completely away. This became the first opportunity in this area on your spiral of life.

A little bit later, you meet someone in college who is majoring in engineering, same as you. You feel that you have taken great care, and learned your lesson from the last relationship. This person, you are sure has the same financial values, as you witness your partner graduate and obtain an entry-level position in an engineering firm. You graduate the following year, and also obtain a new position as an engineer as well. You feel like both of you are creating the partnership of your dreams, and get married. You are happy to give back the 12 year old hand-me-down car that you shared with one of your other siblings. Impressing yourself and others that you could buy a new BMW, you also pushed your spouse to buy a new car too. Although your partner really wanted to buy something less expensive, and practical, you insisted, until there was a new Lexus in the driveway. Just as everything couldn't seem more perfect, suddenly your spouse was terminated at the engineering firm. After months of searching, and simply no other firm making any offers, your spouse gets a job as a server in a restaurant. Now that the household income is about 70% of what it was before, you both decide to sell the Lexus. Although the payment on your BMW is still a stretch on the finances, you insist to keep your car regardless. After sharing with you that your spouse was accepted to become trained for an assistant manager position, you are bewildered. When your partner relates how much s/he is enjoying the restaurant business, this creates the same feelings within you as once before. You begin to push your mate, having more arguments over finances, and what your expectations are for a successful marriage. You both eventually divorce. Again, here is another wonderful example being shown to you, how it is possible for a person to live life in a different, less restricted way. Also, that happiness may not be found simply in material things, or a certain type of career. However, you are just still not able to see this concept from this second example given to you. On our life spiral you'll notice that we have moved up some, as we have been given a more elaborate example and chance to understand a major lesson we have come here to learn.

After a couple of years, you finally feel that you have recovered from the "mess that your last marriage made in your life." You meet someone new. This time you think that you will be *really* cautious, so you know that this person matches up to all of your expectations. You feel that you have found someone who you are more attracted to than any of your previous partners. But you are still careful, and since your partner is steadfast in employment, likes better clothing, fine dining, and everything that is important to you, it seems like a perfect match. So you become married. You notice that your partner is a little bit controlling over finances, but this doesn't really bother you. You are able to see that in every other aspect, you feel you are living the life of your dreams. So you both decide to have a child. You are the one who feels it is the logical next step, even though your partner wanted to wait a little bit. You were also taught that having a child is also another important sign of a successful life. You already have gotten one promotion at your job, and this seems like perfect timing. After the baby comes, you find out your spouse has been controlling the household finances for a major reason. You discover that your partner has put your name on several credit cards as a joint cardholder without your permission, and nearly maxed all of the credit out. You find out that you are behind on payments, and are in a bigger financial mess than you ever thought possible. And now you are responsible for a baby as well. After many fights, counseling, and taking bankruptcy, you both divorce. This relationship on the spiral houses the same lesson, only at an even greater, ramped up level. So it is higher on the spiral. This time it is an even more intense scenario. Even though there is a trust issue in that your partner was dishonest to you, there are still the same underlying currents. At this level, the stakes have become higher, as now there is a child involved too. So the recovery time from this situation will take much longer than the other two times. We can see another message from this situation involving honesty. In this case, analyzing this from a distance, when we are not being fully honest with ourselves, we draw others to us who are not honest with us either. This demonstrates how all relationships simply mirror back to us whatever energies we are putting out. The level of intensity and extra time that it takes to resolve this situation, gives us a greater opportunity to see all that we need to learn. At the end of this marriage, there was not as quick of a fix as there had been previously. This time the financial concerns will linger afterwards, and continue to persistently attempt to win your attention. This financial struggle is still a mere symptom of the underlying causes. It is simply a tool, which is attempting to help you to understand specific life lessons that you still need to learn.

It is now at least a year after your last divorce, and you feel that you are finally settled into living alone, and being a mostly single parent. Your former spouse felt that you had the greatest stability, so you have the primary responsibility for raising your daughter. She is in day care, and your spouse gets her every other weekend. You decide that your lesson from this string of failed relationships is that you can't really rely on others. You feel that you will avoid intimate relationships, and *if* you ever get married again it will only be after dating for at least five years. You be*lie*ve that you are really the victim of being in relationships with three people, who didn't have any control of their lives and were financially losers. After your company gets downsized, you are caught off-guard as you are cut from your job. During your unemployment you use up all of your savings to keep up with your payments on your bankruptcy, your car, home, and day care expenses. You grabbed the best job available just before your unemployment ended working in sales. This income is about half of what you earned previously, so you take another part-time job at a retail store. You simply can't believe this happened to you. Now you are forced to give more responsibility for your daughter back to your ex-spouse because you can't pay for daycare. After losing your part-time job, you find yourself in a situation that you never imagined. Now, into your early

30's you may need to move back in with your parents. You feel like you have completely failed to meet your own expectations of yourself during your life. At this juncture, many of us are simply ready to throw in the towel, asking,"What did I do wrong, why can't I be successful?" Now we have nobody else to blame in this situation than ourselves. So this forces us again to look now at the relationship with ourself, and it is higher on our spiral of life. This situation moves us even higher up on the spiral, because we are now dealing with a full spectrum of complex conditions in our life. We have been given yet another chance to examine what may be the underlying cause of these events. Once we can *really* see, then we can allow ourself to shift our way of thinking. This will allow us to be able to make new decisions in our life. Then these new decisions would ultimately serve us better.

If we examine each of these four relationships carefully at a distance, we can identify the underlying current which flows as a strong river under each of these. If we do this we can distinguish that at the core, we were taught that expensive, nice things, a well-paying career, marriage, and children are all of the keys to a successful, and happy life. Yet each of the four relationships displays the opposite to be true. Each time that you placed all of your energy into acquiring these things, it brought only short-lived happiness. Every time that you grasped at maintaining greater control by focusing singly upon financial success, it shortly thereafter slipped away. This lead you to heartache, and financial distress in each case. Your first two relationships showed wonderful examples of how there may be greater happiness in finding your true calling and purpose in life. Both of these partners demonstrated that it served each of them better to select a career that they enjoyed, rather than one with the highest pay. It is apparent that each time you attempted to accumulate more in each subsequent relationship, there was a greater struggle and more of a loss each time.

What *are* we being shown here that we need to learn? (1) That sometimes concepts we learned in our families may be incorrect, and we need to become open to investigate other possibilities. (2) Each of us has a purpose, which is often a career field in which we have greater talent, and enjoy the most. It doesn't *have* to be in a high-paying career field. (3) Material wealth is not the key to happiness and success. (4) *Divine love* for another one is not based upon the person's financial condition. (5) Having children is not a *requirement* for having a successful and happy marriage and life. (6) It is likely we will continue to have these same experiences again, unless we take some active steps in our life to *awaken* and begin to shift our be*lief*s.

Insanity: doing the same thing over and over again and expecting different results.

-Albert Einstein

We may expect that if there is no progress made by us to learn anything in our situation, that another experience will be coming again right on its heels. We must know that it will continue on and on, until we finally are able to recognize and resolve our lesson. This example shows us what this may look like in a relationship, but we can have several different areas of our life that events are spiraling around for us to recognize, understand, and shift in our life. These may show up in any area, and we can have multiple events occurring seemingly all at once. When this happens, this is when it is time for us to *really* pay attention to all that is going on.

As we begin to advance in our spiritual journey, it is important to know that even as we make progress, other similar situations will come. You might wonder, "If I am understanding my lessons and making progress, why are there more similar situations coming to me?" It is because when we are actively pursuing our own spiritual growth, more opportunities will be energetically drawn to us to assist in expanding our awareness. Most of us need multiple practices to fully learn and master anything that is new. This is the same concept. The first time we have a needed challenge, we may blow it and completely not get what we need to learn. So it spirals around again coming towards us once more. This time we recognize it, and handle the situation and are able to get through it. A little later another event comes, maybe with an additional aspect, and you handle it even better and a little bit faster. Here it comes again, disguised and more complex. This time you still are able to recognize it and move through the challenge much easier than ever. Possibly this might be the last time you face this particular challenge, because you really *got* the lesson these events were attempting to teach you. Because you now have reached a greater level of *awareness* from this series of events, you are now ready to handle greater challenges which will bring you even greater growth. Ultimately, this is why we are here. We must grow from our experiences, and eventually assist others to do the same.

What are the steps we need to take to identify these situations which are occurring in our life? How may we understand them so we are able to take the necessary action to create a shift in our life?

First, we must pick an area of our life that seems to be the greatest area of struggle for us right now. Let's say it is your career. Look at what is challenging you now. Is it a relationship with a boss? A co-worker? Something else? Determine what it is, and write down your perception of the conflict. Ask yourself if you have ever experienced a similar kind of conflict before in your past? Was it at another job? Did it occur in your family? Somewhere else? Write any of these you notice down as well. What was your perception of these, and what was the outcome? Simply gather all of the information, and avoid making any judgments. Afterwards, it is time to move over to our bleachers to separate ourselves and obtain a better view of our game. Our *going to the bleachers,* this time involves us taking our paper in which we have just written to our meditation place. Just before moving into meditation look at your paper, and each situation you have described. Read all that you have written, then set the intention that you will be guided to *discern* everything you need to understand, and handle your situation *now*. Request that you may be able to see the pattern, and understand and see the steps available to help you move towards a higher resolution. Then practice your regular meditation with this intention. Then simply allow and let go. Do this same thing for at least the next three days. You may also choose to invoke the *violet flame* to move into this situation during your meditation. Then it is important to simply release it all. Finally, make sure that you *pay attention* to everything that you notice, especially after your meditations. Also, all that occurs throughout your days. Often, one thing or a chain of events may occur, which will give you a greater level of clarity. As you begin to notice these, try to stay as detached as possible emotionally. It could be another person may say something that gives you insight, or it could be that you get a flash of intuition that allows you to see everything in a different way than before. Remain open to all of the possibilities. The ways you may receive guidance are varied, and may come from anywhere depending upon your needs. A friend might invite you to go to a spiritual workshop or retreat. A stranger at a store notices you are buying a book, and tells you about a great spiritual study group in the city. You are out walking, and you suddenly get a different way of seeing your situation you never considered before. You watch three little children in the park playing ball together, and as you laugh at their fun, an idea pops into your mind for a new project. Just as you are waking in the morning, you experience a dream that seems vivid, showing you a whole different way to look at the events in your life.

It is important to *listen* in this same way for any ideas that you get, no matter how different they may seem. *Take action* and do whatever you feel best guided to do. Once again, *release* all expectations for a certain outcome to occur. Realize that taking *any action,* even if it doesn't work out perfectly is much better than taking no action at all. Taking action will always move you forward if your intentions are for the highest and greatest good for everyone involved. We continue repeating these steps until we are able to see that there has been some noticeable resolution.

Once we have taken these steps to work to resolve our most difficult area, then we look at the other areas of our life. Make sure to examine all of our relationships, romantic, family, friends, career, and self. We choose the next place we are having difficulties, and repeat all of these steps again. We continue doing this again and again, until our life experience mostly has a greater level of peace.

Being armed with the understanding that *spirals* are affecting our lives inside and outside of us, gives us yet another advanced tool. Along with everything else, and some practice, we may add yet another way which assists us to acquire greater *wisdom.* This will allow us to move into a greater level of mastery in our lives on our journey of *awakening.*

AFTERWORD

As I finish this, I am able to see distinctly how this book parallels the recommendations I give my patients in my clinic. It is just like when I give one of my new patients a new diet which lists the healthy foods s/he needs to consume regularly, and the list of ones which are to be avoided and eliminated. Oftentimes, I see them look at the list like a deer caught in headlights, and are quiet for a few moments. They break their silence usually with something like, "But I *love* wheat bread, and eat it with nearly every meal." I smile and tell them to relax, as they don't have to change it *all* overnight. I assure them that I realize that they have been in the habit of eating whatever food choices they have made for years, and simply didn't really know. However, now that they are educated and *know* to stop buying the unhealthy foods, they may start focusing upon buying the heathier selections. The foods that need to be eliminated, they now know to stop buying. Rather than attempting to do everything all at once, I suggest that each week they should *take action* to change one or two things at a time. Gradually, there is a shift towards eating the healthier foods most of the time. Although I have some patients who simply take all of my recommendations at once, it is easier for them take the more gradual approach. There is usually a greater level of success when we make gradual changes, than large drastic ones all at once. The important thing is to take one step, then another, and keep moving forward. Eventually, over a period of time these healthy dietary changes will allow for the gradual shift of increased health.

One of the greatest discoveries a man makes, one of his great surprises, is to find he can do what he was afraid he couldn't do.

-Henry Ford

The other day, I had a patient who called to my office I hadn't seen in well over a year. I recalled that this man, in his sixties, had multiple conditions, including anxiety and depression, diabetes, irritable bowel problems, multiple joint pains, and was obese. When he first came to me his health was spiraling out of control(pun intended); and similar to many of my patients had already been through all of the traditional medical care. My treatment recommendations for him included my typical methods of Chiropractic, enzyme therapy, nutritional supplementation, affirmation exercises, and special dietary changes. I recall that this patient was enthusiastic, and wanted to receive *every* treatment that I offered in my clinic, so he had a couple of energetic healing sessions as well.

He spoke with me on the phone and said that he wanted to thank me for all of the care he had received. He said that he did continue to completely change his diet, and now he has lost over 100 pounds. Not only this, but is no longer diabetic, and is completely off all of his old medications. He said that he just took it one step at a time, like I suggested and now he now feels healthier than he could ever remember during his life.

This is *exactly* how slow steady *action* can create transformative changes in our lives. It works the same way regardless of what we are working to improve in our lives.

Similarly, try to not allow yourself to feel overwhelmed with, "Where do I start?" This is why I highly suggest using the workbook along with this book. I will have this available within a couple of months after the publication of this book.

I encourage you during the first week to take *one action step* forward. Then next week take *another step* forward, and so forth. If some of it feels a little uncomfortable, that is great, as this is when we have the highest level of growth. Within a few short months, you will begin to see the transformations in your life. This book paired up with the workbook, will give you the fundamental knowledge, tools, and advanced tools to help you make as much progress in your spiritual growth as you choose.

We can easily forgive a child who is afraid of the dark; the real tragedy of life is when men are afraid of the light.

-Plato

My analytical mind didn't think that this book would move too much into the more advanced topics, such as the *violet transmuting flame*. I thought that this topic, or other advanced areas would most likely come later in a subsequent book. One morning, towards the end of meditation, I was apparently being resistant to the message of including the *violet flame* in this book. Next thing, I felt and heard what seemed like a loud commotion from my divine assistants telling me, *the violet flame belongs in **this** book!*. I felt and *heard* this over and over for several minutes, until I finally put my own controlling ideas aside and agreed.

I also had a certain set deadline in my mind, and decided it was absolutely necessary that I finish this book before a certain date. I really pushed, and after having the extra chapter added, I realized that I simply wouldn't make it. Another day later during meditation, I was reminded that I am on a *journey*, and *not* simply attempting to reach a destination. So I was reminded of the essence this book attempts to teach us, which are constant concepts to be applied to *everything* throughout our life. It is not just for the bigger things, but also for the smaller details. These are concepts for us to continuously use, and remember in every aspect of our daily life.

I'm not a teacher: only a fellow traveler of whom you asked the way. I pointed ahead - ahead of myself as well as you.

— George Bernard Shaw

As I finally finish this book, it is important for me to share with all of you, the readers, that I am travelling in my own spiritual journey same as everyone. Every day I am learning and growing, and within this book I have simply shown you that which I have come to know in my own life. Many of the concepts I learned through my own inquiry, experience, and the teaching and guidance of a living Spiritual Master. The rest of the information simply *came through,* and I was divinely guided and given much information to share with all of you. I realize that this *guidance* was just as much for me, as for everyone else. So realize that much of this material is new for me to consider and learn as well. I have shared with everyone who is close to me and some in my spiritual community; that I can't wait to get a copy of my book and workbook, as I know that I need to do this work in my life too. They act surprised as though I am kidding them, yet I am not at all.

I harbor my suspicions that this book and workbook will most likely be a perpetual book. This means it is one that a person can read the book, and work through the exercises the first time and gain much growth. Then a few months later, one can pick it up and re-read the book and work through the exercises again, and gain new insights and grow some more. Then this may be done each year, and every time there will be new areas of life to work upon. Eventually, you will know all of the applications so well that you have moved into mastery. I know that this is the design, and I feel this is the divine intention of this book.

I remember when Sai Maa finally wrote her book, *Petals of Grace,* after many students begged her to put some of her main teachings into writing. I anxiously read her book the first time, and learned so much. Then I read it again. The second time through, I had at least a couple of aha's and garnered new understanding. I was sure I didn't see it in her book the first time. Then I read it yet again, and again, until I lost count of how many times I had read it. Each time I picked up yet another nugget, that I hadn't noticed the times before. Today, I still make a point to read her book again each year to keep a strong foundation of these teachings.

So it is important in our lives to frequently make important inquiries. Who am I? Why am I here? What is my purpose? What is happening right now in my life and why? Then it is just as important to frequently analyze what is happening in our life. And we must learn to use our *love, power, discipline,* and *wisdom.* We must take an active step forward *regularly*, using *every* tool we have available. This is when we will begin to witness the incredible transformation of our lives. *Then* we will move further into our spiritual journey with great joy, and *Awakening.*

REFERENCES

Chapter 1

http://www.ucmp.berkeley.edu/geology/tecmech.html

Chapter 2

The Center for the Study of Global Christianity (CSGC) at Gordon-Conwell Theological Seminary in South Hamilton, Mass. CSGC researchers generated their estimates based in large part on figures provided by Christian denominations and organizations around the world. CSGC has obtained denominational membership information from about 41,000 organizations worldwide.

Chapter 3

Cannon, Delores. *The Convoluted Universe: Book IV.* Ozark Mountain Publishing, 2012.

Stevenson, Ian. *20 Twenty Cases Suggestive of Reincarnation.* The University of Virginia Press, 1974.

Chapter 4

Hawkins, David R. Power vs. Force: The Hidden Determinants of Human Behavior. Veritas Publishing, 1998.

Walther, David S. *Applied Kinesiology Synopsis.* Triad of health publishing, 1988.

http://en.wikipedia.org/wiki/The_Beatles_in_India

Chapter 5

Attila Andics, Marta Gacsi, Tamas Farago, Anna Kis, Adam Miklosi. Voice-Sensitive Regions in the Dog and Human Brain Are Revealed by Comparative fMRI. *Current Biology*, Volume 24, issue 5, (pp.574–578), 3 March 2014.

http://www.heartmath.org/research/science-of-the-heart/entrainment-coherence-autonomic-balance.html?submenuheader=3

http://www.hsperson.com/

http://en.wikipedia.org/wiki/Hachik%C5%8D

Chapter 6

http://4tprosperity.com/

http://www.biography.com/people/thomas-edison-9284349#synopsis

http://www.history.com/news/ford-and-edisons-excellent-camping-adventures

http://www.motherteresa.org/layout.html

Chapter 7

https://www.biblegateway.com/quicksearch/?quicksearch=meditation&version=NKJV&resultspp=25

https://www.biblegateway.com/quicksearch/?quicksearch=meditate&qs_version=NKJV

https://www.biblegateway.com/quicksearch/?quicksearch=meditate&qs_version=OJB

https://www.biblegateway.com/quicksearch/?quicksearch=meditation&qs_version=OJB

http://www.chron.com/life/houston-belief/article/Perlman-makes-his-music-the-hard-way-2009719.php

http://quran.com/search?q=meditate

http://www.restoredgospel.com/scriptures/Results.asp?R1=V3&SearchString=meditation&B1=Search&OrText

http://www.restoredgospel.com/scriptures/Results.asp?R1=V3&SearchString=meditate&B1=Search&OrText

Watkins, P. C., Grimm, D. L., Whitney, A., & Brown, A. (2005). Unintentional memory bias in depression. In A. V. Clark (Ed.), Mood state and health (pp. 59-86). Hauppauge, NY: Nova Science.

http://en.wikipedia.org/wiki/Sanskrit

Yale University. "Meditation Associated With Increased Grey Matter In The Brain." Science Daily, 11 November 2005.

Yogananda, Paramahansa. *Man's Eternal Quest: Collected Talks and Essays on Realizing God in Daily Life, Volume 1*. The International Publications Council of The Self-Realization Fellowship, 2002.

Chapter 8

http://en.wikipedia.org/wiki/Pareto_principle

Chapter 10

Oprah Winfrey ,O Magazine (January 2007), pages 160 & 217

http://parade.condenast.com/50135/parade/a-day-in-oprah-life

http://en.wikipedia.org/wiki/Oprah_Winfrey%27s_Legends_Ball

http://en.wikipedia.org/wiki/Oprah_Winfey

Chapter 11

http://dshannahan.hubpages.com/hub/Levitation-Revealed-Levitation-Trick-Used-for-Centuries

http://fox41blogs.typepad.com/wdrb_weather/2012/08/oakland-city-indiana-was-hit-hard-by-a-storm-three-days-ago-was-it-a-tornado.html

Jones, Aurelia Louise. *The Seven Sacred Flames.* California: Mount Shasta Light Publishing, 2007.

Chapter 12

2004 Study commissioned by *Smart Money magazine* and *Redbook magazine,* What is the #1 reason couples argue?

Suggested Reading

Although I could easily create a list of probably 100's of spiritual books which I have either read, or know are highly valuable, I am keeping it simple with my top ten list. These are the top books in an approximate order in which I would attempt to study them.

Devi, Sai Maa Lakshmi. *Petals of Grace: Essential Teachings for Self-Mastery*. HIU Press, 2005.

Luk, A.D.K. *Law of Life (Volumes 1 and 2)*. A.D.K. Luk Publications, 1959

King, Godfrey Ray. *Unveiled Mysteries*. Saint Germain Press, 2001.

King, Godfrey Ray. *The Magic Presence*. Saint Germain Press, 1974.

Germain, Ascended Master. *The "I AM" Discourses*. Saint Germain Press, 1940.

Yogananda, Paramahansa. *Autobiography of a Yogi*. Self-Realization Fellowship, 2001.

Jones, Aurelia Louise. *The Seven Sacred Flames.* California: Mount Shasta Light Publishing, 2007.

Spalding, Baird T. *Life and Teaching of the Masters of the Far East (Volumes 1-6).* Devorss and Company, 1964.

Cannon, Delores. *The convoluted UNIVERSE: Book IV.* Ozark Mountain Publishing, 2012.

The URANTIA BOOK. Urantia Foundation, 1993.

About The Author

Dr. Jane E. Rackley is a Chiropractic Physician, who has been in active private practice over 16 years. She has offered many cutting-edge treatments for her patients throughout the years including Chiropractic, clinical nutrition, and energetic medicine. As a healer, she is dedicated to bringing the greatest level of health and well-being into as many lives as possible.

For over 13 years, she has been graced with the direct teachings of a living Spiritual Master in her life, H.H. Sai Maa Lakshmi Devi. She fully embraces and teaches core spiritual concepts to help direct others to heal. She is dedicated in assisting others to learn how to actively participate in healing themselves.

She recently developed a specialty energetic water, *Doc's Elixir of Life,* which is designed to restore balance and health throughout all aspects of the body. It utilizes the newer quantum energetic frequencies.

She speaks for various groups, and facilitates classes on health, healing, and spirituality.

Her website: www.DrJaneRackley.com

Printed in Great Britain
by Amazon.co.uk, Ltd.,
Marston Gate.